A Specimen Portfolio of Wood Type in the Cary Collection

A Specimen Portfolio of Wood Type in the Cary Collection

Melbert B. Cary, Jr. Graphic Arts Collection
Rochester Institute of Technology

RIT CARY
GRAPHIC ARTS
PRESS

Cary Graphic Arts Press
Rochester Institute of Technology
90 Lomb Memorial Drive
Rochester, New York 14623-5604
http://carypress.rit.edu

Library of Congress Control Number: 2009939763

ISBN 978-1-933360-44-7
Printed in the United States

Contents

Contents

Foreword

In 1967, the esteemed design educator and wood type scholar, Rob Roy Kelly, used the title "Addendum to the Victorians: Wood Letters in the Twentieth Century," to head an article he composed for an RIT publication. At that time Kelly, along with graphic designers, typographers, scholars, and others were spearheading a revival of the wood type fonts of the late 1800s. Whether they were appropriate or not, these designers were dipping into the past to use antique style fonts for advertisements, printed matter and book design. Many fonts soon became available through photocomposition by Headliners International, Inc. Private press printers were scouring the country grabbing up wood types from letterpress shops that were about to become extinct. Kelly fueled the fire with the limited edition publication of specimens from his own extensive collection, with his issue of *Design Quarterly* magazine on wood type and with his book *American Wood Type 1828–1900*. In this writing, Kelly recounted a detailed documentation of the history of wood types in America; how they were made, what companies produced them, and what many of them looked like. He informed me at one point that, in its heyday, there were over 20,000 different styles of wood type available. Fortunately, this interest in historic wood type fonts has been sustained by many private press printers and designers.

This historic richness will be celebrated in this new book published by the RIT Cary Graphic Arts Press. We see in these pages, the variety and depth of the wood type collection at RIT in the Cary Library. Graphic designers, students and scholars, as well as other imaging professionals, will benefit from this reference volume in their libraries. Kudos to all of those people who were involved in this project at RIT–for this important reminder of the rich resources of our graphic arts past.

R. Roger Remington
Massimo and Lella Vignelli Distinguished Professor in Design
School of Design
Rochester Institute of Technology

Curator's Note

Over the course of the last thirty years, the Cary Graphic Arts Collection has assembled an impressive collection of wood type fonts. Some have been acquired from old commercial print shops, some from antique dealers and collectors, and some from amateur printers or graphic designers who saved them from the fireplace. The compositional possibilities these fonts still offer as letterforms, and even as abstract shapes, is timeless. Today, the wood type collection includes some 400 fonts, making it one of the larger institutional repositories in the United States.

The bulk of this collection was described and featured in a master's thesis prepared by David Wall, a graduate student at RIT in the early 1990s. His principle objective was to devise an effective classification system for wood type, and then test it on the holdings owned by the Cary Collection. David's classification system–along with a companion finding aid–was supplemented by a comprehensive portfolio of alphabet proofs, pulled directly from the wood types. This part of the project, all by itself, was a painstaking and arduous task that took almost a year to complete. Only a few copies of the portfolio were produced, however, and historians and wood type enthusiasts have until now been forced to travel to RIT in order to examine the proofs, as well as the types themselves.

This reworked edition of the portfolio, in a handy new, print-on-demand format, now provides an exciting opportunity to broaden its reach. Each page in the original portfolio was carefully photographed and then reworked into a series of double-page spreads for this publication. The left-hand page shows the full alphabet (reduced as necessary), while the right-hand page features selected characters at full size along with descriptive information about the font, including size, style and manufacturer, when known. Eventually, online access to digital images of the type proofs will also be offered through the Cary Collection website.

The page layouts and design work for this new edition were created by Jackie Clements and Candice Reese, graduate assistants in the Cary Collection and students in the Graphic Design program at RIT. They have produced an elegant, simple and beautifully designed new tool for accessing and appreciating this marvelous collection. Their work, together with David Wall's original research and careful type proofing, demonstrates the quality of work produced by students in the graduate programs at RIT. This is an example of what can happen when bright and motivated students are given access to original source material in the graphic arts.

David Pankow, Curator
Cary Graphic Arts Collection

Introduction

Wood type brought commercial advertising to life more than 160 years ago, and continues today to influence the signs, posters, and billboards that adorn the face of every town. In the introduction to his 1964 portfolio *American Wood Type, 1828–1900*, Rob Roy Kelly emphasized the importance of recognizing the role played by wood type in American typography and printing history, a role he felt was yet to be fully understood and appreciated. Kelly deemed essential an effort to preserve records of the type styles that had been manufactured and in common use, so that future generations would have access to this important heritage. In the twenty-eight years that have passed since these sentiments were first expressed, many printers and printing historians have been inspired to start collections of wood type on their own. As many of these collections have grown beyond the bounds of basements, garages, and storerooms, they have been generously bestowed upon those "proper archives" which Kelly felt should be the final resting place for such artifacts.

The Melbert B. Cary, Jr. Graphic Arts Collection at Rochester Institute of Technology has been fortunate in acquiring a number of private collections of wood type. To date it has accumulated almost three hundred fonts, ranging from the most plain of Plain Gothics to the very unique and colorful Chromatic French Clarendon Ornamented. Until recently, limited space dictated that most of this collection be housed in storage, and therefore out of the reach of most students and scholars. With the opening of the new and expanded facilities of the Cary Collection, [in 1991], however, has come improved accessibility to all of the library's archives, including the collection of wood type. The need for a thorough and descriptive catalogue of the collection has thus become more imperative. The volume before you now is a response to this need, the result of more than twelve months of cleaning, sorting, identifying, organizing, cataloging, and printing, and the culmination of my graduate studies at RIT.

The portfolio contains specimens of all complete and near complete fonts of wood type, as well as incomplete samples of some unusual designs found in the Cary Collection. One hundred sixty of the 286 fonts in the collection have manufacturer's marks imprinted on one or more sorts, or possess some other distinguishing mark or feature, allowing for positive identification by name, manufacturer, and approximate date. This information is given with the printed specimen of each font. The remaining 126 fonts have been supplied with names that best describe each font based on commonly used typographic language. These names are given enclosed in brackets, and are followed by entries which indicate a manufacturer and type design shown in a catalog of that manufacturer, which closely resembles the specimen shown here.

Also included with each specimen is a decimal number, or in some instances a group of numbers, which refers to a particular font's placement within the organizational scheme developed for the collection. This scheme arranges fonts into specific classes, subclasses, and groups, and assigns each font its own unique number, making the location of fonts within the collection, and the information that is available on them, easily pinpointed. This arrangement is based not on the names of type designs, which tended to be somewhat ambiguous, but rather on the structure of the letterforms themselves, the result being that many designs of similar form can be found grouped together. Each decimal number can be used to refer to an entry within the separate reference manual, which includes information on the completeness of character sets, manufacturers' marks found on the font, the bibliographic source used to identify the font and the location of that source, the location of the font within the Cary Collection's archives, and the donor of that particular font.

For both aesthetic and logical purposes, the portfolio's specimens are arranged within their particular groups in a progression from smallest to largest in size, and when possible within a size, from most condensed to most expanded. Decorated or ornamented fonts such as inlines and outlines are included at the end of the group sections, as are oblique or italic fonts. The organizational scheme has been designed to be open-ended, making the incorporation of new acquisitions into their proper locations as easy as possible. Fonts that are added to the collection in the future are to be included at the end of each group section, no matter what their size or degree of ornamentation.

The reference manual explains in greater detail the organization of the collection, and contains an outline of the organizational scheme along with descriptions of each category and letterform structure diagrams for each font group within the collection. The manual's main reference listing is also accompanied by three cross-reference lists, which allow information about each typeface and manufacturer to be accessed in a number of useful ways.

It should be noted that all of the specimens within this portfolio have been printed from the original wood type, a task which Professor David Pankow, principle advisor for the project, predicted would use up every ounce of patience that I possessed. This assessment was found, at times, to be not too far off the mark. Most of the wood type in the collection ranges from fair to excellent in condition, but much of it also dates from the mid 1800s, and has aged accordingly. And there are a number of fonts which appear to have withstood relentless use and abuse. The purpose of this project has been to render the collection accessible to students and scholars in the spirit of the ideas expressed by Rob Roy Kelly in 1964. Every effort has been made to produce clear images of each letter in every font, but in a number of cases, the type stubbornly resisted these efforts. The most noteworthy examples of some fonts' reluctance to print properly can be seen in the Fat Face designs (4.01.01.00), and in the typefaces manufactured by the Celluloid Stereotype Company of New York.

Finally, as in all projects of this scope, grateful acknowledgments are due to the many people who offered and provided their assistance, suggestions, knowledge, and expertise. I sincerely hope that all of them will discover in this volume their own contributions, and recognize that without their generosity this project could not have been seen to completion.

David P. Wall
July 1992

Classification System

A person faced with the task of organizing a large collection of wood type is faced with a daunting one at best. The method used by Rob Roy Kelly in classifying wood type designs was based on the evolution of these typefaces from three primary models: the roman, the antique, and the gothic letterforms. Almost all designs, he found, were derived from these three basic forms, with the exception of some truly independent inventions which he grouped in a fourth class, called the tuscan class. This method of classification works well for a great number of wood type designs, but begins to falter the further down the evolutionary line one looks, as the differences between gothic tuscan, antique tuscan, and plain tuscan become somewhat garbled, and the relation of these designs to the original parent letterform becomes less and less obvious.

The classification system used in organizing the wood type in the Cary Collection is based not on the evolution or derivation of typeface designs, but rather on the structure of the letterforms themselves. This system was developed under the guidance of Professor Archie Provan in the School of Printing Management and Sciences at RIT, and is modeled after the Typeface Design Grouping scheme of the I.S.O. 9541-1, Annex A, Electronic Font Interchange. The wood type classification system consists of a four level hierarchical structure which groups together type designs having similar characteristics, and uniquely identifies each individual font within the collection. The highest, most general level of the hierarchy is the Class, followed at the second level by the Subclass, at the third level by the Group, and at the fourth and most specific level, by the Font. Descriptions of all levels and categories within the levels are given on the following pages. At the Font level, the individual fonts are numbered sequentially in the order that there were acquired.

In the future, as more fonts of wood type are obtained by the Cary Collection, it is likely that some type designs will not fit reasonably within any of the groupings presently described. This classification system has been tailored specifically for the wood type now on hand, with the intent and understanding that new Group levels can and will be added to the system's structure, to allow for the incorporation of new acquisitions. It therefore becomes the responsibility of the person given the task of cataloguing the new acquisitions to decide whether a Group level is needed, and to take the appropriate measures in each situation. Similarly, it may be found that some wood type designs seem to be associated with more than one grouping within the classification system. On these occasions it is again the responsibility of the cataloger to choose the one Group level which, overall, is most appropriate.

1.00 Inscriptional Class: Upper case only. Based on proportions of Roman Inscriptional letterform (Narrow E, F, L; sweeping tail on R).

2.00 Uncial Class: Based on the writing hands of the 6th-9th Centuries.

3.00 Blackletter Class: Based on the writing hands of the German monasteries and the typeface designs based on those writing hands by printers of Germany, circa 12th-15th Centuries.

3.01 Formal Style Subclass: Characters have a condensed and angular appearance, with few or no curves, and a large x-height.

3.01.01 Serif Group: With Serifs.

4.00 Serif Class: Typefaces which have serifs or ornamented terminals and which are not classed in the above three categories.

4.01 Fine Subclass: Serif thickness is approximately ¼ of stem width or less, and serifs may or may not be bracketed.

4.01.01 Fat Face Group: Stems are straight with unbracketed serifs and great contrast between thick and thin strokes.

4.01.02 Flared Stem Group: Serifs are very short and stubby, and stems flare at ends.

4.01.03 Bracketed Oldstyle Group: Stems are straight with bracketed serifs, and characters E, F, L, T, and Z have bracketed arm serifs.

4.01.04 Bracketed Geometric Group: Stems are straight with bracketed serifs, and characters E, F, L, T, and Z have triangular arm serifs.

4.02 Egyptian Subclass: Serif thickness is more than approximately ¼ of stem width, and serifs are unbracketed.

4.02.01 Antique Group: Serif thickness is equal to or thinner than the stem width of the character, and strokes are either straight or curved.

4.02.02 Grecian Group: Serif thickness is equal to or thinner than the stem width of the character, and bowls of characters are made up of short straight strokes.

4.02.03 French Antique Group: Serifs are thicker then the stem width of the character.

4.03 Clarendon/Tuscan Subclass: Serif thickness is more than approximately ¼ of stem width, and serifs are bracketed.

4.03.01 Clarendon Group: Serif thickness is equal to or thinner than the stem width.

4.03.02 Stub Serif Group: Serifs are very short, and serif thickness is equal to or thinner than the stem width of the character. Also, the terminal at the apex of A is sheared, and the lower stem of the G has a spur itself.

4.03.03 French Clarendon Group: Serifs are thicker then the stem width, and are bracketed.

4.03.04 Ætna Group: Serif thickness is equal to or thinner than the stem width, and serifs are sheared.

4.03.05 Tuscan Group: Serifs are thicker than stem width and are spurred, giving the appearance of having points turned back upon stem.

4.04 Pointed Subclass: Serifs end in a point.

4.04.01 Bracketed Group: Serifs are bracketed to point.

4.04.02 Angled Group: Serifs have angled fillets which give the appearance of triangular shaped serifs.

4.04.03 Combination Group: Both of the above serif structures can be found on characters in this group.

4.05 Rounded Subclass: Serifs are rounded or bulbous.

4.05.01 Traditional Group: These typefaces are based on designs from historical models dating between the 15th and 17th Centuries. In large sizes these designs appear to have rounded serifs.

4.05.02 Modern Group: These typefaces are not based on historical models, and have rounded or bulbous serifs.

4.06 Cupped/Indented Subclass: Serif/terminals are notched, cupped, or indented in some way.

4.06.01 Slab Group: Serif thickness is more than ¼ of stem width, and serifs are bracketed.

4.06.02 Flared/Lobed Group: Serifs/terminals flare out from stem and have two distinct and rounded lobes.

4.06.03 Flared Pointed Group: Serifs/terminals flare out from stem and are pointed.

4.06.04 Curved Point Group: Serifs/terminals are points that are turned back upon stem.

4.06.05 Multi-Pointed Group: Serifs/terminals are made up of many elaborately curved and upturned points.

4.07 Protruding Subclass: Serifs/terminals have ornamentation that protrudes or projects from stem end.

4.07.01 Slab Serif/Dotted Group: Serif thickness is greater than stem width and serifs have half-round ornaments that extend outward from stem end.

4.07.02 Flared/Dotted Group: Serifs/terminals flare outward from stem and have half-round ornaments that extend outward from stem end.

4.07.03 Flared/Pointed Group: Serifs/terminals flare outward from stem and have points extending outward from stem end.

4.07.04 Flared/Ornamented Group: Serifs/terminals flare outward from stem and are adorned with ornamentation, other than dots or points, which extends outward from stem end.

4.07.05 Straight/Pointed Group: Stems are straight, with points extending from stem end. (Essentially a sans serif with a pointed or spurred terminal).

5.00 Sans Serif Class: Typefaces that have no serifs or otherwise ornamented terminals, and are not classed as scripts.

5.01 Square Stem Subclass: Stem ends are square.

5.01.01 Plain Gothic Group: These are the earliest of the sans serif designs (circa 1815). Characters may have some stress variation, but are generally monotone, and the tail of the R is curved.

5.01.02 Unit Gothic Group: Characters may have slightly more stress variation than Plain Gothic. Also, the tail of the R is straight, and some terminals may be sheared.

5.01.03 Geometric Group: These designs are monotone, and are basically composed of circles and straight lines.

5.01.04 Angled Group: Bowls of characters are made up of sort straight strokes, and some terminals may be sheared.

5.02 Rounded Stem Subclass: The ends of the stems are rounded.

5.02.01 Rounded Plain Group: A Plain Gothic design with rounded stem ends.

5.03 Flared Stem Subclass: The ends of the stems flare outward.

5.03.01 Flared Plain Group: The bowls of characters are made up of one rounded stroke.

5.03.02 Flared Tuscan Group: The bowls of characters are made up of more than one stroke.

6.00 Script Class: Typefaces that are designed to appear as handwriting.

6.01 Joined Subclass: Characters are connected.

6.01.01 Monotone Group: Strokes of characters have little or no stress variation. Characters appear to be drawn with a pen which is not broad edged.

7.00 Miscellaneous Class: Typefaces that are highly stylized or decorated, and which do not fit into any of the above classes.

7.01 Neat Ends Subclass: Characters have long appendages extending from the end of a stroke.

7.01.01 Serif Group: With serifs.

Using the Type Specimen

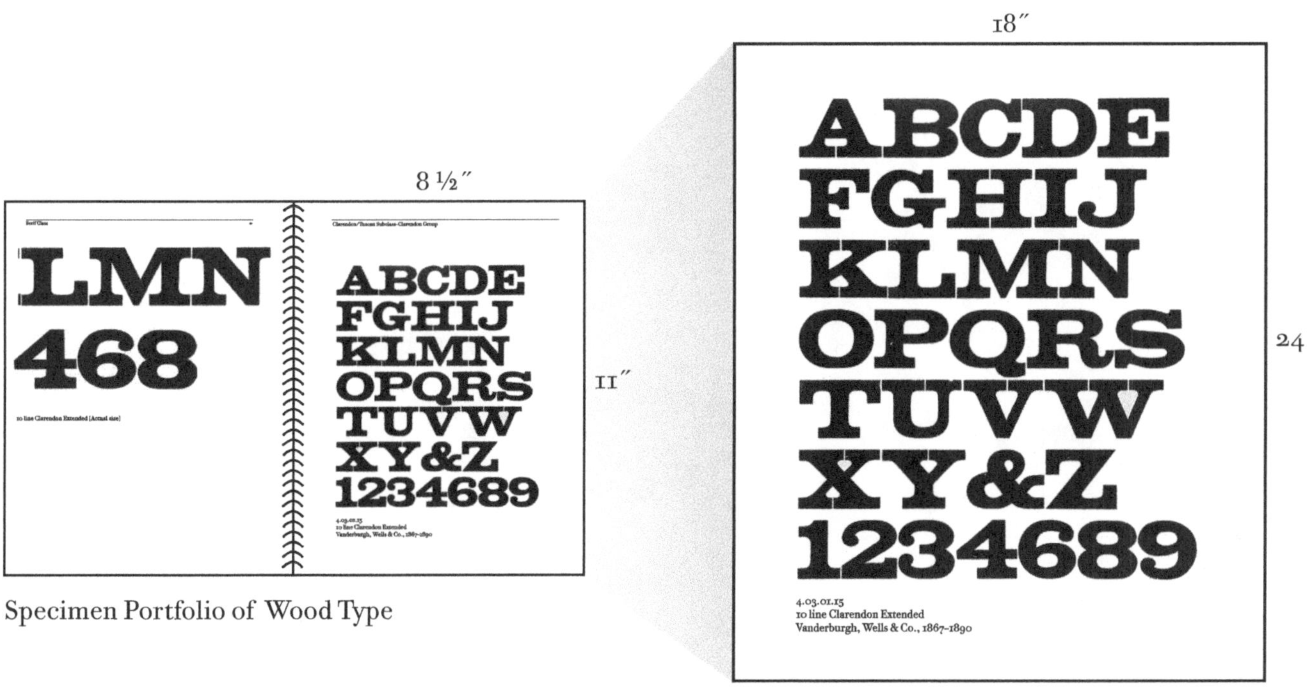

Specimen Portfolio of Wood Type

Original Specimen

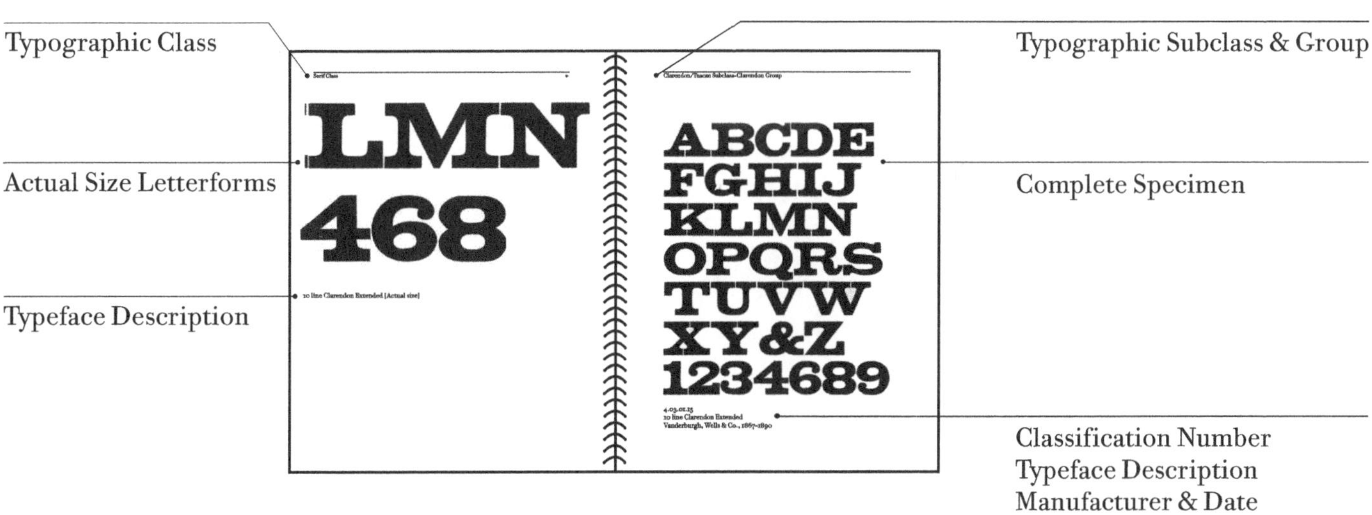

Blackletter Class

Based on the writing hands of the German monasteries and the typeface designs derived thereof by German printers, circa 12th–15th centuries.

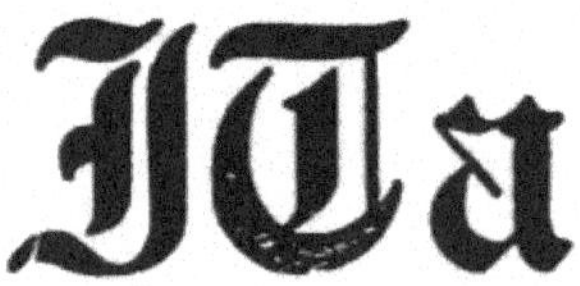

4 line [Blackletter] cf. Hamilton: No. 613 [Actual Size]

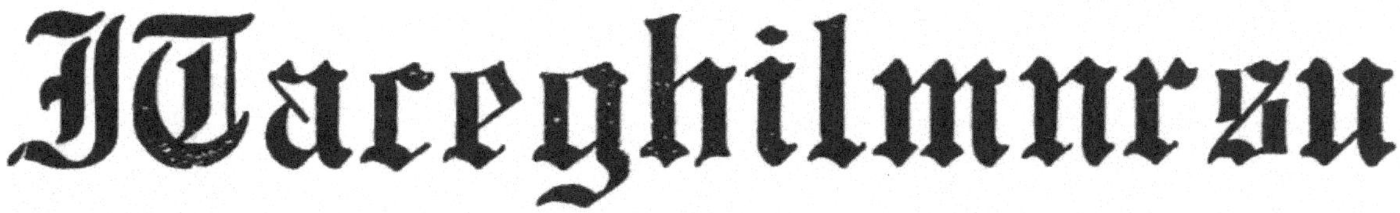

3.01.01.01
4 line [Blackletter] cf. Hamilton: No. 613
Manufacturer and date unknown

Serif Class

Typefaces which have serifs or ornamented terminals.

WXYZ!

4 line [Roman Fat Face] cf. Hamilton: No. 241 [Actual size]

JKL
cdefg

4 Line [Roman Fat Face Extended] cf. Hamilton: No. 5151 [Actual size]

ABCDEFGHIJKLMNOP
RSTUVWXYZ!

4.01.01.01
4 line [Roman Fat Face] cf. Hamilton: No. 241
Manufacturer and date unknown

ABCDEFG
HIJKLM
NOPQRS
TUVWXY
Z& ÆŒ
abcdefghi
jklmnop
qrstuvw
xyz!æœ
ff fi fl ffi ffl

4.01.01.02
4 Line [Roman Fat Face Extended] cf. Hamilton: No. 5151
Manufacturer and date unknown

OPQRST

5 line [Roman Modern] cf. Page: Roman Condensed Light Face [Actual size]

KLMNOPQ

4 line Hamilton: No. 5151 [Actual size]

ghik 789

5 Line [Roman Fat Face] cf. Hamilton: No. 241 [Actual size]

ABCDEFGHIJKLMN
OPQRSTUVWXY&Z

4.01.01.03
5 line [Roman Modern] cf. Page: Roman Condensed Light Face
Manufacturer and date unknown

ACDEIKLMNOPQ
RSTUVXYZ&
abdefghiklmno
qrstuvwxy
ff fl ffi fi ffl œ
$1234567890

4.01.01.04
5 Line [Roman Fat Face] cf. Hamilton: No. 241
Manufacturer and date unknown

Y&Z!

5 line [Roman Fat Face] cf. Page: Roman No. 2 [Actual size]

IFG
134

6 Line [Roman Fat Face] cf. Hamilton: No. 5151 [Actual size]

ABCDEFGHIJKL
MNOPRTUVWX
Y&Z!

4.01.01.05
5 line [Roman Fat Face] cf. Page: Roman No. 2
Manufacturer and date unknown

ABC
DFG
HIJL
MNO
PRS
TUV
WXZ
13456

4.01.01.06
6 Line [Roman Fat Face] cf. Hamilton: No. 5151
Manufacturer and date unknown

ABCD efgh

æœﬀﬁﬂﬄ $1234

7 line [Roman Fat Face] cf. Page: Roman Extra Condensed [Actual size]

HIJKL 6789

8 line [Roman Fat Face Condensed] cf. AWT (Conn): No. 2017 [Actual size]

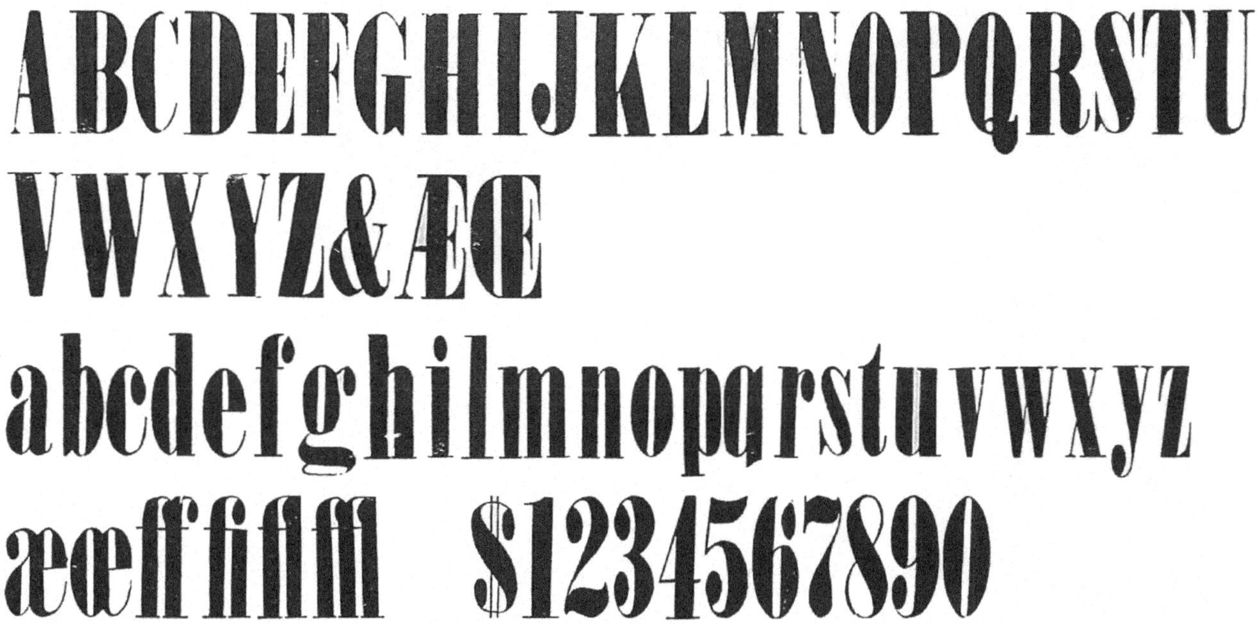

4.01.01.07
7 line [Roman Fat Face] cf. Page: Roman Extra Condensed
Manufacturer and date unknown

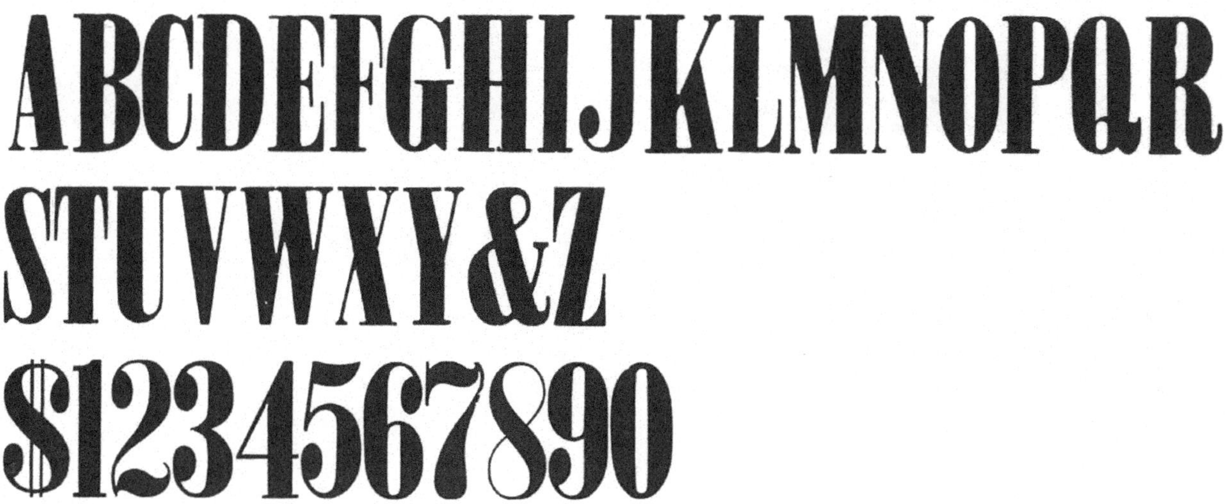

4.01.01.08 & 4.01.01.09
8 line [Roman Fat Face Condensed] cf. AWT (Conn.): No. 2017
Manufacturer and date unknown

NOPQ Æ

fghi

ffiffl œ

8 line [Roman Fat Face] cf. Hamilton: No. 242 [Actual size]

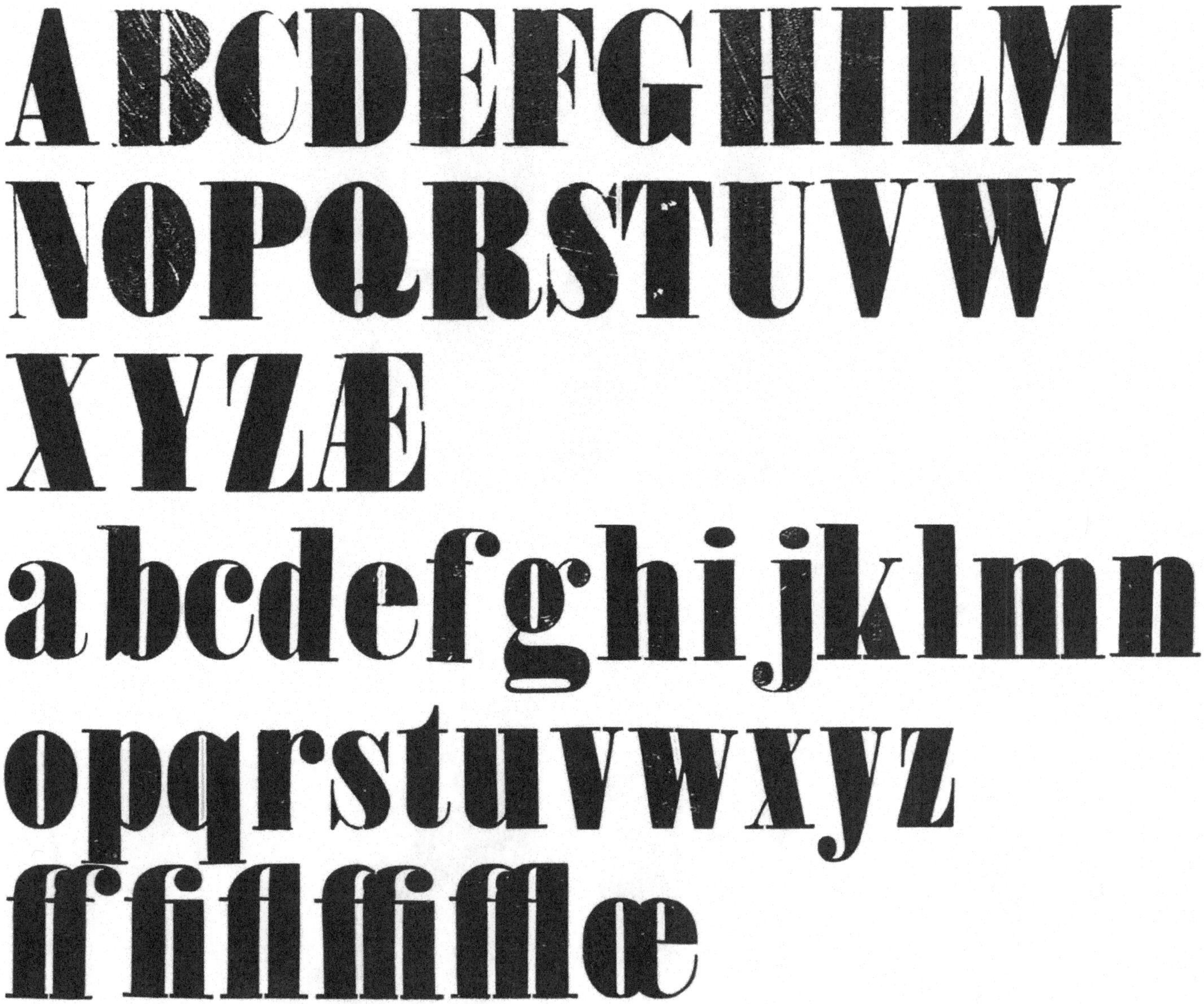

4.01.01.10
8 line [Roman Fat Face] cf. Hamilton: No. 242
Manufacturer and date unknown

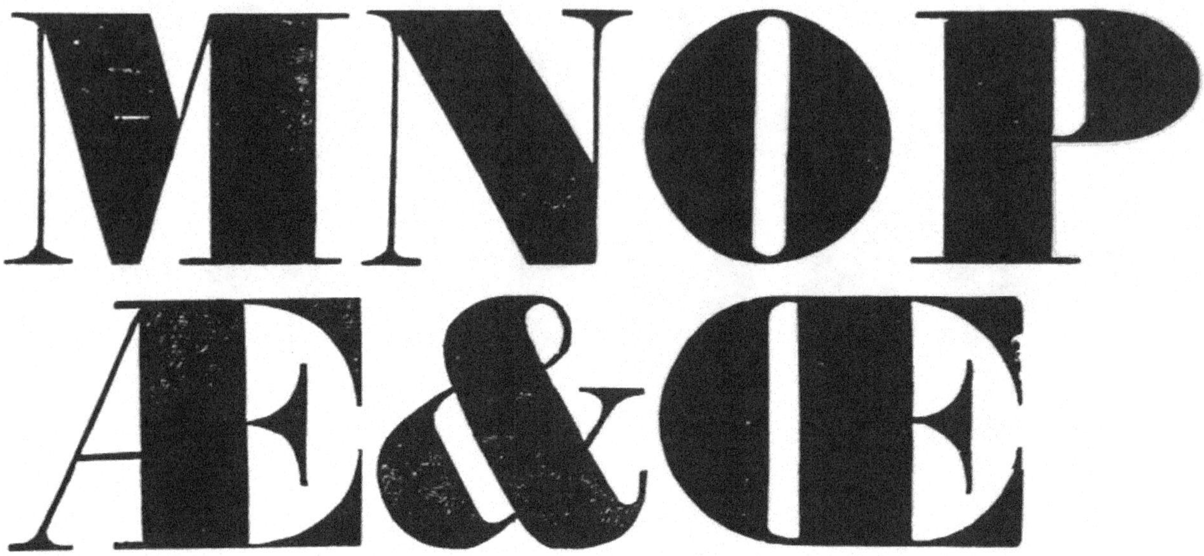

8 line [Roman Fat Face] cf. Page: Roman [Actual size]

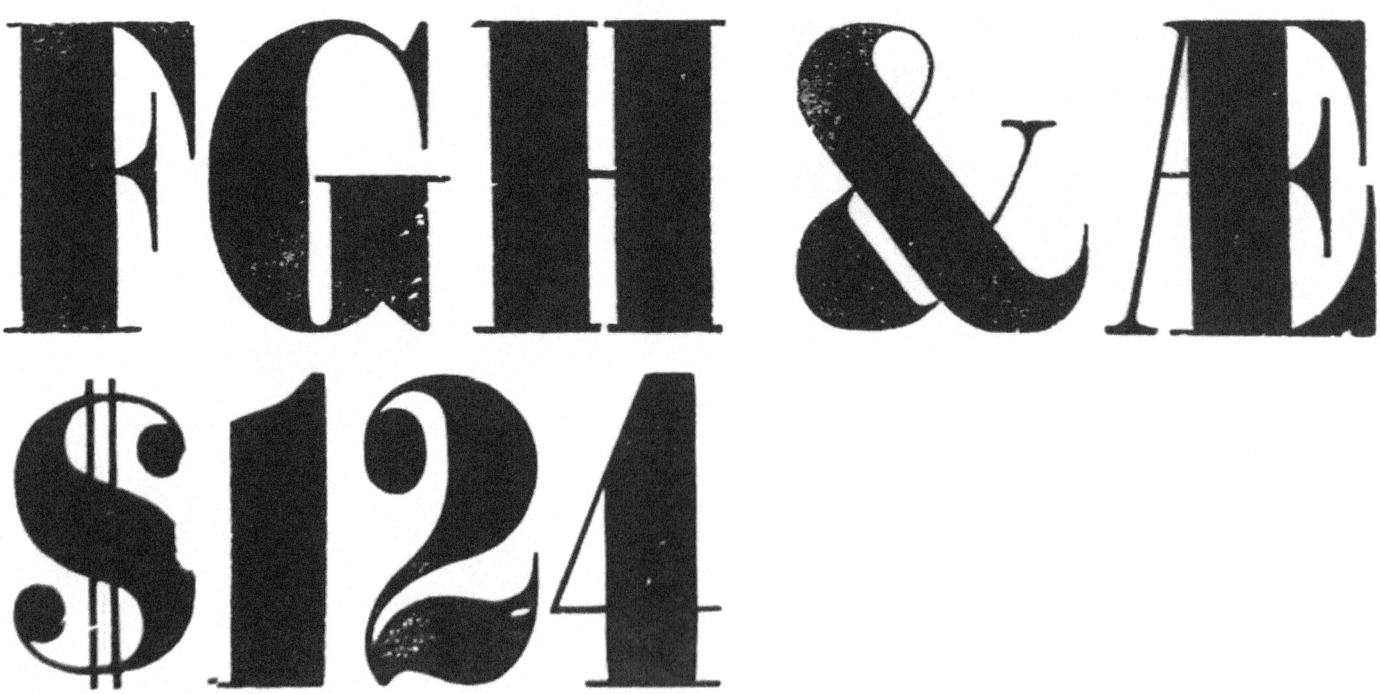

10 line [Roman Fat Face] cf. Hamilton: No. 212 [Actual size]

ABCDEFGH
IJKLMNOP
QRSTUVW
XYZÆ&Œ

4.01.01.11
8 line [Roman Fat Face] cf. Page: Roman
Manufacturer and date unknown

ABCDEFGHI
JKLMNOPQR
STUWXYZ&Æ
$124567890!

4.01.01.12
10 line [Roman Fat Face] cf. Hamilton: No. 212
Manufacturer and date unknown

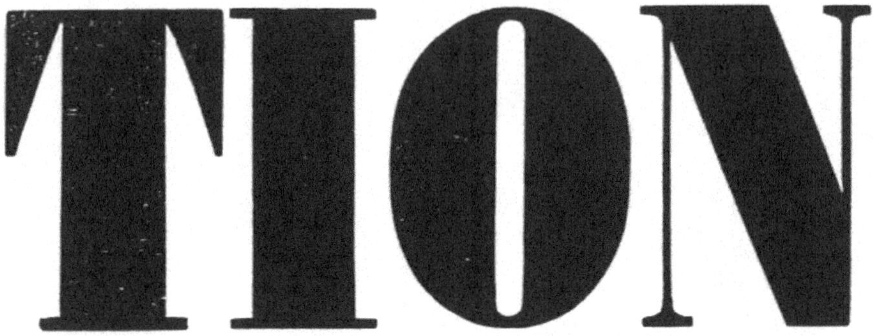

10 line [Roman Fat Face] cf. Page: Roman Condensed [Actual size]

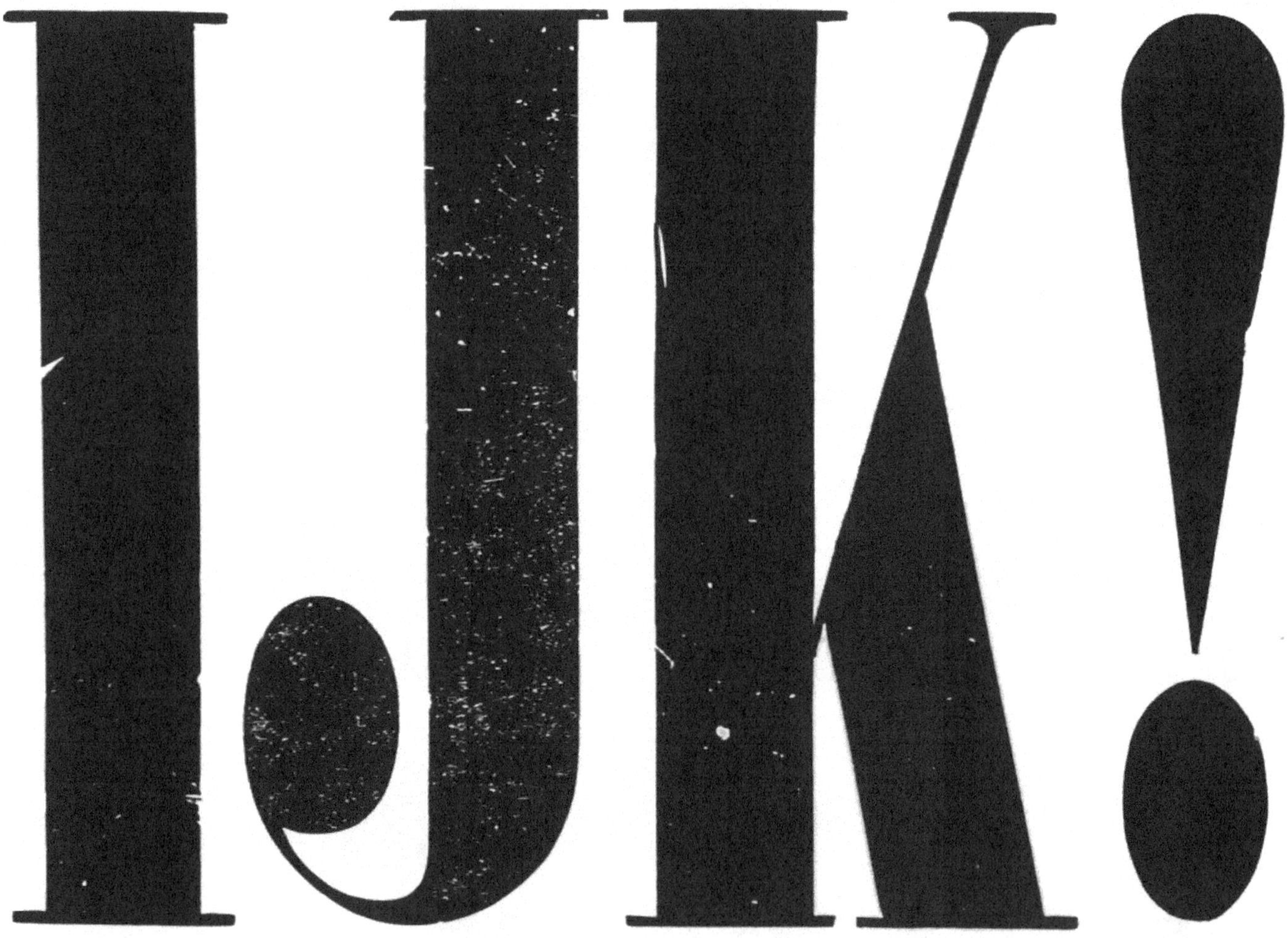

30 line Roman Extra Condensed [Actual size]

AUCTION

4.01.01.13
10 line [Roman Fat Face] cf. Page: Roman Condensed
Manufacturer and date unknown

ABCDEFGHIJK
LMNOPQRSTU
VW!

4.01.01.14
30 line Roman Extra Condensed
William H. Page & Co., 1859 or later

EFG
&ÆŒ

8 line [Roman Fat Face Open Shade] [Actual size]

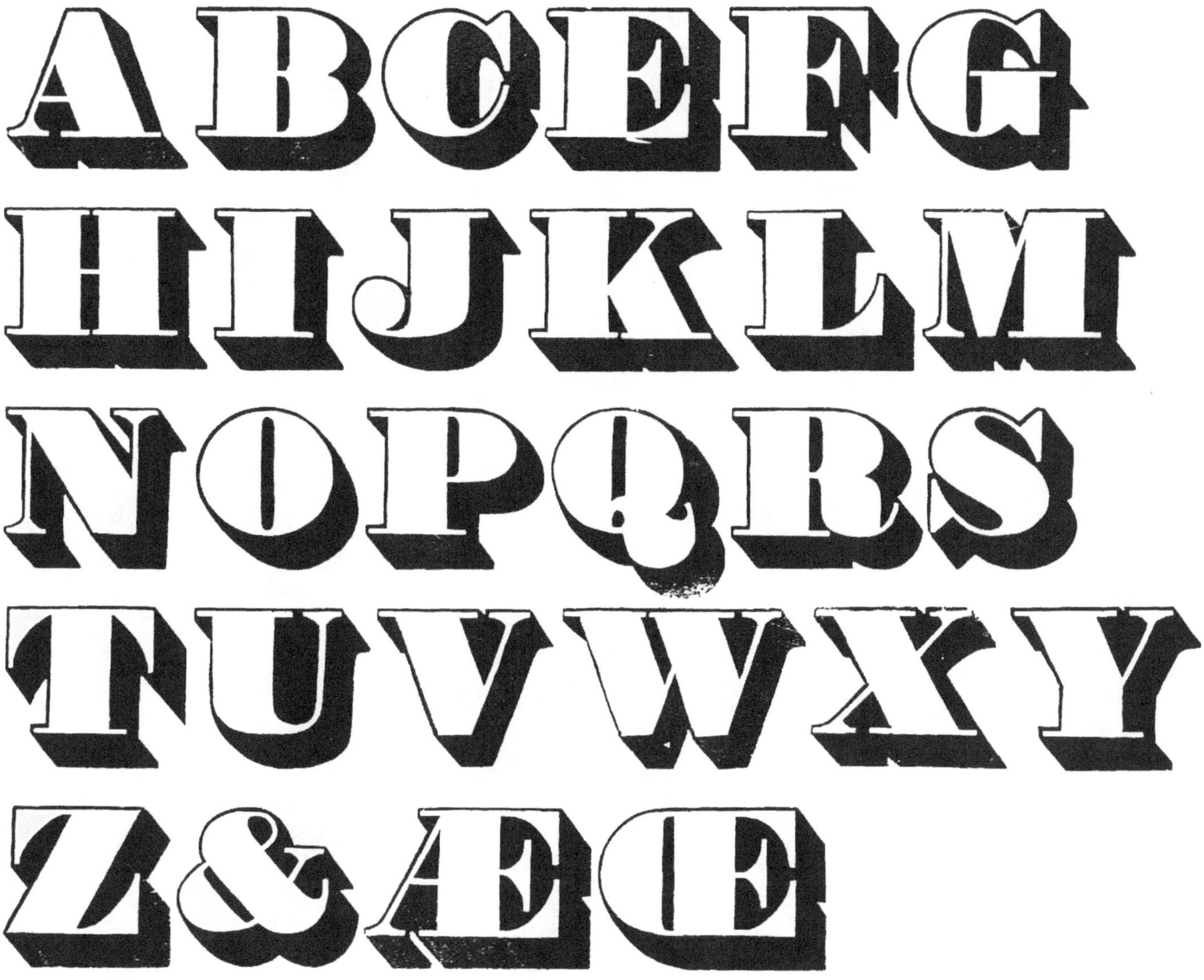

4.01.01.15
8 line [Roman Fat Face Open Shade]
Manufacturer and date unknown

RSTU
XY&Z!

15 line No. 2158 [Actual size]

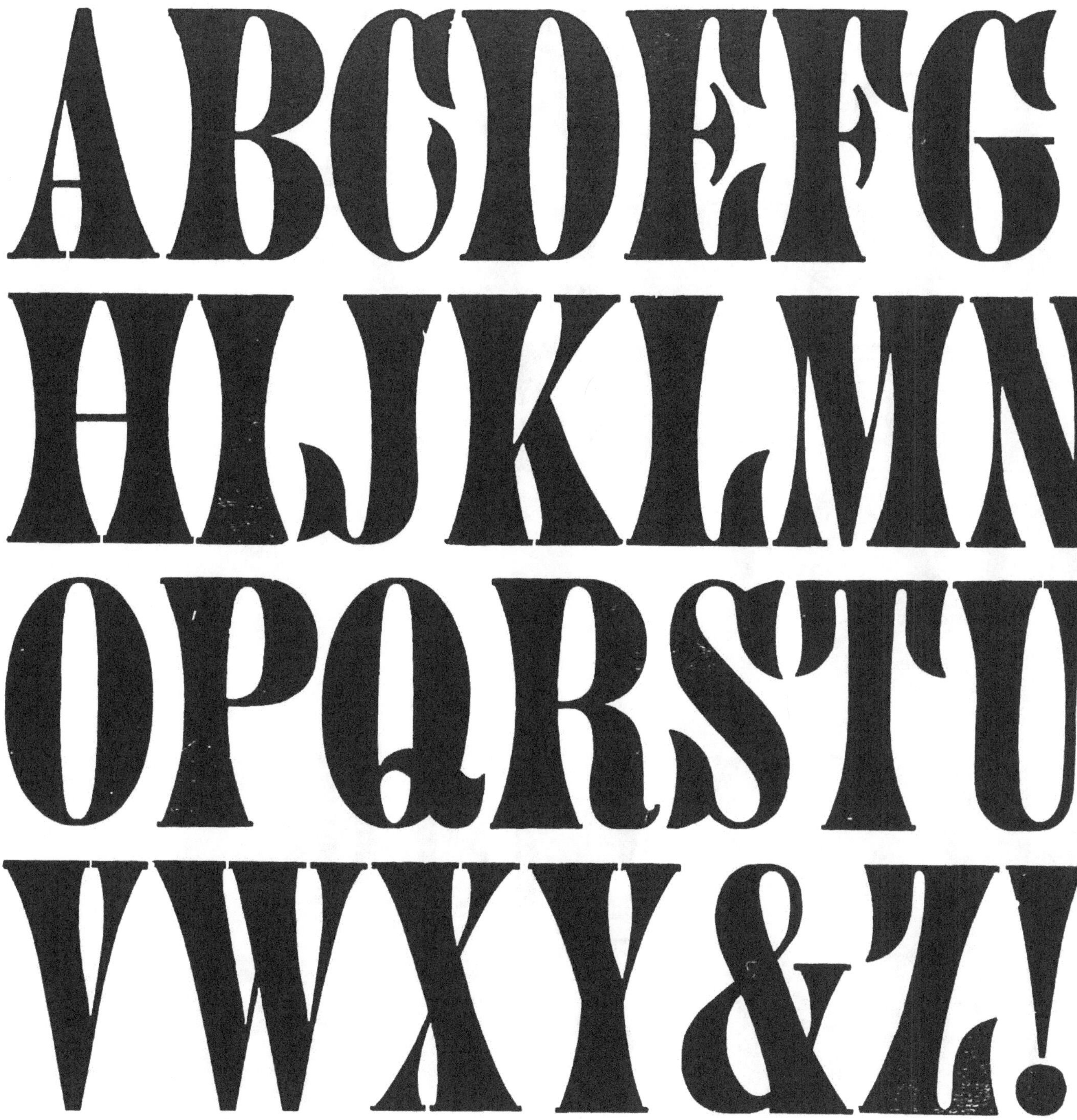

4.01.02.01
15 line No. 2158
American Wood Type Co. (Conn.), after 1885

ABCDE
ddefgghij
ffiffiffifflffl&
$1234

5 line [Roman] cf. Page: Old Style [Actual size]

OPST ghijk
flfflffi $134.56¢

6 line Old Style Condensed [Actual size]

ABCDEFGHIJKLMN
OPRSTUVWXYZ
abcddefgghijkklmn
oopqqrrrstuvwxyz
ff ff fi fi fl fl ffi ffi ffl ffl &
$1234567890

4.01.03.01
5 line [Roman] cf. Page: Old Style
Manufacturer and date unknown

ABCDEFGHIJKLMN
OPSTVWXYZ
bcdefghijklmnopq
stuvwxy
ff fi fl ffl ffi $134.56¢

4.01.03.02
6 line Old Style Condensed
William H. Page & Co., 1857–1859

WXY&Z

8 line [Roman Modern Condensed] cf. AWT (LI): Old Style No. 6 [Actual size]

ABCDEF

8 line [Roman Modern Condensed] cf. Hamilton: No. 231 [Actual size]

WY&78

12 line [Roman Condensed] cf. Hamilton: No. 629 [Actual size]

ABCDEFGHIJKLMNO
PQRSTUVWXY&Z

4.01.03.03
8 line [Roman Modern Condensed] cf. AWT (LI): Old Style No. 6
Manufacturer and date unknown

ABCDEFGHIJKLMN
OPRSTUVWXY&Z

4.01.03.04
8 line [Roman Modern Condensed] cf. Hamilton: No. 231
Manufacturer and date unknown

BCFGIJLNOS
VWY&
13467890

4.01.03.05
12 line [Roman Condensed] cf. Hamilton: No. 629
Manufacturer and date unknown

LMNOPQ
ghijklm
$1234567890

4 line [Roman Inline] cf. Hamilton: Cameo Highlight, No. 834 [Actual size]

ABCDEFGHIJKLMNOPQ
RSTUVWY&Z
abcdefghijklmnopqrstuv
wxyz $1234567890

4.01.03.06
4 line [Roman Inline] cf. Hamilton: Cameo Highlight, No. 834
Manufacturer and date unknown

PQRST
cdefghij ﬀﬁﬂ
$123456

4 line [Ætna] cf. Hamilton: No. 62 [Actual size]

XY&Z

6 line Painters' Roman [Actual size]

HIJKL

12 line [Ætna Condensed] cf. Hamilton: No. 253 [Actual size]

ABCDEFGHIJKLMN
OPQRSTUVWXY&Z
abcdefghijklmnop
qrstuvwxyz ﬀﬁﬂﬃ
$1234567890

4.01.04.01
4 line [Ætna] cf. Hamilton: No. 62
Manufacturer and date unknown

ABCDEFGHIJ
KLMNOPQRS
TUVWXY&Z

4.01.04.02
6 line Painters' Roman
Vanderburgh, Wells & Co., 1867-1890

ABDEFGHIJKLM
NOPRSTVWXY&Z

4.01.04.03
12 line [Ætna Condensed] cf. Hamilton: No. 253
The Celluloid Stereotype Company, 1885-1900

XYZ&
abcdef
4567

12 line Painters' Roman Condensed [Actual size]

ABCDEFGH
IJKLMNOP
QRSTUVW
XYZ&
abcdefghi
klmnopqr
stuvwxyz
1234567890

4.01.04.04
12 line Painters' Roman Condensed
Vanderburgh, Wells & Co., 1867–1890

WXY&Z

3 line [Antique Extended] cf. M&W: Antique Extended [Actual size]

NOPQ

3 line [Antique Extended] cf. M&W: Antique Extended [Actual size]

JKLM

4 line No. 51 [Actual size]

RSTU&$34

4 line No. 51 [Actual size]

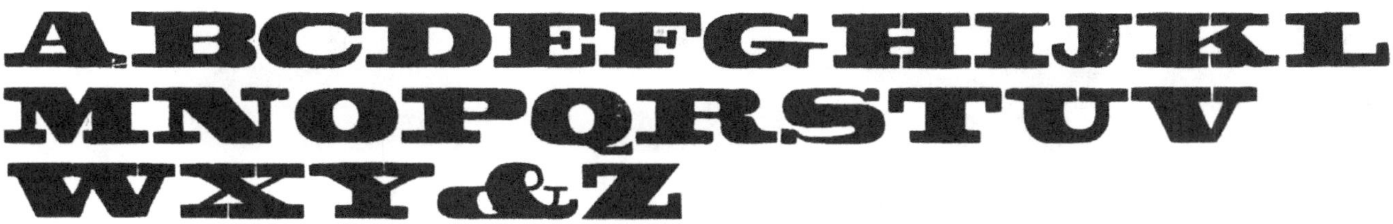

4.02.01.01
3 line [Antique Extended] cf. M&W: Antique Extended
Manufacturer and date unknown

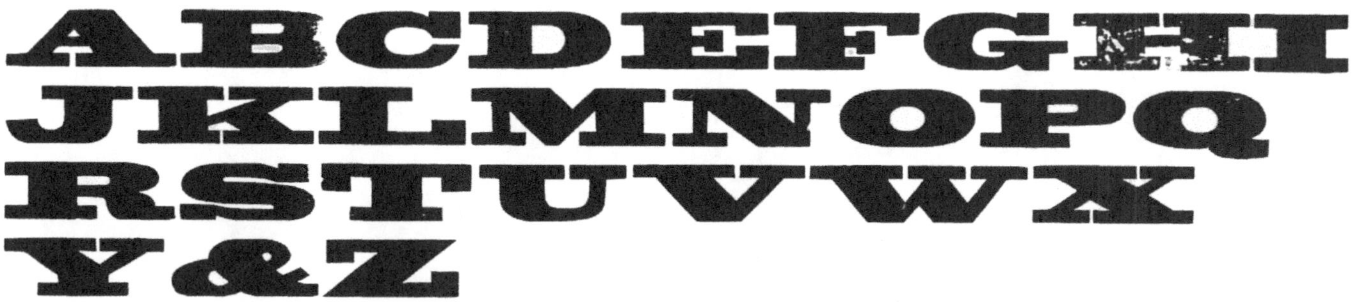

4.02.01.02
3 line [Antique Extended] cf. M&W: Antique Extended
Manufacturer and date unknown

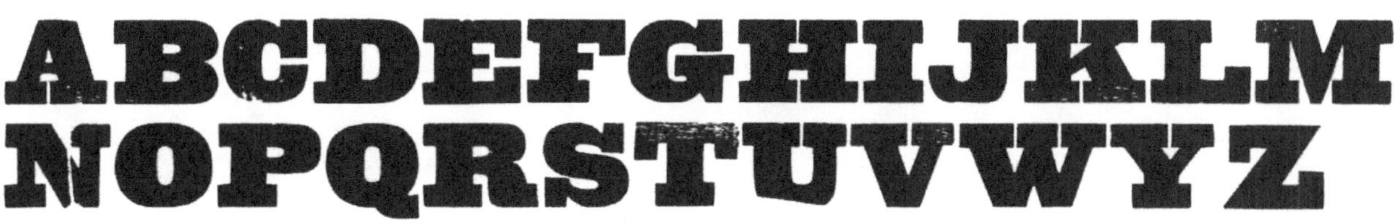

4.02.01.03
4 line No. 51
Hamilton Manufacturing Co., 1880–1889

4.02.01.04
4 line No. 51
Hamilton Manufacturing Co., 1880–1889

OPQS
1234

4 line [Antique Extended] cf. Hamilton: No. 254 [Actual size]

ABC

4 line Antique Extended [Actual size]

DEGHIJKLM

5 line [Antique Condensed] cf. Hamilton: No. 87 [Actual size]

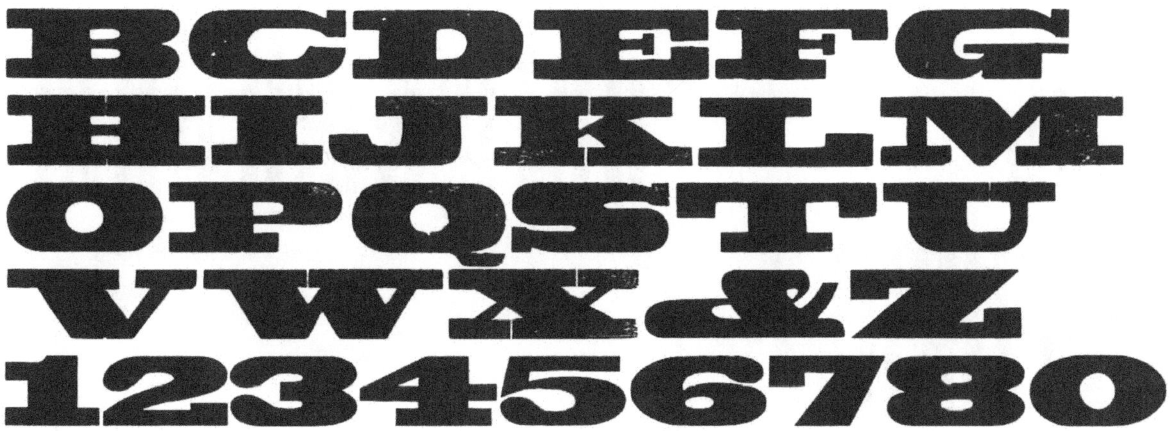

4.02.01.05
4 line [Antique Extended] cf. Hamilton: No. 254
Manufacturer and date unknown

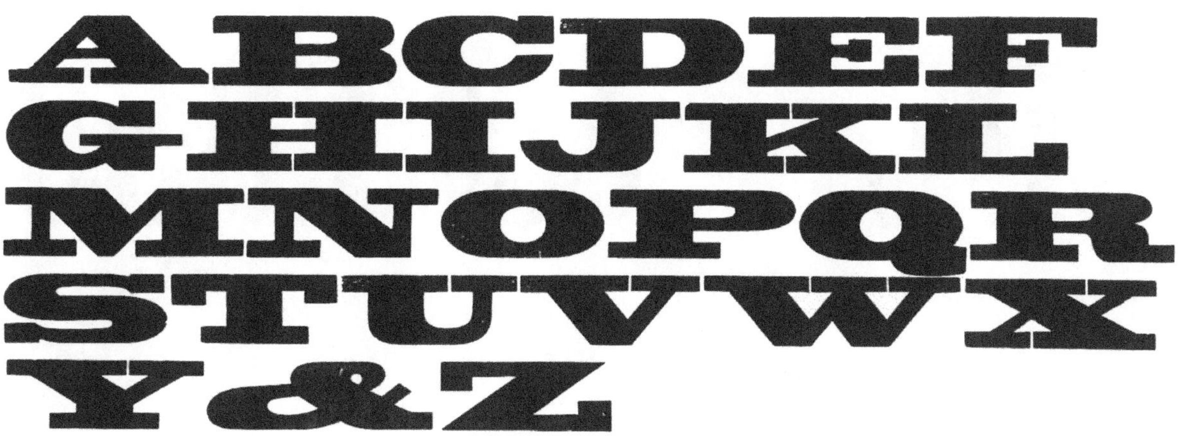

4.02.01.06
4 line Antique Extended
Vanderburgh, Wells & Co., 1867-1890

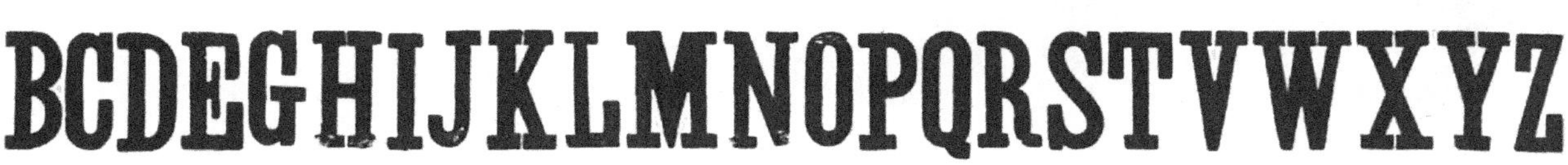

4.02.01.07
5 line [Antique Condensed] cf. Hamilton: No. 87
Manufacturer and date unknown

XYZ&ÆŒ defg&æfffiflffi

$1234567890

6 line Antique Double Extra Condensed No. 2 [Actual size]

ABCDE &$12356

6 line [Antique Condensed] cf. Hamilton: No. 87 [Actual size]

7890

6 line [Antique] cf. Hamilton: No. 5013 [Actual size]

ABCDEFGHIJKLMNOPQRSTUVWXYZ&ÆŒ
abcdefghijklmnopqrstuvwxyz&æfffiflffifflœ
$1234567890

4.02.01.08
6 line Antique Double Extra Condensed No. 2
Vanderburgh, Wells & Co., 1864-1867

ABCDEFGHIJKLMNOPQRST
UVWXYZ&$123567890

4.02.01.09
6 line [Antique Condensed] cf. Hamilton: No. 87
Manufacturer and date unknown

1267890

4.02.01.10
6 line [Antique] cf. Hamilton: No. 5013
Manufacturer and date unknown

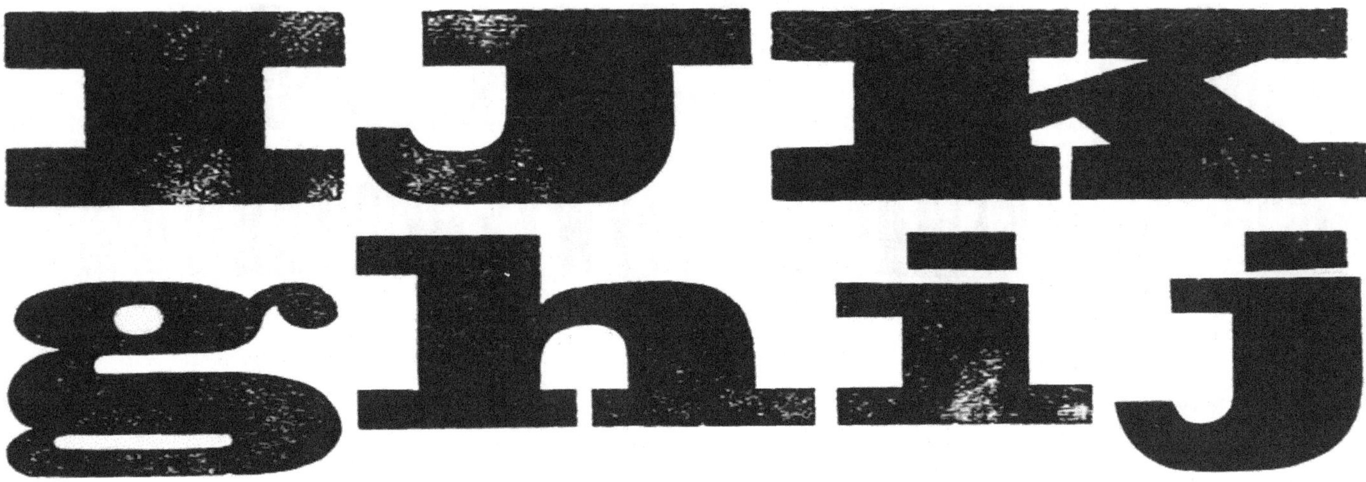

6 line [Antique Extended] cf. Hamilton: No. 77 [Actual size]

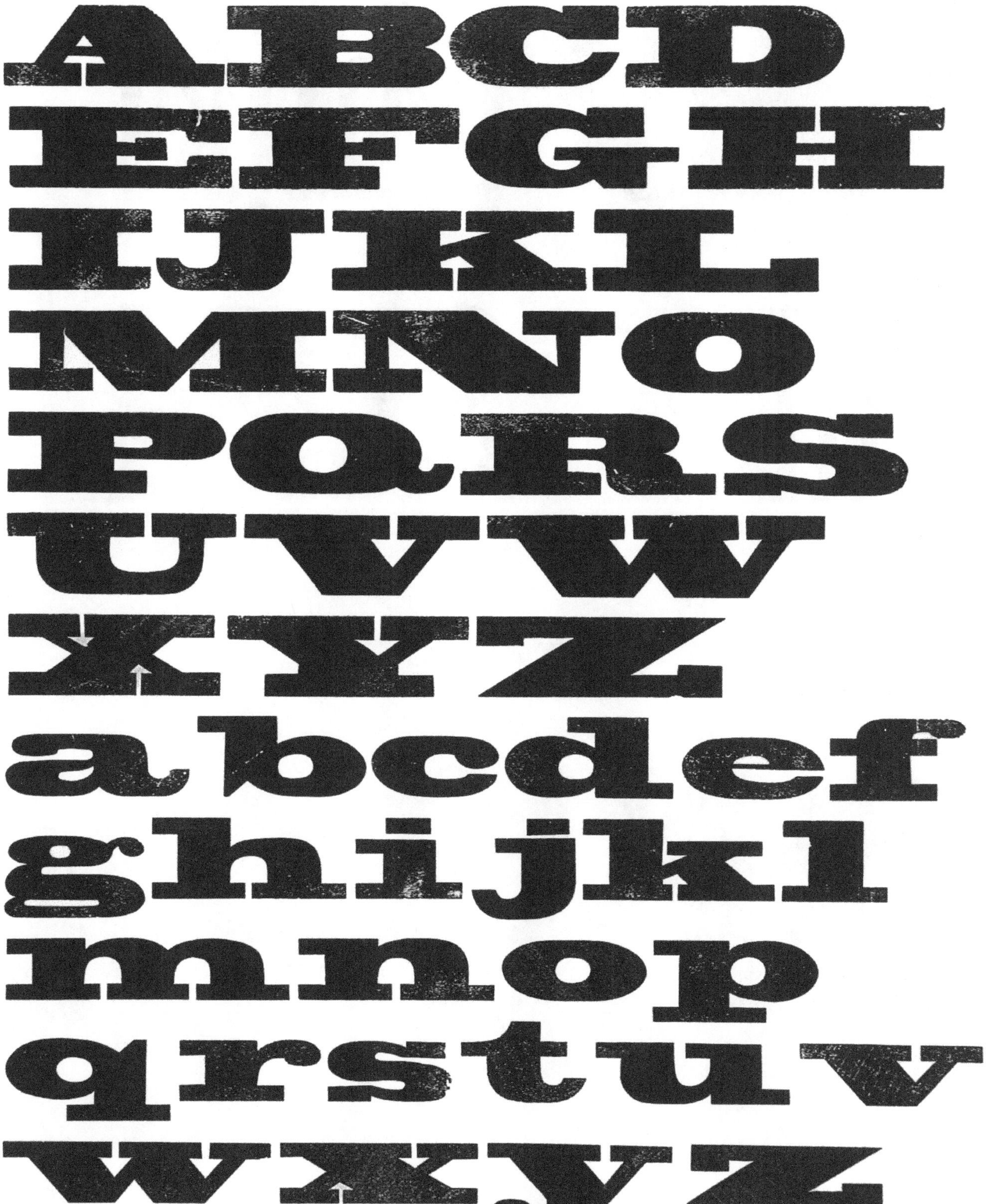

4.02.01.11
6 line [Antique Extended] cf. Hamilton: No. 77
Manufacturer and date unknown

EFGHI ghijkl

ff fi ffi $1234

8 line No. 2044 [Actual size]

MOP

10 line [Antique Condensed] cf. Hamilton: No. 87 [Actual size]

ABCDEFGHIJKLMNOPQ
RSTUVWXY&Z
abcdefghijklmnoprstuvw
xyz ff fi ffi $1234567890

4.02.01.12
8 line No. 2044
American Wood Type Co. (Conn.), after 1885

BCDEFGJKMOP
TUVWYZ

4.02.01.13
10 line [Antique Condensed] cf. Hamilton: No. 87
Manufacturer and date unknown

acdefg ff fi fl ffi ffl

10 line [Antique Condensed] cf. Hamilton: No. 87 [Actual size]

EFGHI
$123456

10 line Antique Extra Condensed [Actual size]

acdefghiklmnoqrstuvx
ffiflffifl

4.02.01.14
10 line [Antique Condensed] cf. Hamilton: No. 87
Manufacturer and date unknown

ABCDEFGHIJKL
MNOPQRSTUVW
XYZ $1234567890

4.02.01.15
10 line Antique Extra Condensed
William H. Page & Co., 1857-1859

w

e 1

10 line Antique Extended [Actual size]

RSTV

14 line Antique Extra Condensed No. 3 [Actual size]

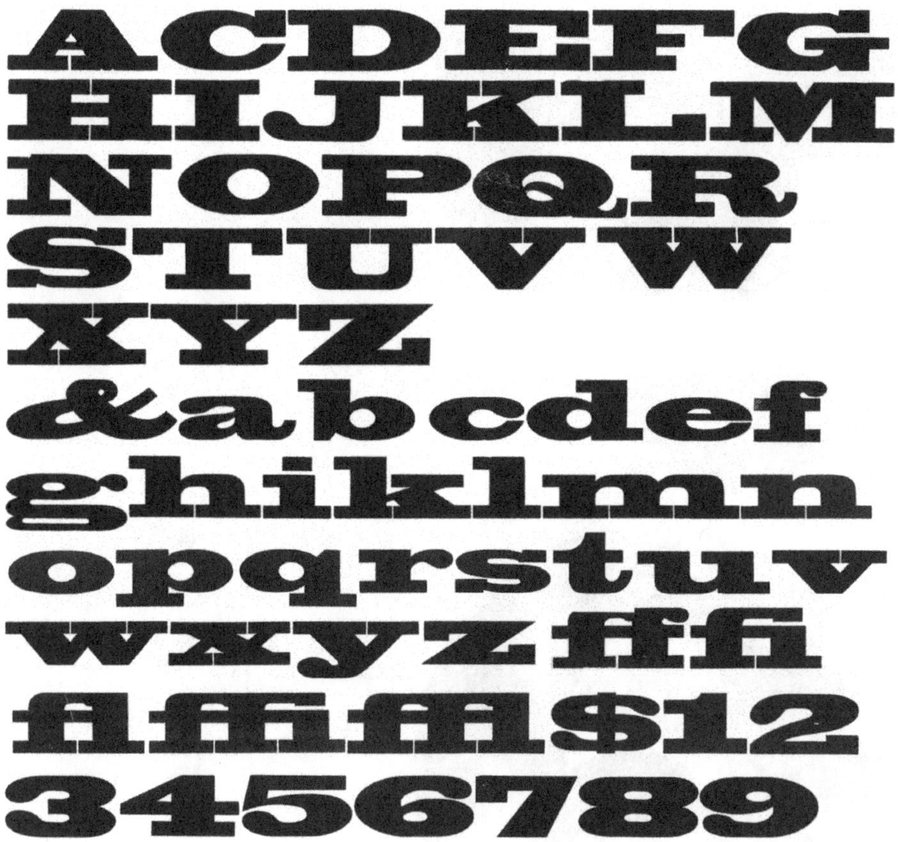

4.02.01.16
10 line Antique Extended
William H. Page & Co., 1859 or later

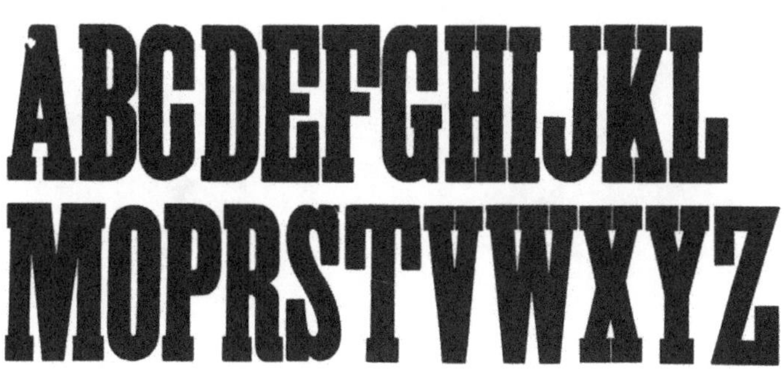

4.02.01.17
14 line Antique Extra Condensed No. 3
William H. Page & Co., 1857–1859

EF
PQ

15 line [Antique] cf. Page: Antique No. 4 [Actual size]

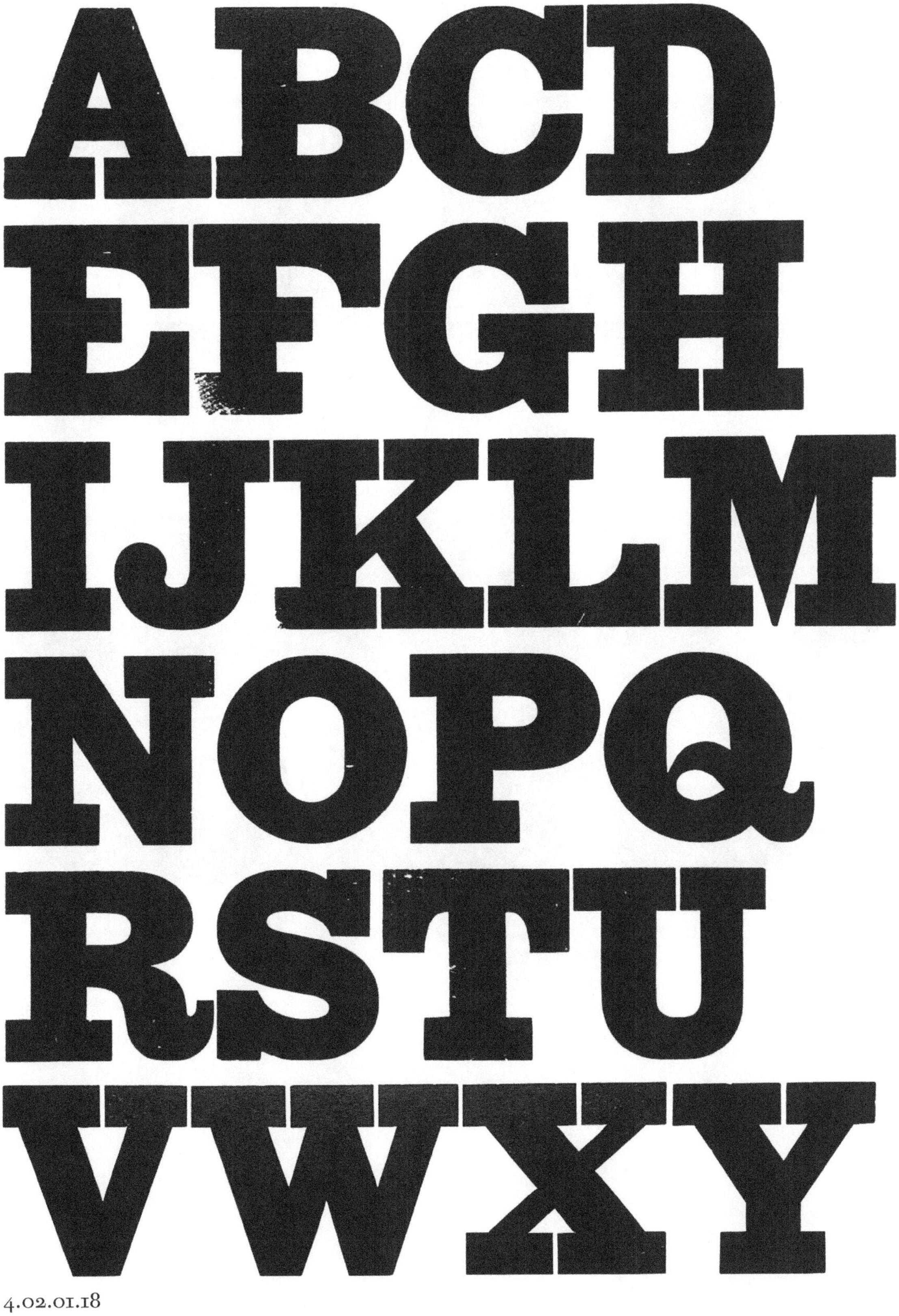

4.02.01.18
15 line [Antique] cf. Page: Antique No. 4
Manufacturer and date unknown

defg
1239

15 line [Antique] cf. Hamilton: No. 178 [Actual size]

abcdefg
hijklm
nopqrs
tuvwx
yzff
12390

4.02.01.19
15 line [Antique] cf. Hamilton: No. 178
Manufacturer and date unknown

PQRST
$123

20 line Antique Double Extra Condensed [Actual size]

ABCDEFGHIJLMNO

PQRSTUVWXY&Z

$1234567890

4.02.01.20
20 line Antique Double Extra Condensed
William H. Page & Co., 1870 or later

ABC
XY&Z

20 line Antique Extra Condensed [Actual size]

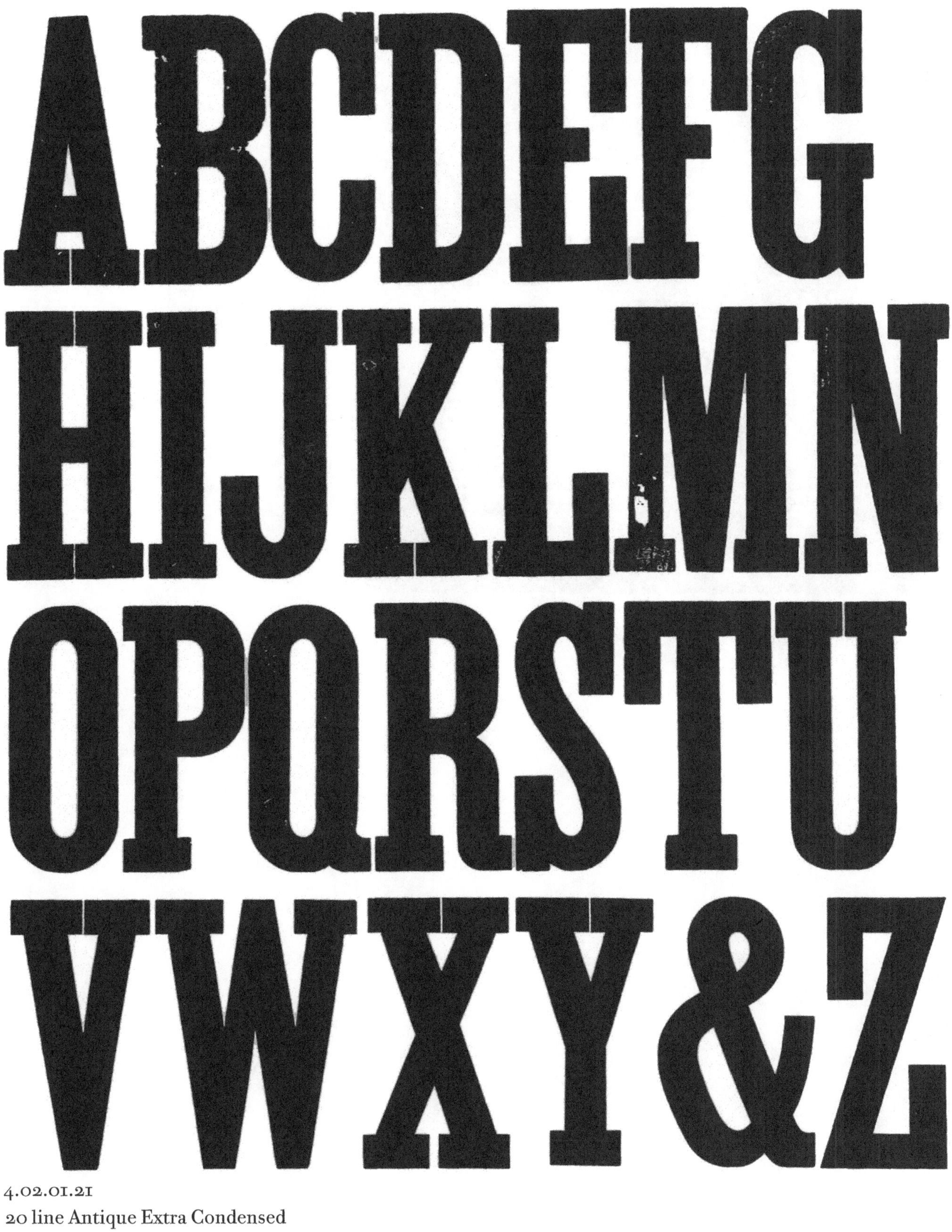

4.02.01.21
20 line Antique Extra Condensed
William H. Page & Co., 1857–1859

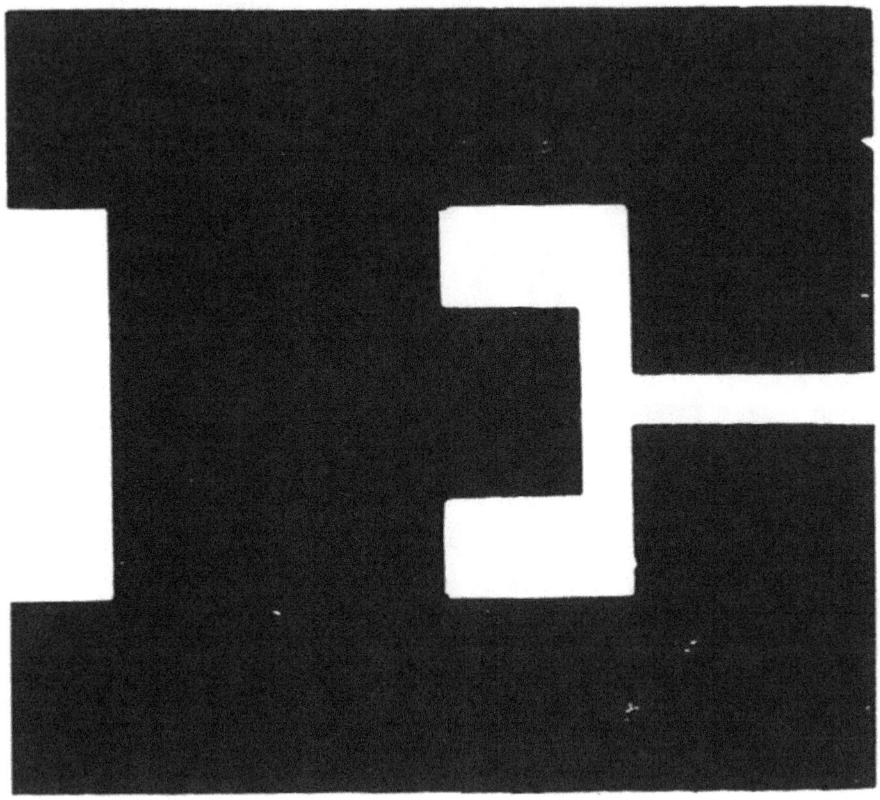

25 line Antique [Actual size]

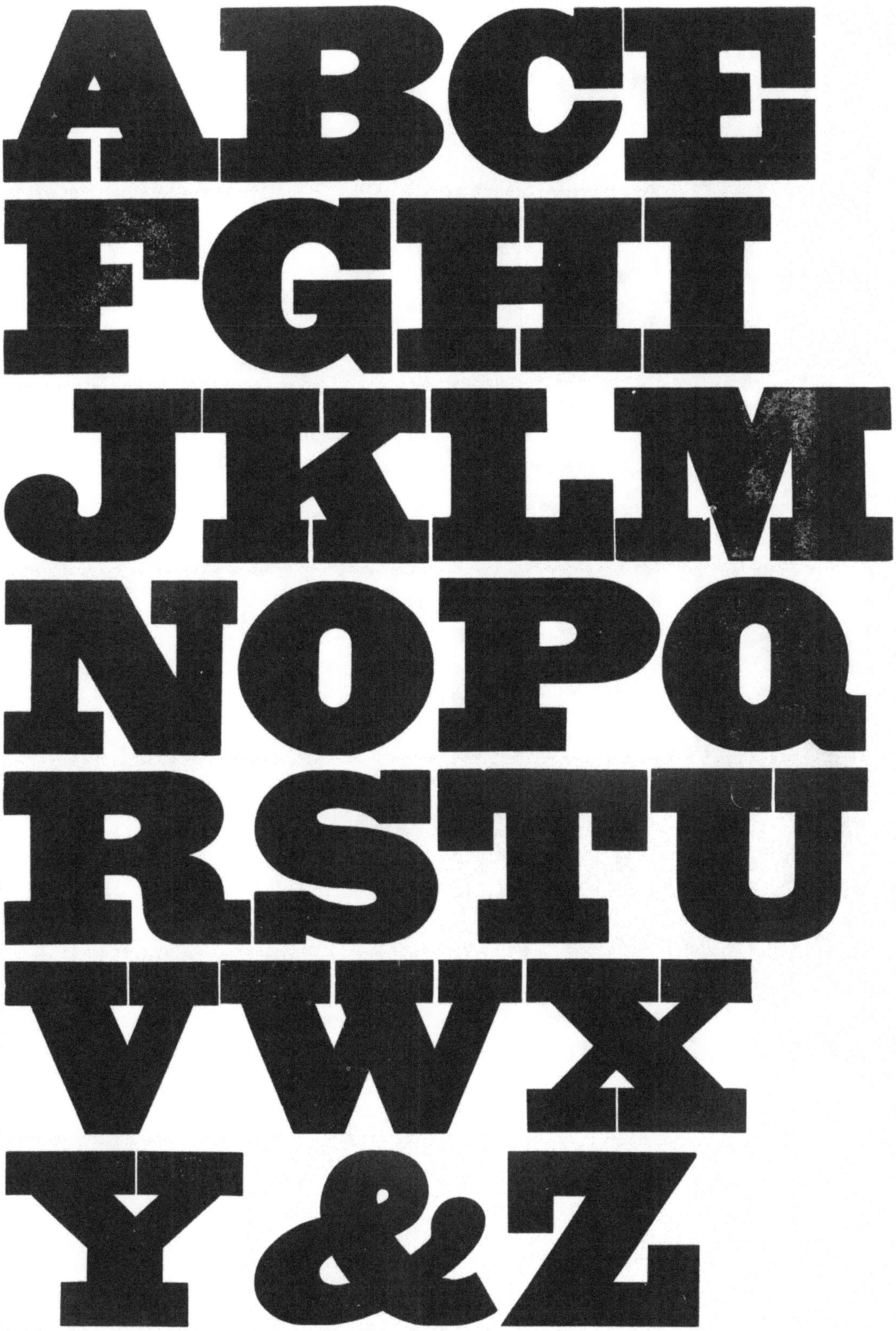

4.02.01.24 & 4.02.01.25
25 line Antique
William H. Page & Co., 1859 or later

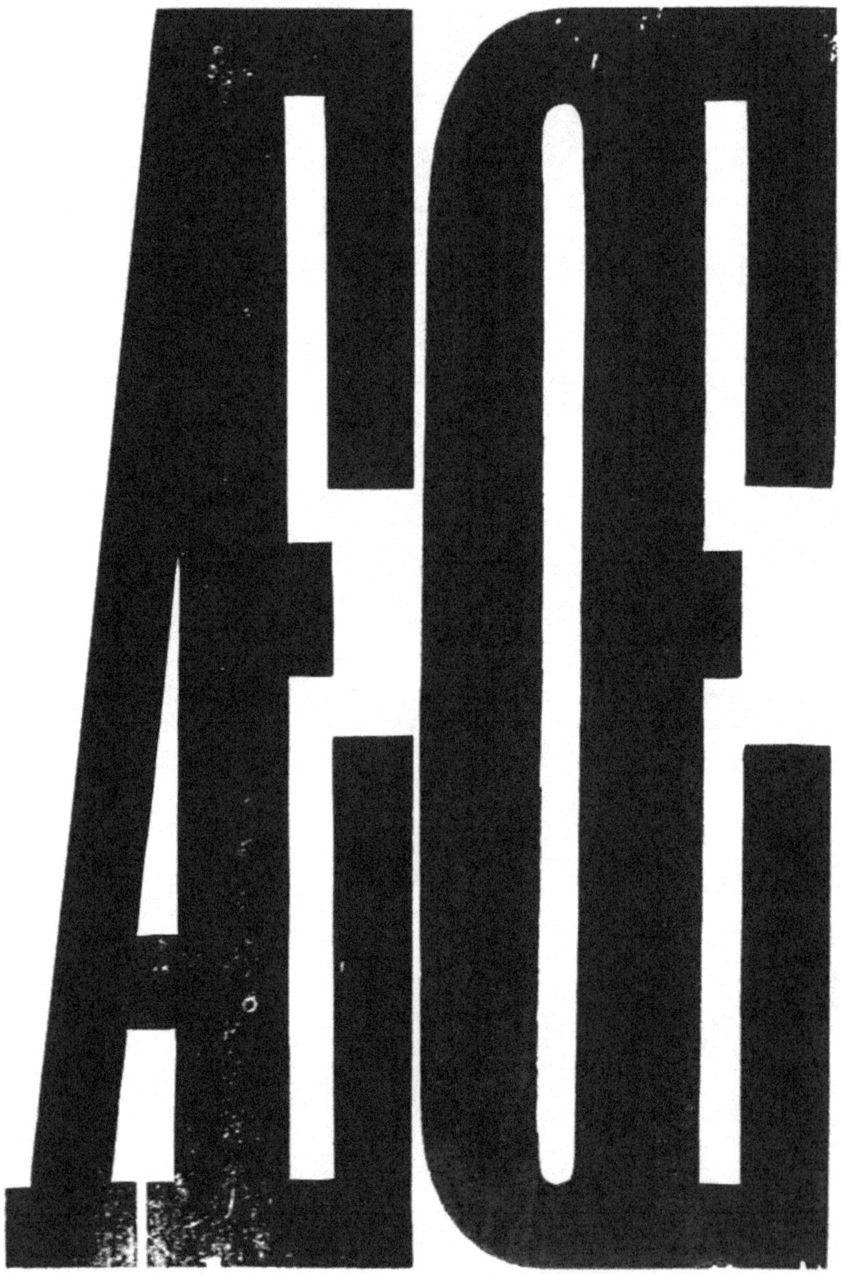

40 line [Antique Extra Condensed] cf. Page: Antique Double Extra Condensed [Actual size]

ABCDEFGHIJK
LMNOPQRSTU
VWXY&ZÆŒ

4.02.01.26
40 line [Antique Extra Condensed] cf. Page: Antique Double Extra Condensed
J.G. Cooley, 1859–1868

ABCD WXY&Z

8 line [Grecian Condensed] cf. AWT (Conn.): No. 2155 [Actual size]

MNOP

10 line [Grecian Condensed] cf. Page: Grecian Condensed [Actual size]

CDEF

10 line [Grecian Condensed] cf. Hamilton: No. 287 [Actual size]

ABCDEFGHIJKLMNOP
RSTUVWXY&Z

4.02.02.01
8 line [Grecian Condensed] cf. AWT (Conn.): No. 2155
Manufacturer and date unknown

ABCDEFGHIJKL
MNOPQRSTUV
WXYZ

4.02.02.02
10 line [Grecian Condensed] cf. Page: Grecian Condensed
J.G. Cooley, 1859–1868

CDEFGIJKLMNOP
QSUVX&Z

4.02.02.03
10 line [Grecian Condensed] cf. Hamilton: No. 287
Manufacturer and date unknown

WXY&Z

12 line [Grecian Condensed] cf. Hamilton: No. 288 [Actual size]

CDE &12

18 line [Grecian Condensed] cf. Page: Grecian Extra Condensed [Actual size]

ABCDEFGHIJKLMNOPRSTUV
WXY&Z

4.02.02.04
12 line [Grecian Condensed] cf. Hamilton: No. 288
Manufacturer and date unknown

CDEFGIJLNO
PQRUVWXYZ
&12569

4.02.02.05
18 line [Grecian Condensed] cf. Page: Grecian Extra Condensed
Manufacturer and date unknown

HIJKL abcdef

ﬀﬁﬂﬃ $123

6 line Egyptian [Actual size]

ABCDEFGHIJKL

8 line No. 55 [Actual size]

MNOPQRS $1234567890

8 line French Antique No. 1 [Actual size]

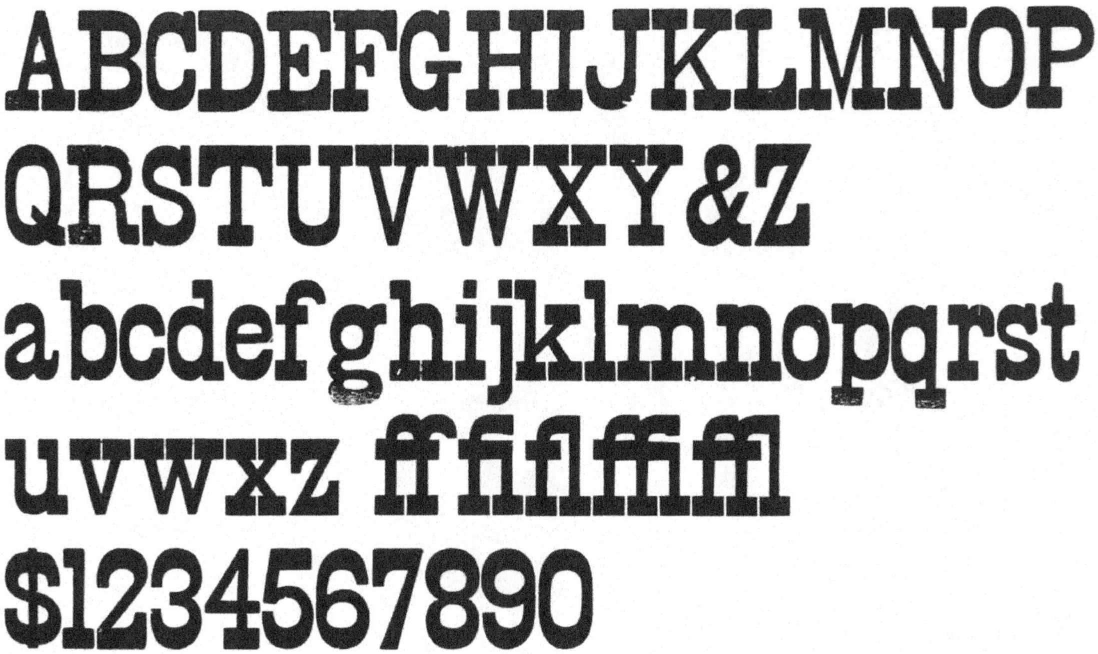

4.02.03.01
6 line Egyptian
Vanderburgh, Wells & Co., 1867–1890

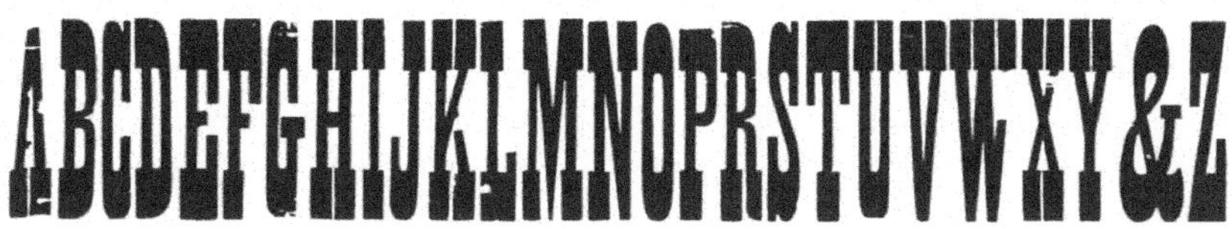

4.02.03.02
8 line No. 55
Hamilton Manufacturing Co., 1880–1889

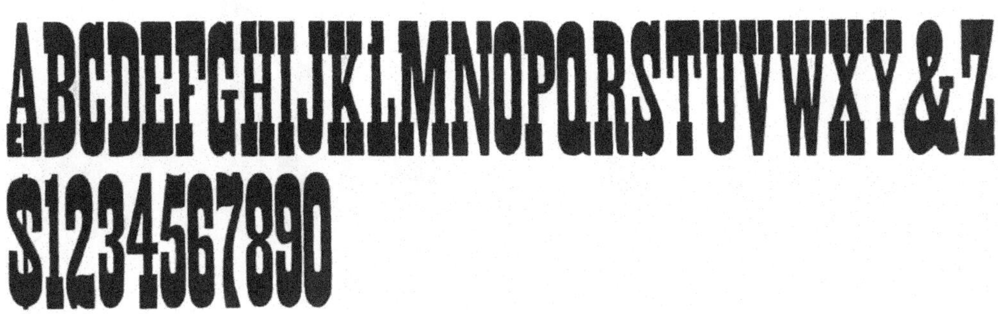

4.02.03.03
8 line French Antique No. 1
Morgans & Wilcox Mfg. Co., after 1881

TUVWXYZ
abcdefg
$12345

8 line [French Clarendon] cf. Hamilton: No. 3013 [Actual size]

XYZ&Æ him ffiffl $1345780

10 line French Antique [Actual size]

ABCDEFGHIJKLM
NOPQRSTUVWXYZ
abcdefghijklmnop
qrstuvwxyz
$1234567890

4.02.03.04
8 line [French Clarendon] cf. Hamilton: No. 3013
Manufacturer and date unknown

ABCDFGHIJKLMNOPQRSTUVWXYZ&Æ
abcdefghimnorstuvwx fffiflffiffl $1345780

4.02.03.05
10 line French Antique
William H. Page & Co., 1870 or later

ABCDEF $12345678

12 line French Antique [Actual size]

P 2

25 line [French Antique] cf. Hamilton: No. 70 [Actual size]

ABCDEFHIJKLMNOPQRSTUVWXY&Z
$1234567890

4.02.03.06
12 line French Antique
William H. Page & Co., 1857–1859

ABCDEFG
HIJKLMN
OPQRSTU
VWXY&Z
$1234567
890

4.02.03.07 & 4.02.03.08
25 line [French Antique] cf. Hamilton: No. 70
Manufacturer and date unknown

40 line No. 55 [Actual size]

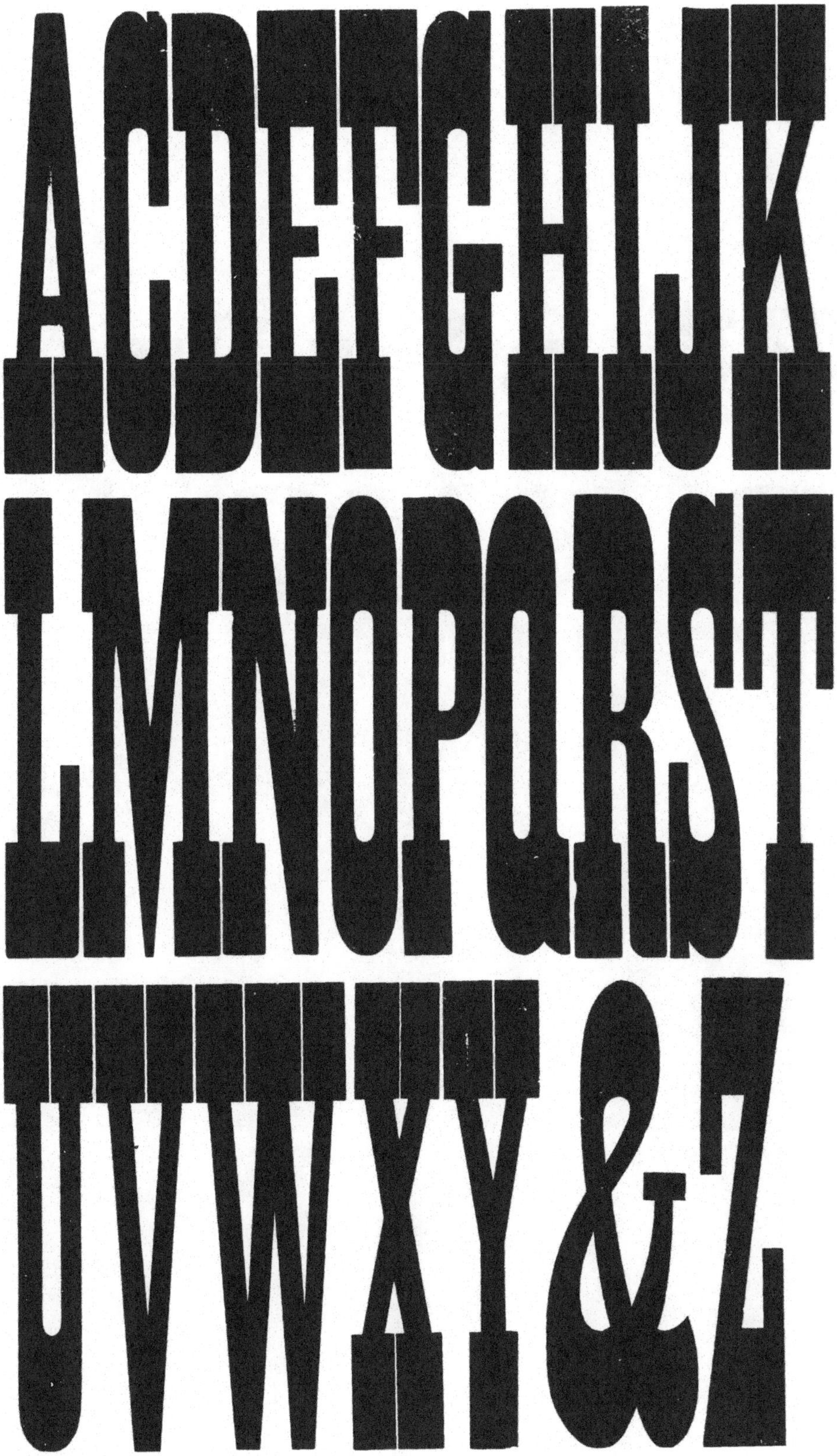

4.02.03.09 & 4.02.03.10
40 line No. 55
Hamilton Manufacturing Co., after 1891

JLMNOPQ

4 line [Clarendon Condensed] cf. Page: Clarendon [Actual size]

GHIJK ghijk

ﬀﬁﬂﬃ \$123

4 line Clarendon Extended [Actual size]

ABCDEF

5 line No. 22 [Actual size]

ABCDEFGHIJLMNOPQRSTUVWXZ

4.03.01.01
4 line [Clarendon Condensed] cf. Page: Clarendon
Manufacturer and date unknown

ABCDEFGHIJKLMNOP
QRSTUVWXY&Z
abcdefghijklmnoprstu
vwxyz ff fi fl ffi ffl
$1234567890

4.03.01.02
4 line Clarendon Extended
Vanderburgh, Wells & Co., 1867-1890

ABCDEFGHIJKLMNOPQR
STUVWXYZ

4.03.01.03
5 line No. 22
Hamilton Manufacturing Co., 1880-1889

PQRS
fghi ffiffl
$12345

5 line Clarendon Extended [Actual size]

$1234567890

6 line [Clarendon] cf. Hamilton: No. 22 [Actual size]

ABCDE $1234567

8 line Clarendon Double Extra Condensed [Actual size]

ABCDEFGHIJ
KLMNOPQRS
TUVWXY&Z
abcdefghijklmn
opqrstuvwxyz
ffifflffiffl
$1234567890

4.03.01.04
5 line Clarendon Extended
William H. Page & Co., 1857-1859

$1234567890

4.03.01.05
6 line [Clarendon] cf. Hamilton: No. 22
Manufacturer and date unknown

ABCDEFGHIJKLMNOPQRSTUVWX
Y&Z $1234567890

4.03.01.06
8 line Clarendon Double Extra Condensed
Vanderburgh, Wells & Co., 1867-1890

XY&Z

8 line Clarendon Condensed No. 1 [Actual size]

DEFGHI

8 line [Clarendon Condensed] cf. Hamilton: No. 105 [Actual size]

PQRST

8 line Clarendon Condensed [Actual size]

ABCDEFGHIJKLMNOPR
STUVWXY&Z

4.03.01.07
8 line Clarendon Condensed No. 1
Vanderburgh, Wells & Co., 1867-1890

ABCDEFGHIJKLM
PQRSTVWXY&Z

4.03.01.08
8 line [Clarendon Condensed] cf. Hamilton: No. 105
Manufacturer and date unknown

ABCDEFGHIJKL
MNOPQRSTUVW
XYZ $12345780

4.03.01.09
8 line Clarendon Condensed
William H. Page & Co., 1859 or later

$123456

8 line [Clarendon] cf. Hamilton: No. 22 [Actual size]

KLMNO
$2346

8 line Ionic [Actual size]

BFG 26

8 line [Clarendon] cf. Hamilton: No 155 [Actual size]

$1234567890

4.03.01.10
8 line [Clarendon] cf. Hamilton: No. 22
Manufacturer and date unknown

ABCDEFGHIJ
KLMNOPQRS
TUVWXY&Z
$234689

4.03.01.11
8 line Ionic
Vanderburgh, Wells & Co., 1867-1890

BFGJLSTV
Y26790

4.03.01.12
8 line [Clarendon] cf. Hamilton: No. 155
Manufacturer and date unknown

QRSTUV
abcdef ff fi fl ffl

10 line [Clarendon Condensed] cf. Hamilton: No. 152 [Actual size]

hijklm ff fi fl ffl

10 line Clarendon Condensed (?) [Actual size]

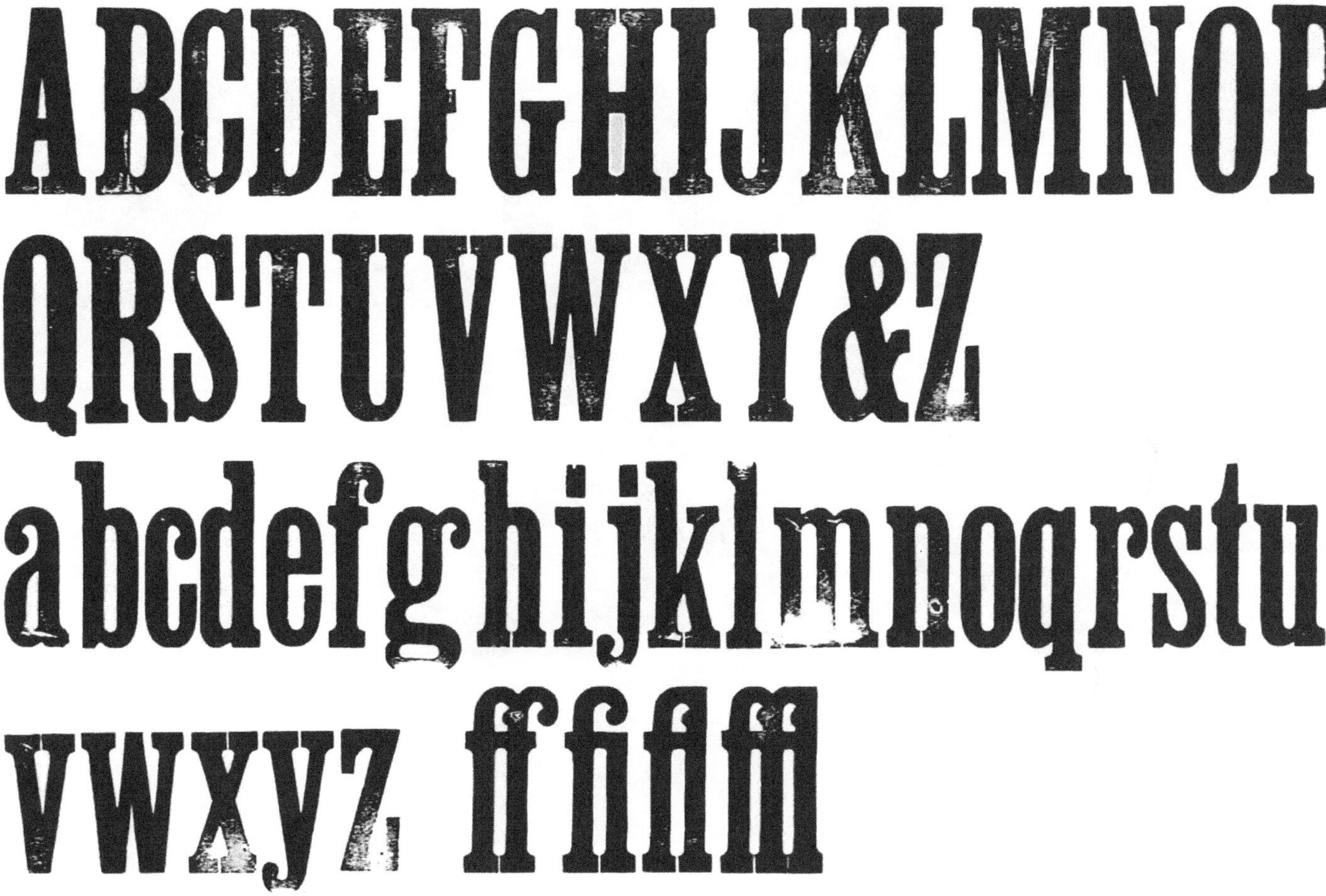

4.03.01.13
10 line [Clarendon Condensed] cf. Hamilton: No. 152
The Celluloid Stereotype Company, 1885–1900

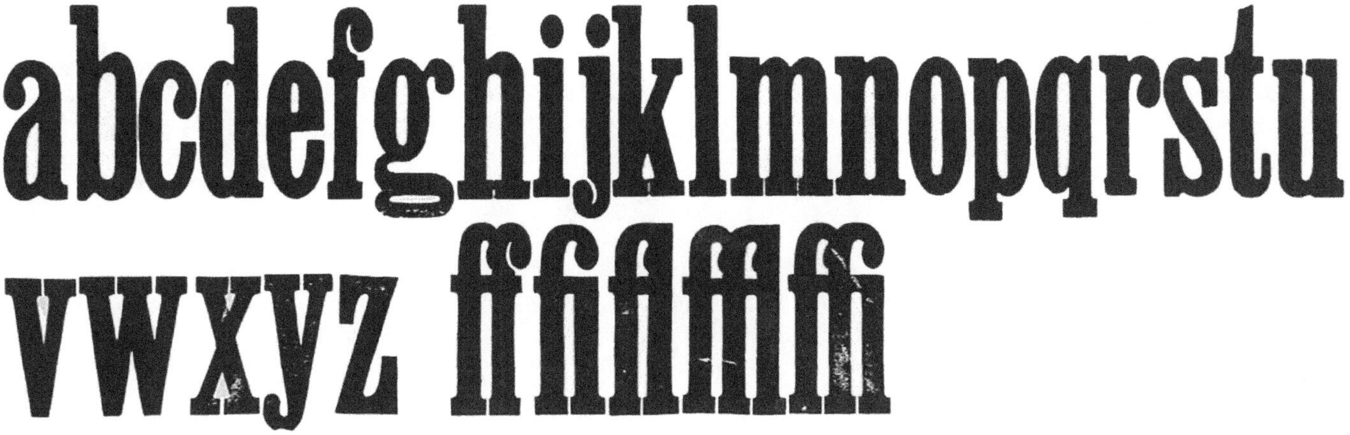

4.03.01.14
10 line Clarendon Condensed (?)
William H. Page & Co., 1859 or later

LMN
468

ABCDE
FGHIJ
KLMN
OPQRS
TUVW
XY&Z
1234689

4.03.01.15
10 line Clarendon Extended
Vanderburgh, Wells & Co., 1867–1890

MNOPQ 67890

12 line Clarendon Double Extra Condensed [Actual size]

BCD $123456

12 line [Clarendon Condensed] cf. Hamilton: No. 153 [Actual size]

ABCDEFGHIJKLMNOPQR
STUVWXY&Z
$1234567890

4.03.01.16
12 line Clarendon Double Extra Condensed
William H. Page & Co., 1870 or later

BCDEFGHIJKLNOPQST
UVWXY&Z
$1234567890

4.03.01.17
12 line [Clarendon Condensed] cf. Hamilton: No. 153
Manufacturer and date unknown

RSTUV
$1234

12 line Clarendon Condensed No. 2 [Actual size]

ABCDEFGHI
JKLMNOPQ
RSTUVWX
Y&Z
$1234567890

4.03.01.18
12 line Clarendon Condensed No. 2
Vanderburgh, Wells & Co., 1867-1890

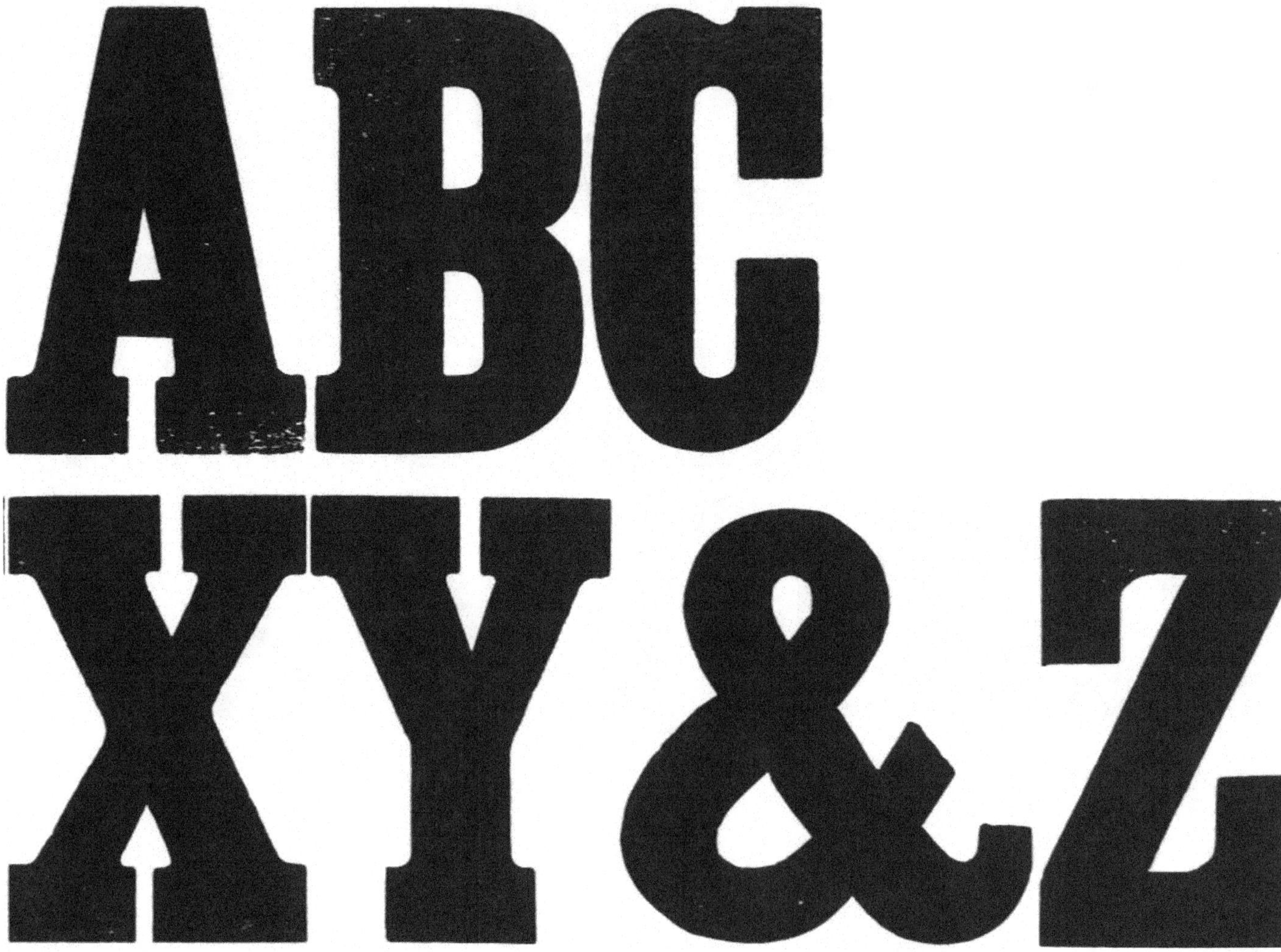

15 line [Clarendon Condensed] cf. Hamilton: No. 105 [Actual size]

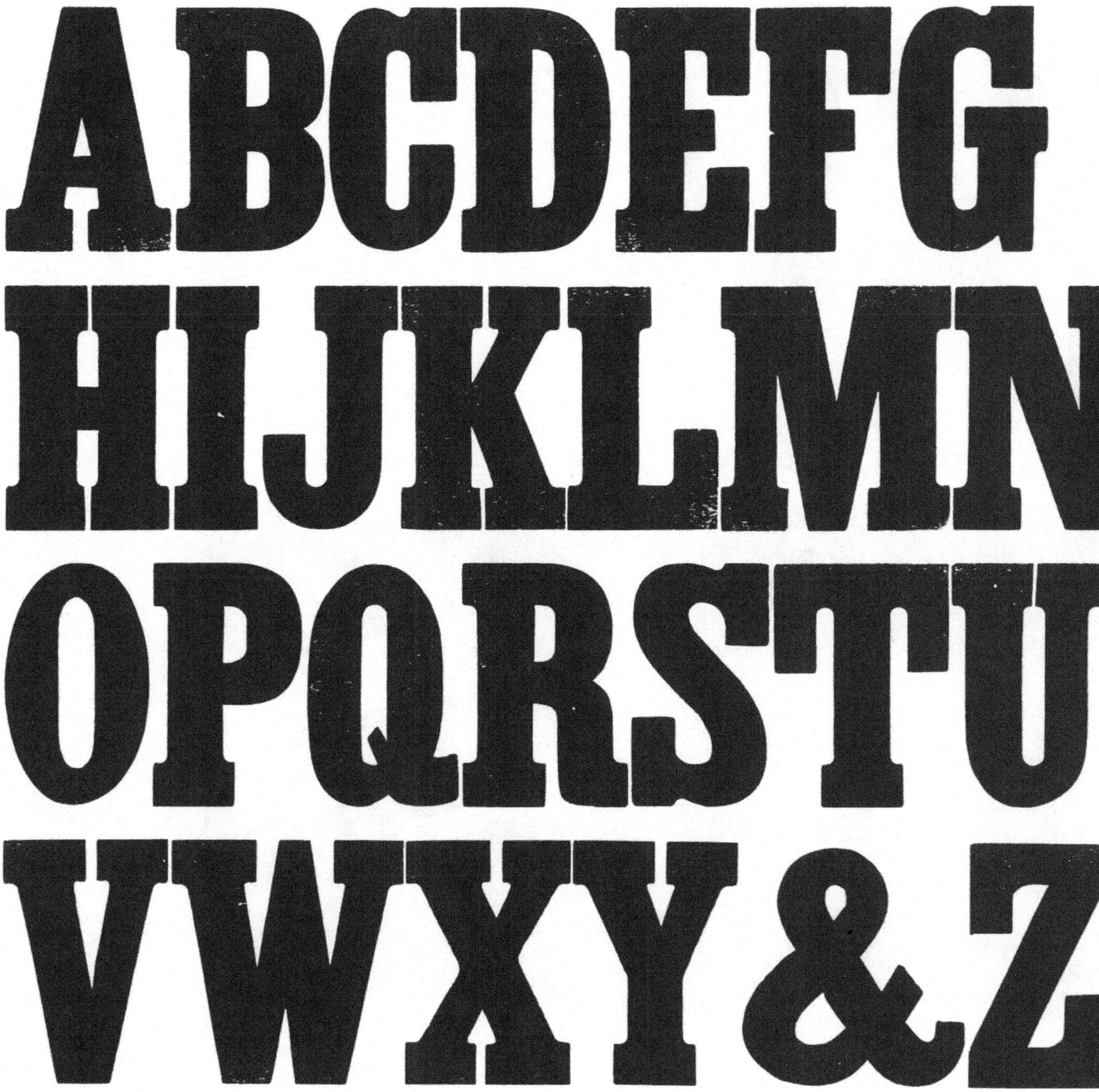

4.03.01.19
15 line [Clarendon Condensed] cf. Hamilton: No. 105
Manufacturer and date unknown

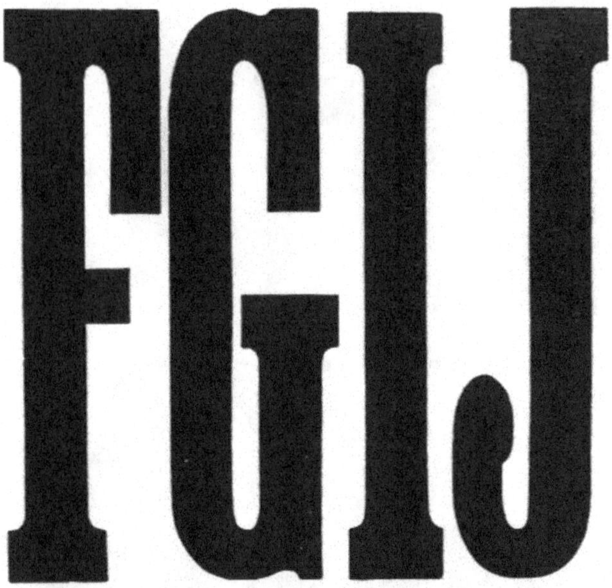

18 line [Clarendon Extra Condensed] cf. Hamilton: No. 153 [Actual size]

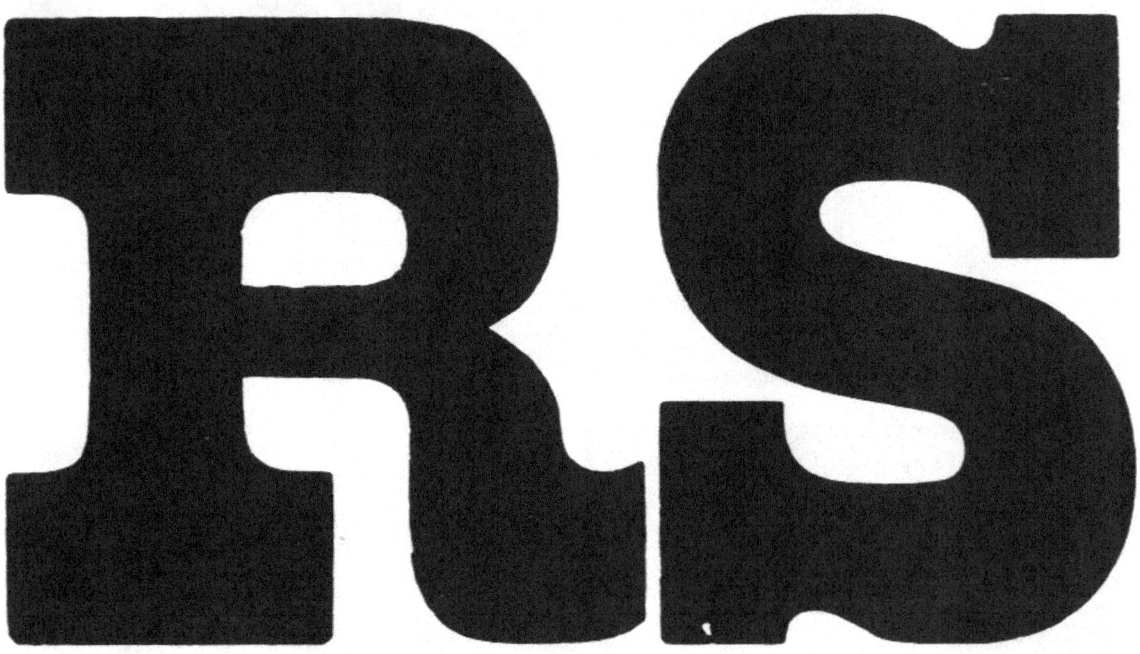

20 line [Clarendon] cf. Hamilton: No. 23 [Actual size]

FGIJNOSW

4.03.01.20
18 line [Clarendon Extra Condensed] cf. Hamilton: No. 153
Manufacturer and date unknown

CDEFGHI
JKLMNO
PQRSTU
VWXYZ

4.03.01.23 & 4.03.01.24
20 line [Clarendon] cf. Hamilton: No. 23
Manufacturer and date unknown

NOPQS

24 line Clarendon Double Extra Condensed [Actual size]

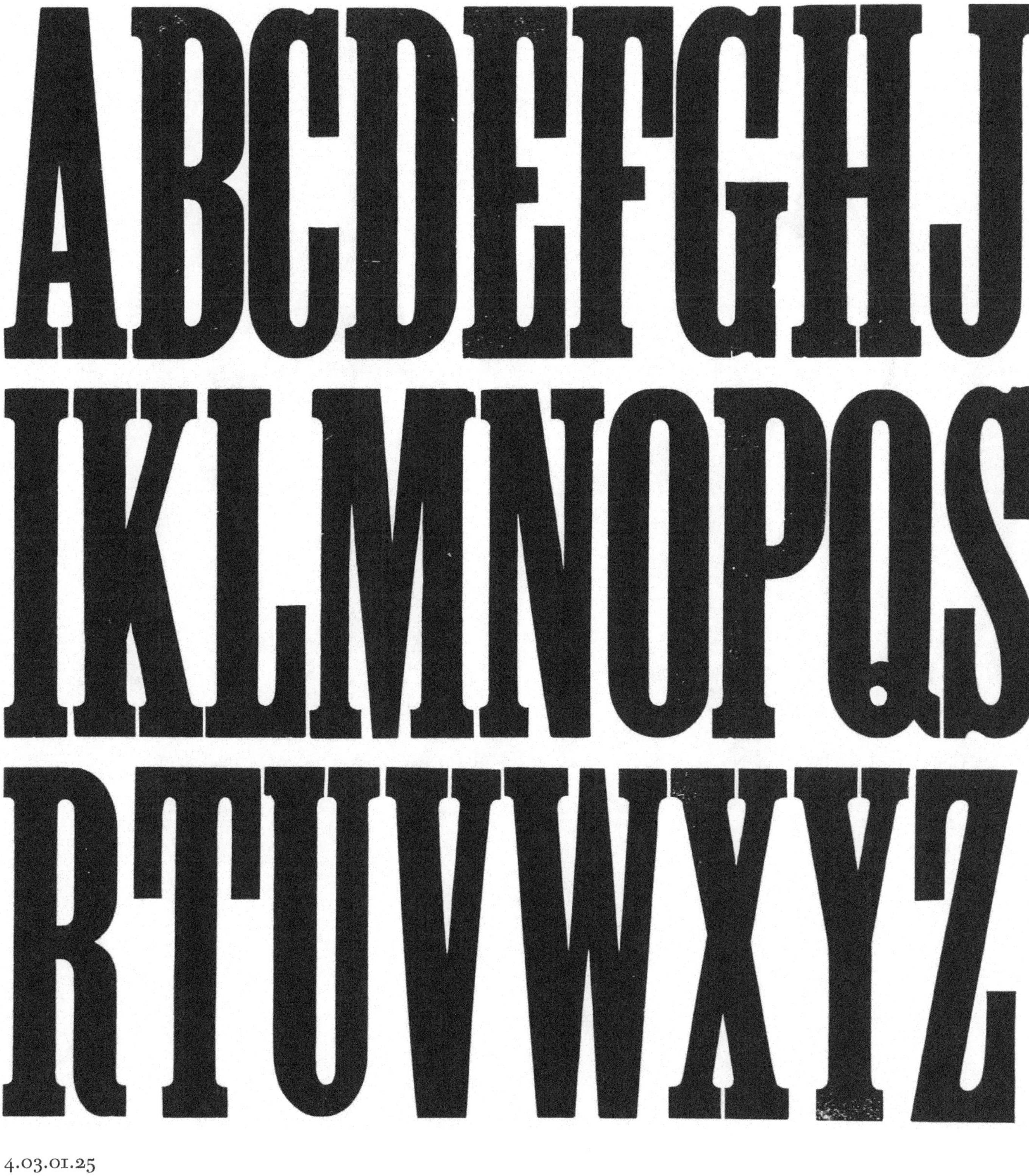

4.03.01.25
24 line Clarendon Double Extra Condensed
Vanderburgh, Wells & Co., 1867-1890

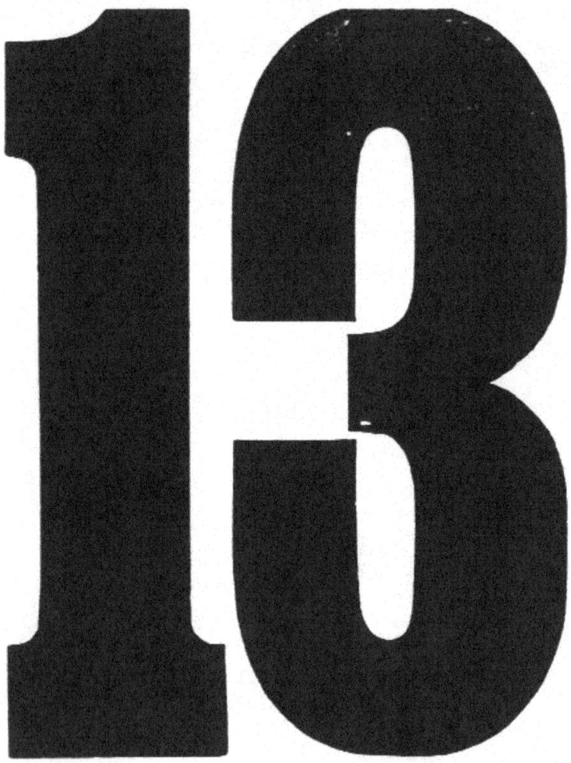

24 line [Clarendon] cf. Hamilton: No. 5031 [Actual size]

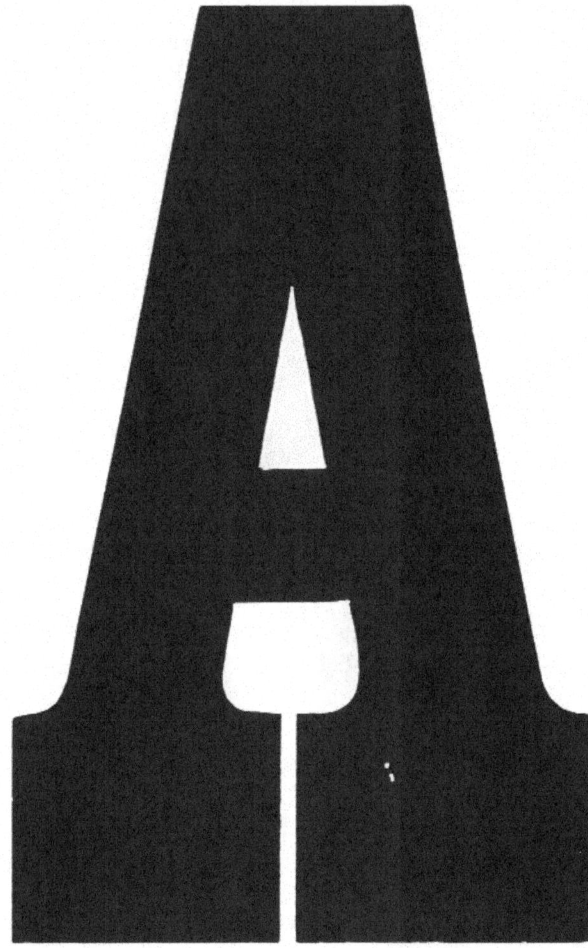

30 line Clarendon Italian [Actual size]

135670

4.03.01.26
24 line [Clarendon] cf. Hamilton: No. 5031
Manufacturer and date unknown

ABCDEF
GHIJKL
MNOPQR
STUVW
XY&Z

4.03.01.27 & 4.03.01.28
30 line Clarendon Italian
Vanderburgh, Wells & Co., 1867-1890

CDEF

36 line Clarendon Double Extra Condensed [Actual size]

ABCDEFGH
IJKLMNOP
QRSTUVW
XY&Z

4.03.01.29 & 4.03.01.30
36 line Clarendon Double Extra Condensed
Vanderburgh, Wells & Co., 1867-1890

QRSTU
fghijk
$12345

10 line [Ionic Oblique] cf. Vanderburgh, Wells & Co.: Ionic [Actual size]

ABCDEFGH
IJKLMNOP
QRSTUVW
XY&Z
abcdefghijkl
mnopqrstuv
wxyz
$123456789

4.03.01.31
10 line [Ionic Oblique] cf. Vanderburgh, Wells & Co.: Ionic
Vanderburgh, Wells & Co., 1867–1890

XY&Z defg
$123456

6 line No. 98 [Cheltenham], cf. Hamilton: No. 706, Cheltenham Bold Condensed [Actual size]

4567

10 line No. 98 [Cheltenham], cf. Hamilton: No. 696, Cheltenham Bold [Actual size]

ABCDEFGHIJKLMNOPQ
RSTUVWXY&Z
abcdefghijklmnopqrstuv
wxyz $1234567890

4.03.02.01
6 line No. 98 [Cheltenham] cf. Hamilton: No. 706, Cheltenham Bold Condensed
Empire Type Foundry (Delevan, NY), 1918-1924

$1234567890

4.03.02.02
10 line No. 98 [Cheltenham] cf. Hamilton: No. 696, Cheltenham Bold
Empire Type Foundry (Delevan, NY), 1918-1924

PQRST

10 line [Cheltenham Bold Condensed] cf. Hamilton: No. 706 [Actual size]

Y&Z

10 line [Cheltenham Bold Condensed] cf. Hamilton: No. 706 [Actual size]

ABCDEFGHIJK
LMNOPQRSTU
VWXY&Z

4.03.02.03
10 line [Cheltenham Bold Condensed] cf. Hamilton: No. 706
Manufacturer and date unknown

DFGIJKLMNPR
STUVWXY&Z

4.03.02.04
10 line [Cheltenham Bold Condensed] cf. Hamilton: No. 706
Manufacturer and date unknown

LMNO
opqrst
$123456

8 line No. 696 [Actual size]

ABCDEFGHIJK
LMNOPQRSTU
VWXYZ
abcdefghijklmn
opqrstuvwxyz
$1234567890

4.03.02.05
8 line No. 696
Hamilton Manufacturing Co., after 1891

ABCDE wxyz

4 line [French Clarendon Condensed] cf. Page: French Clarendon No. 2 [Actual size]

PQRS nop 56789

4 line [French Clarendon] cf. Hamilton: No. 157 [Actual size]

EFG ghi 45678

5 line Egyptian Condensed [Actual size]

EFGH rst $123

6 line French Clarendon [Actual size]

ABCDEGHIJKLMNOPQRSTUVWXY&Z
abcbefhijklmnpqrstvwxyz ffffiflffiffl

4.03.03.01
4 line [French Clarendon Condensed] cf. Page: French Clarendon No. 2
Manufacturer and date unknown

ABCDEFGHIJKLMNOPQRSTUVWXY&Z
abcdefghiklmnopqrstuvwxyz ffffiflffiffl
$1234567890

4.03.03.02
4 line [French Clarendon] cf. Hamilton: No. 157
Manufacturer and date unknown

ABCDEFGHIJKLMNOPQRSTUVWXYZ
abcdefghijklmnopqrstuvwxyz&ffffiflffiffl
$1234567890

4.03.03.03
5 line Egyptian Condensed
Vanderburgh, Wells & Co., 1867–1890

ABCDEFGHIJKLMNOPQRSTUVWXYZ ffffiflffiffl
abcdefghijklmpqrstvwxyz $1234567890

4.03.03.04
6 line French Clarendon
Vanderburgh, Wells & Co., 1867–1890

WXY&Z 12456789

6 line [French Clarendon] cf. Hamilton: No. 24 [Actual size]

ABCDEFGH xyz&fffifl

$1234

6 line [French Clarendon Condensed] cf. Page: Egyptian Condensed [Actual size]

JKLMN 6789!

6 line Egyptian Condensed [Actual size]

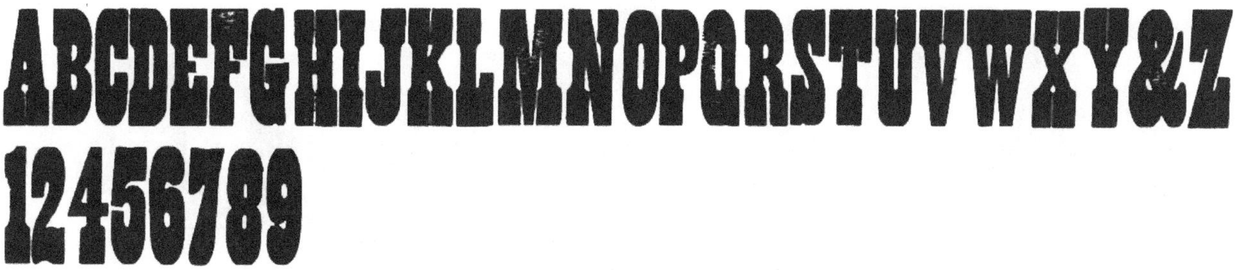

4.03.03.05
6 line [French Clarendon] cf. Hamilton: No. 24
The Celluloid Stereotype Company, 1885–1900

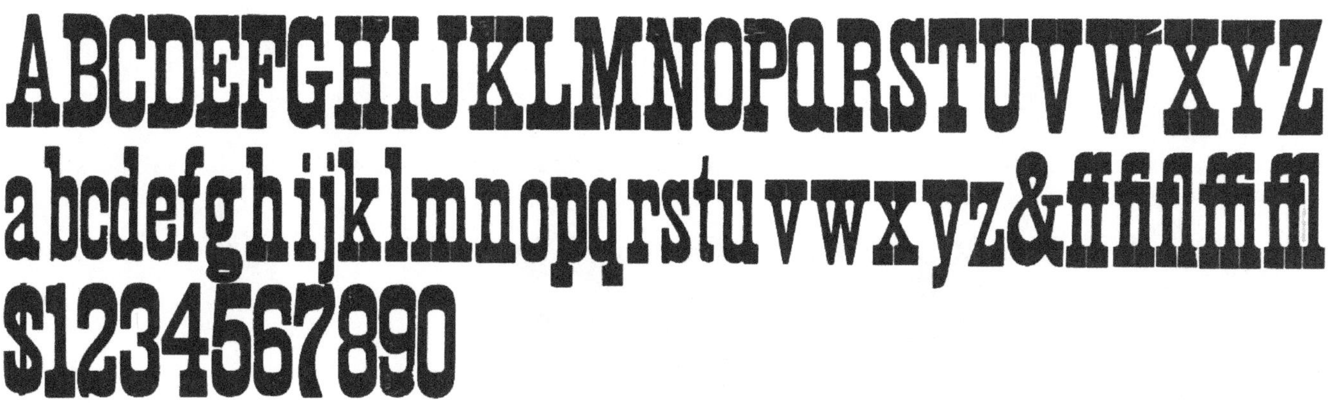

4.03.03.06
6 line [French Clarendon Condensed] cf. Page: Egyptian Condensed
Morgans & Wilcox Mfg. Co., after 1881

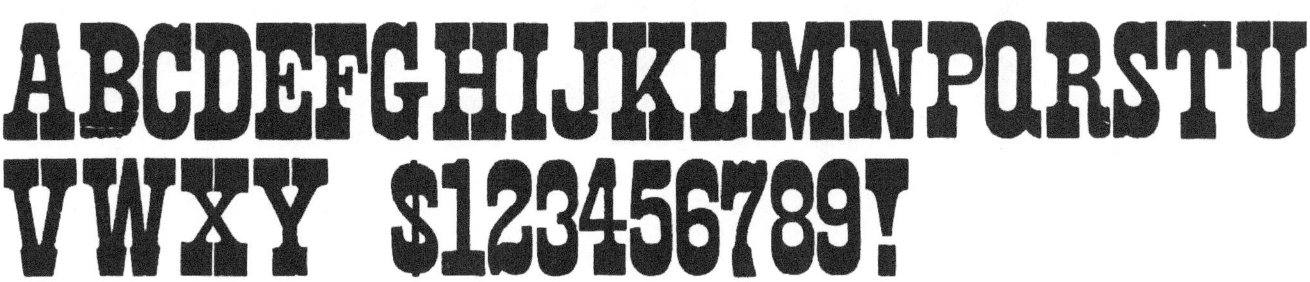

4.03.03.07
6 line Egyptian Condensed
Vanderburgh, Wells & Co., 1867–1890

ABCD befgh
$12470

6 line Yorkaldine [Actual size]

1256789

6 line [French Clarendon] cf. Hamilton: No. 5056 [Actual size]

QRST

6 line Aldine Expanded [Actual size]

ABCDEFGHIJKLM
NOPQRSTUVWXYZ
adcbefghiklmnqorst
uvwxyz $12470

4.03.03.08
6 line Yorkaldine
Vanderburgh, Wells & Co., 1867–1890

1256789

4.03.03.09
6 line [French Clarendon] cf. Hamilton: No. 5056
Manufacturer and date unknown

ABCDEFGH
IJKLMNOP
QRSTUVW
XY&Z

4.03.03.10
6 line Aldine Expanded
Morgans & Wilcox Mfg. Co., after 1881

HIJKLM &$1234

8 line French Clarendon [Actual size]

ABC &ffi
efgh $123

8 line Norwich Aldine [Actual size]

ABCDEFGHIJKLMNOPQRSTUVWXYZ
&$1234567890

4.03.03.11
8 line French Clarendon
Vanderburgh, Wells & Co., 1867–1890

ABCDEFGHIJK
LMNOQRSTUV
WXYZ&fffiflffiffl
abcdefghiklmnopq
rstuvwxyz
$1234567890

4.03.03.12
8 line Norwich Aldine
William H. Page & Co., 1870 or later

PQRSTUVWXY&Z $234568

10 line French Clarendon Treble Extra Condensed [Actual size]

ABCD $123456

10 line No. 24 [Actual size]

VWXY&Z 1234567

10 line No. 502 [Actual size]

ABCDEFGHIJKLMNOPQRSTUVWXY&Z $234568

4.03.03.13
10 line French Clarendon Treble Extra Condensed
Morgans & Wilcox Mfg. Co., after 1881

ABCDEGHIJKLMNOPQRSTU
VWXYZ $1234567890

4.03.03.14
10 line No. 24
Hamilton Manufacturing Co., 1880-1889

ABCDEFGHIJKLMNOPQRSTU
VWXY&Z 1234567890

4.03.03.15
10 line No. 502
William H. Page & Co., 1887-1891

BEF 680 wyzff

10 line [French Clarendon] cf. Hamilton: No. 24 [Actual size]

PQRS

10 line No. 69 [Actual size]

ABCD adgij

10 line No. 154 [Actual size]

BEFJKLNOPQSUVW 135680
abcdefghiklmnopqrsuvwyzff

4.03.03.16
10 line [French Clarendon] cf. Hamilton: No. 24
Manufacturer and date unknown

ACDEFGHIJKLMNO
PQRSTUVWXYZ

4.03.03.17
10 line No. 69
Hamilton Manufacturing Co., after 1891

ABCDEFLMNORSU
adgijlnopqrstuvwxyz

4.03.03.18
10 line No. 154
Hamilton Manufacturing Co., after 1891

XY& prstu

fffifl 5678

10 line No. 154 [Actual size]

ABCDEFGHIJKLMN

OPQRSTUVWXY&Z

abcdefghiklmnoprstuv

wxyz ff fi fl

$1234567890

4.03.03.19
10 line No. 154
Hamilton Manufacturing Co., after 1891

PQRS
$1234567

12 line Egyptian [Actual size]

bef fffifl

12 line [French Clarendon Condensed] cf. Hamilton: No. 157 [Actual size]

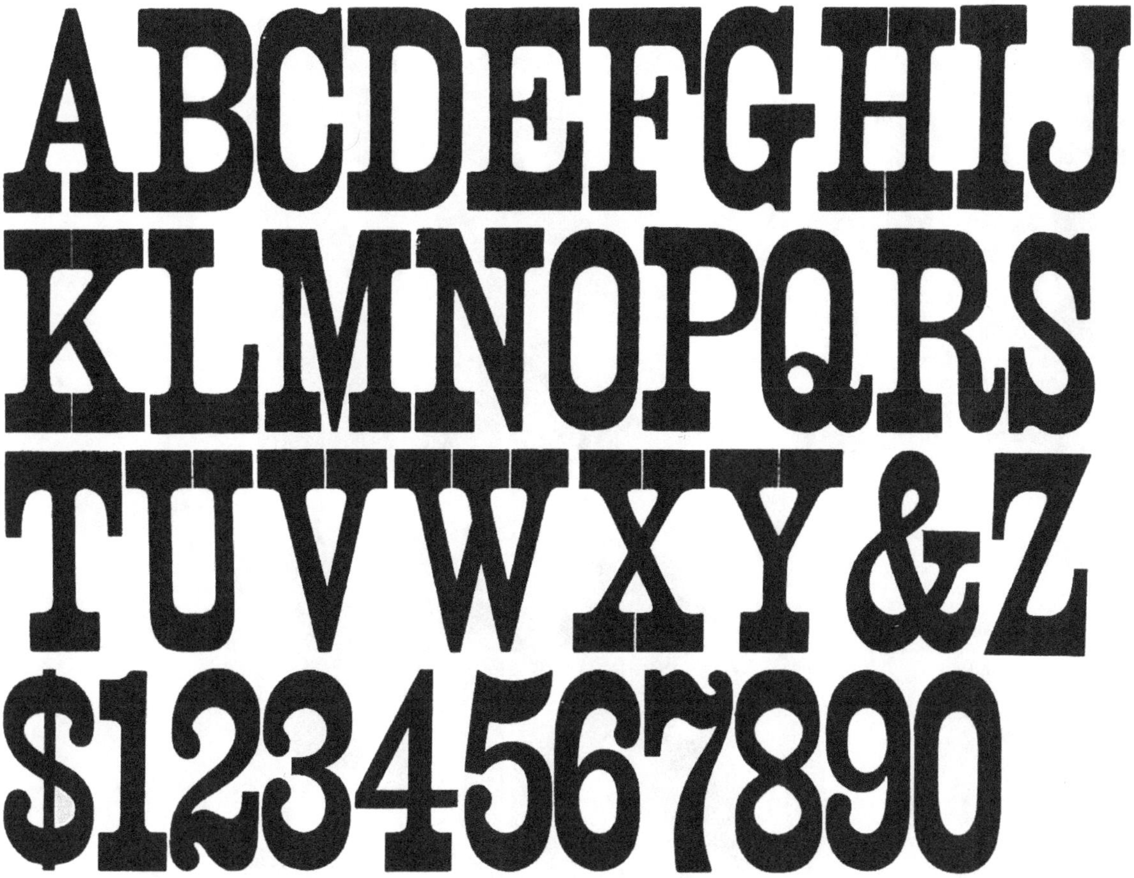

4.03.03.20
12 line Egyptian
William H. Page & Co., 1857–1859

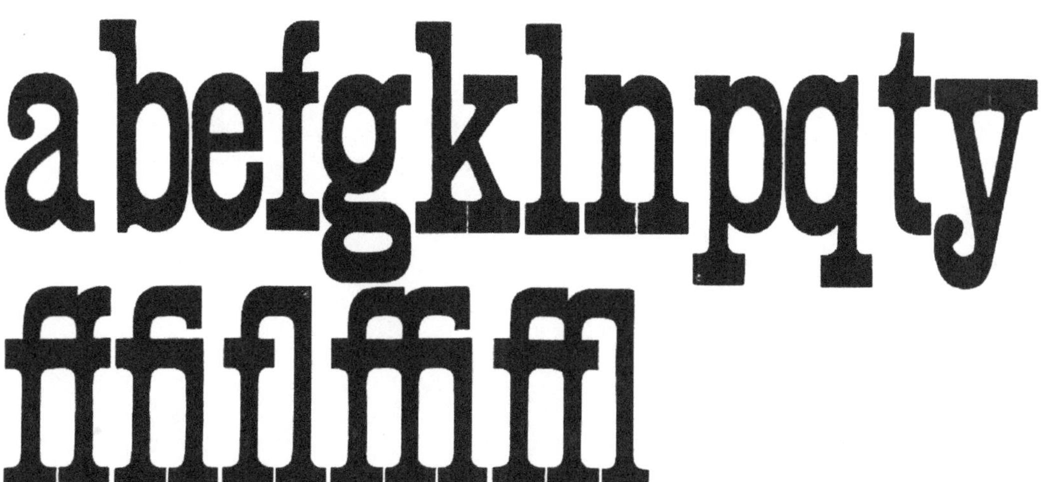

4.03.03.21
12 line [French Clarendon Condensed] cf. Hamilton: No. 157
Manufacturer and date unknown

EFGH &Z
34567890£

15 line [Antique Condensed] [Actual size]

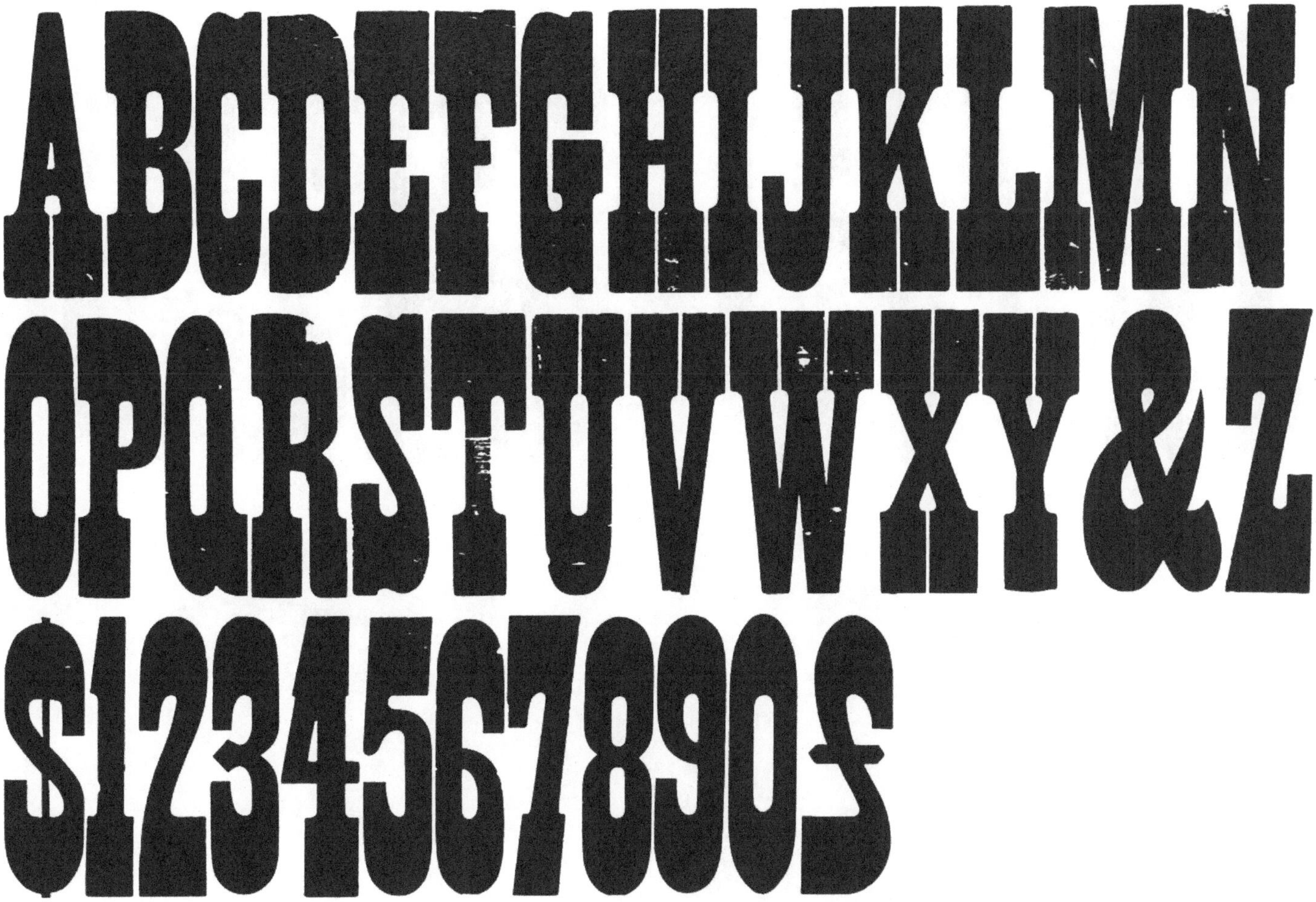

4.03.03.22
15 line [Antique Condensed]
Hamilton Manufacturing Co., 1880–1889

MNO $123

15 line No. 2117 [Actual size]

GHIJ

16 line [French Clarendon Condensed] cf. Hamilton: No. 24 [Actual size]

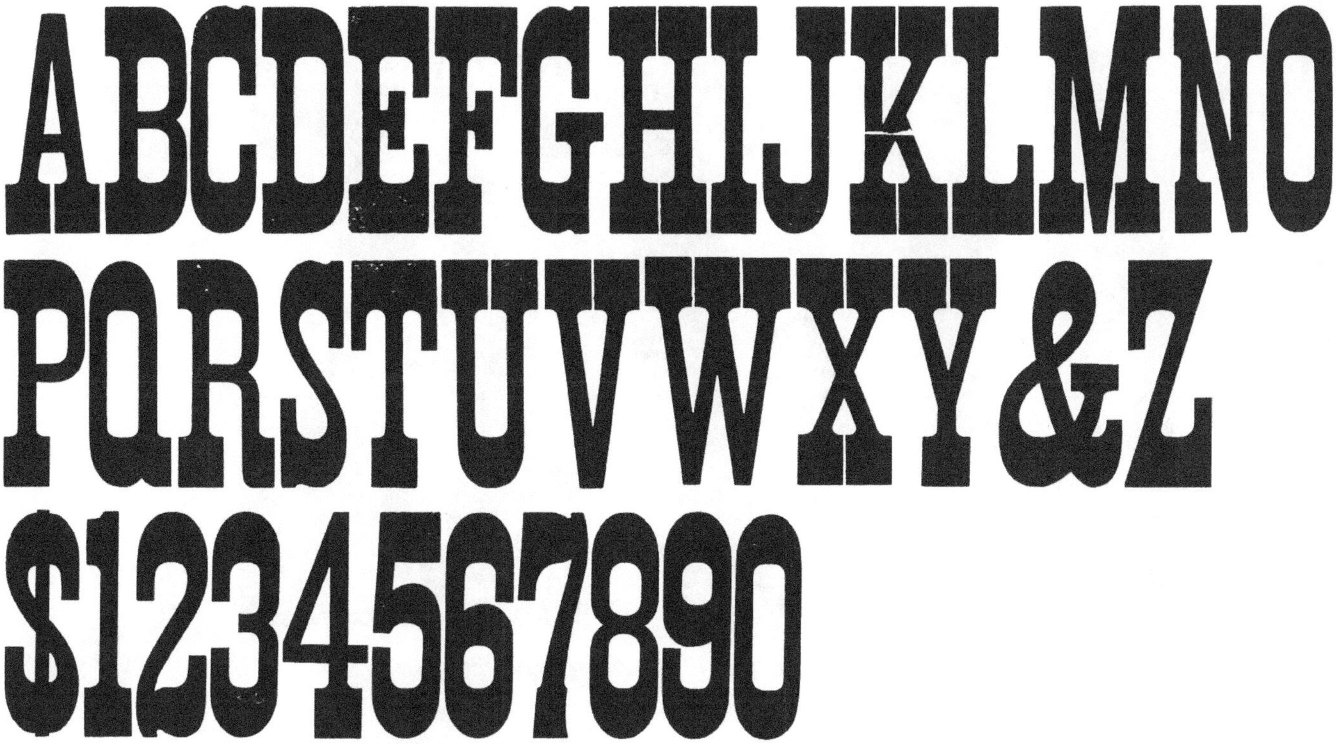

4.03.03.23
15 line No. 2117
American Wood Type Co. (Conn.), after 1883

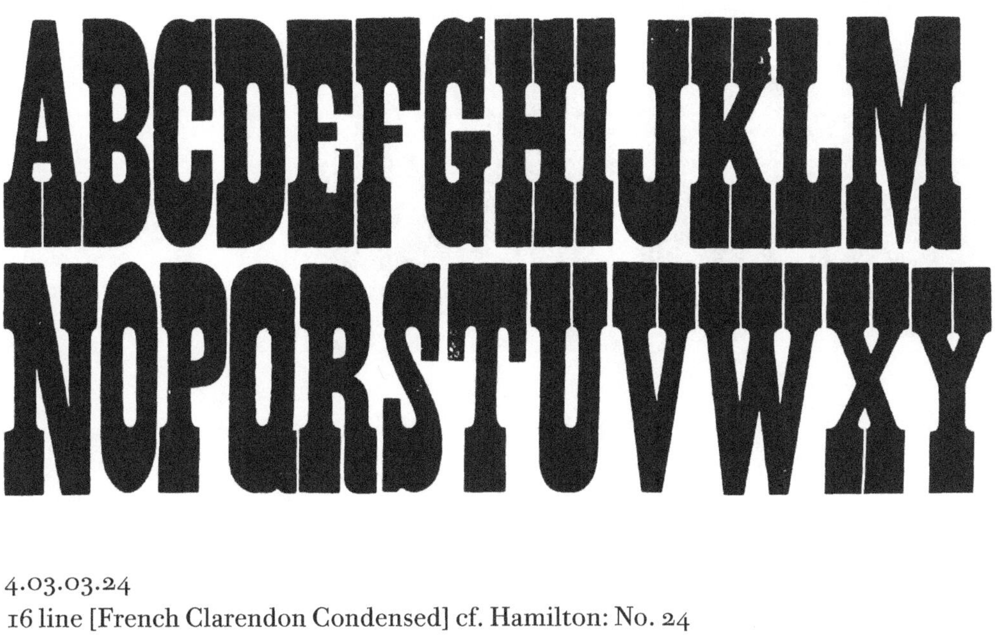

4.03.03.24
16 line [French Clarendon Condensed] cf. Hamilton: No. 24
Manufacturer and date unknown

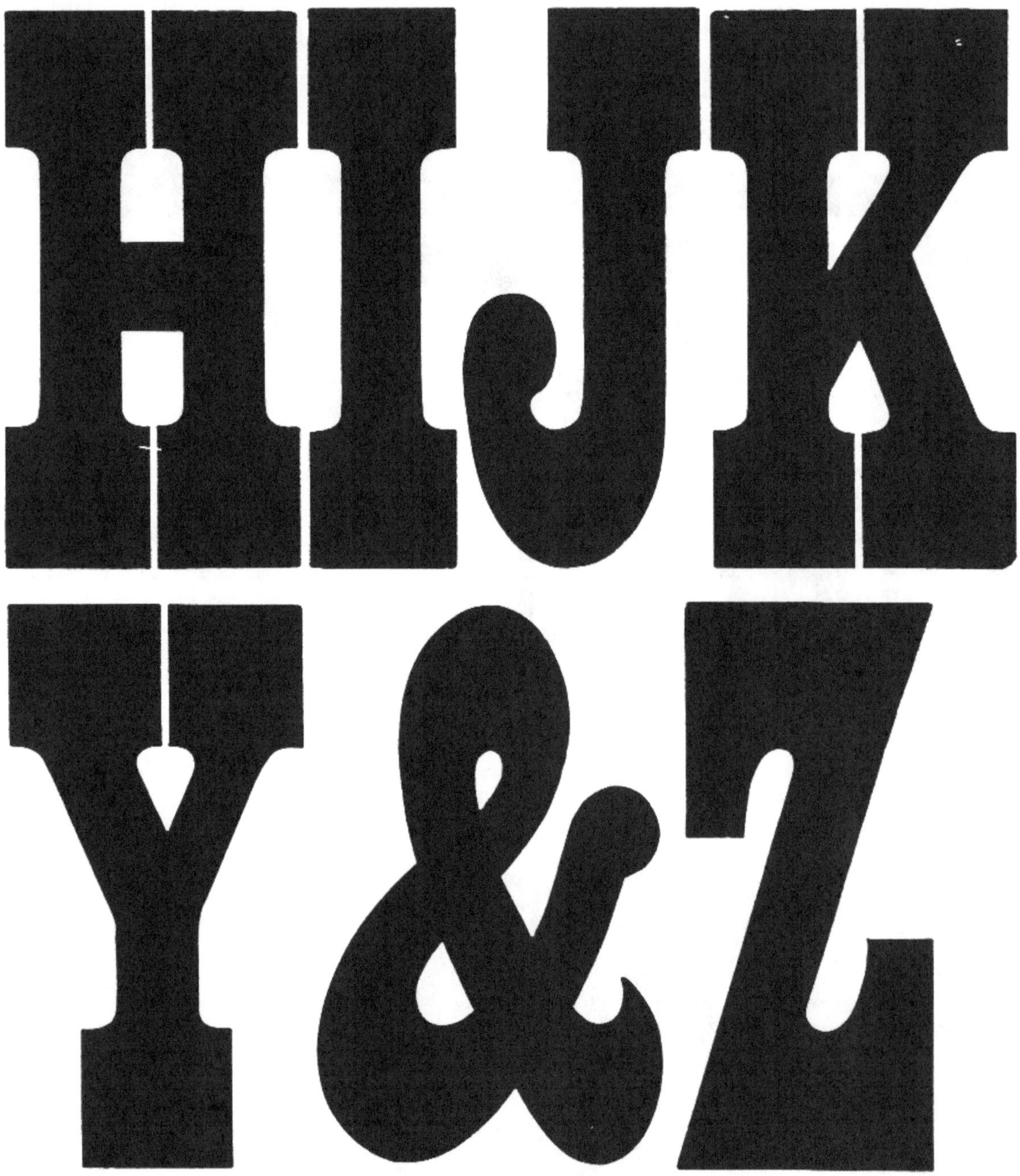

20 line [French Clarendon Condensed] cf. Hamilton: No. 154 [Actual size]

ABCDEFG
HIJKLMN
OPQRSTU
VWXY&Z

4.03.03.25
20 line [French Clarendon Condensed] cf. Hamilton: No. 154
Manufacturer and date unknown

20 line French Clarendon]
cf. Hamilton: No. 37 [Actual size]

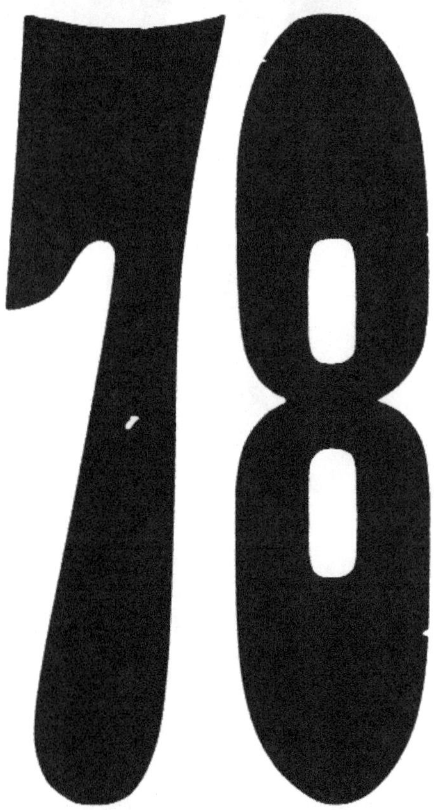

25 line No. 24 [Actual size]

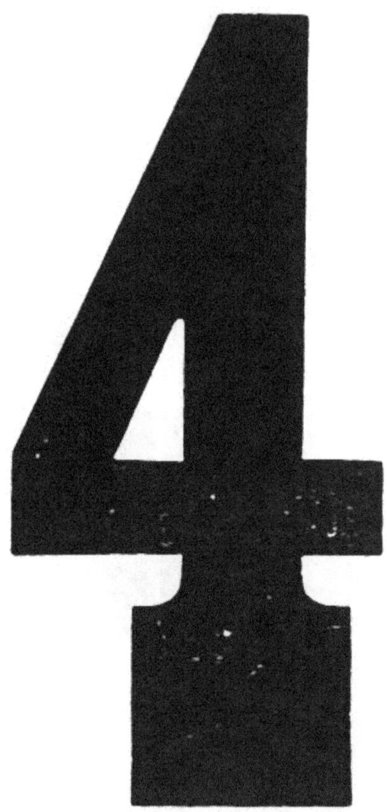

25 line [French Clarendon]
cf. Hamilton: No. 4154 [Actual size]

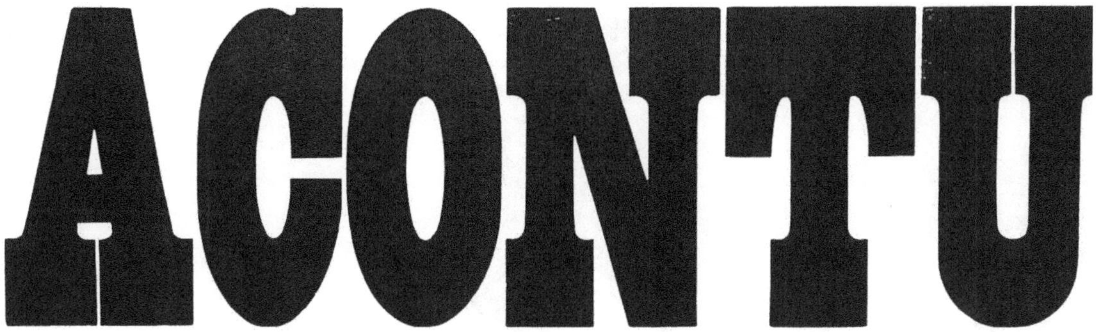

4.03.03.26
20 line [French Clarendon] cf. Hamilton: No. 37
Manufacturer and date unknown

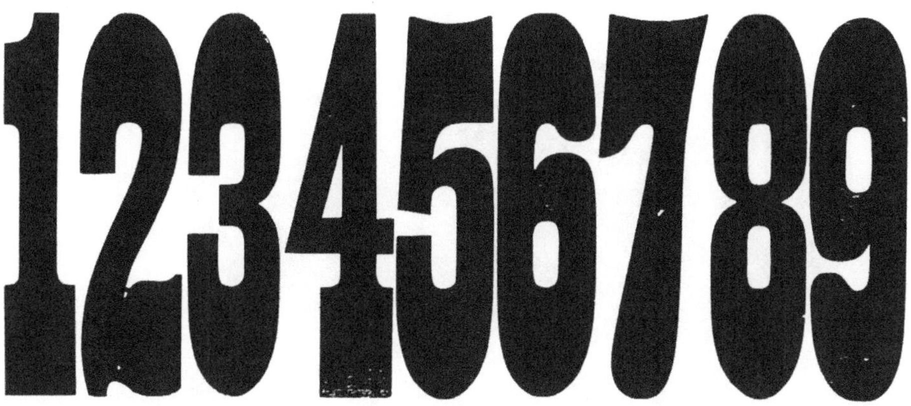

4.03.03.27
25 line No. 24
Hamilton Manufacturing Co., 1880–1889

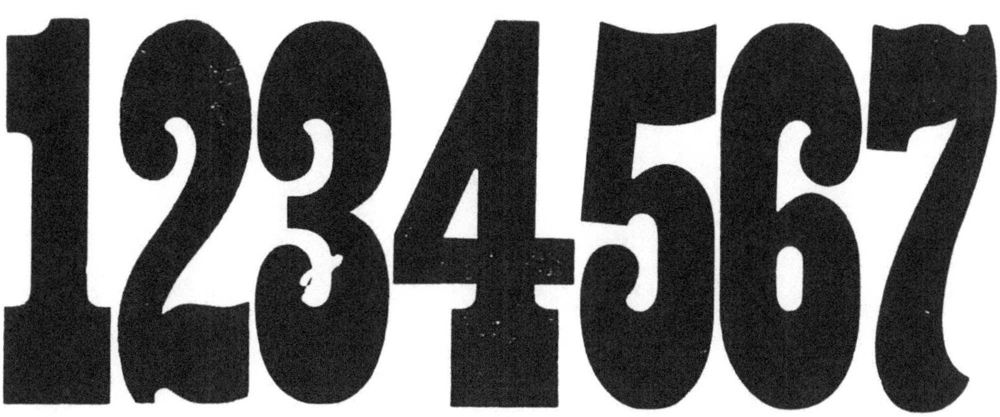

4.03.03.28
25 line [French Clarendon] cf. Hamilton: No. 4154
Manufacturer and date unknown

Y&

30 line No. 69 [Actual size]

ABCDEF
GHIJKL
MNOPQ
RSTUV
WXY&Z

4.03.03.29, 4.03.03.30, 4.03.03.31 & 4.03.03.32
30 line No. 69
Hamilton Manufacturing Co., after 1891

FG

30 line No. 37 [Actual size]

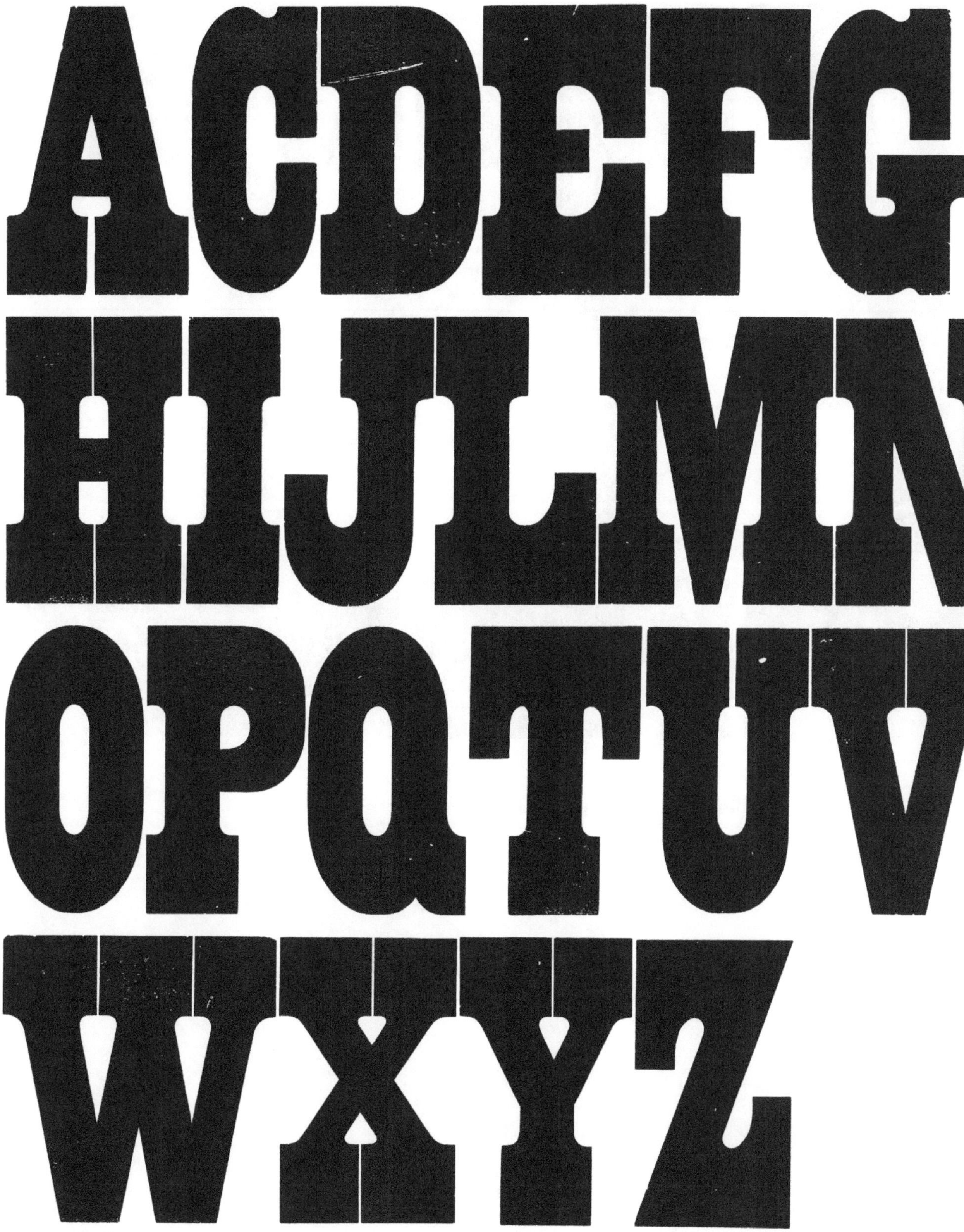

4.03.03.33 & 4.03.03.34
30 line No. 37
Hamilton Manufacturing Co., after 1891

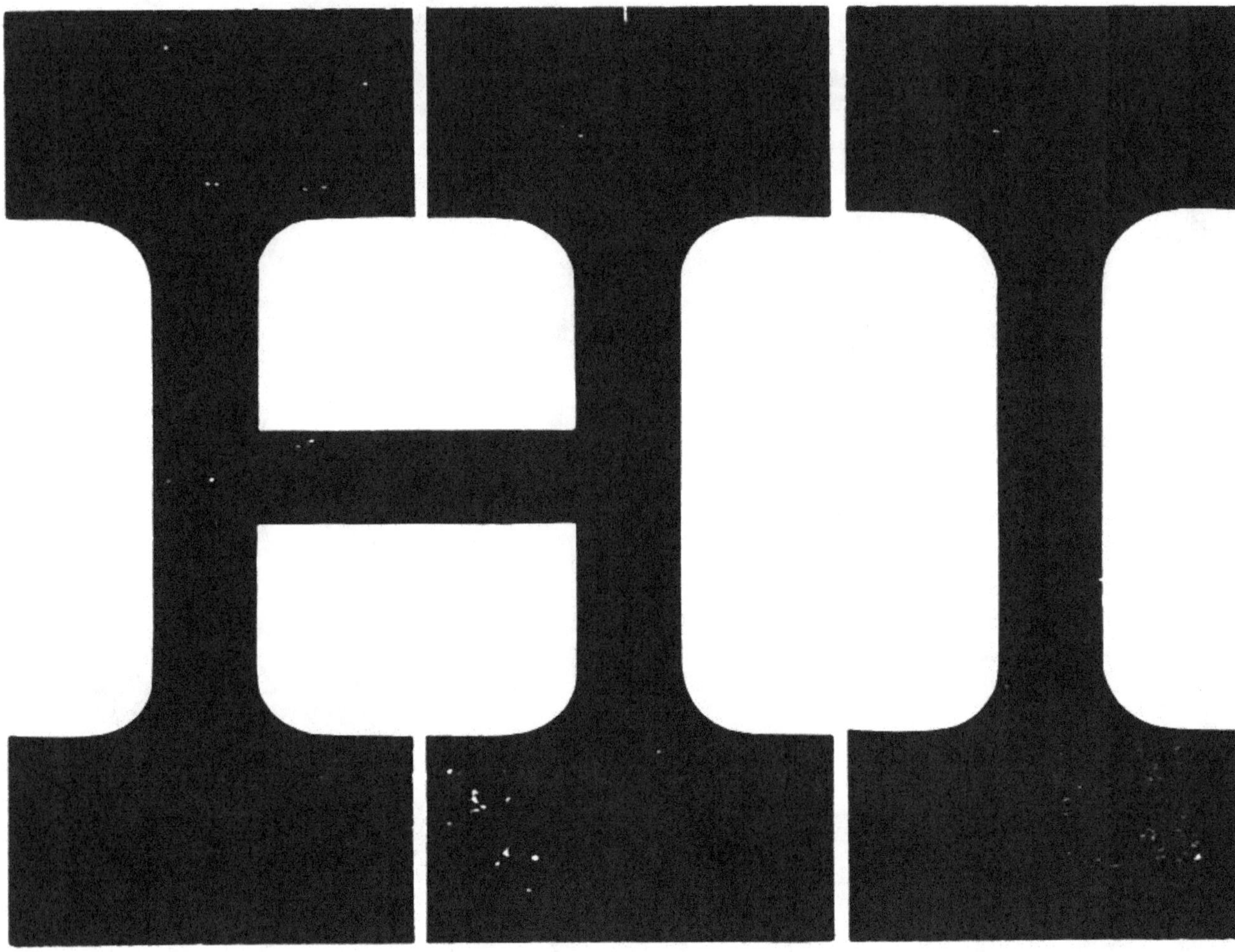

30 line [French Clarendon] cf. Hamilton: No. 116 [Actual size]

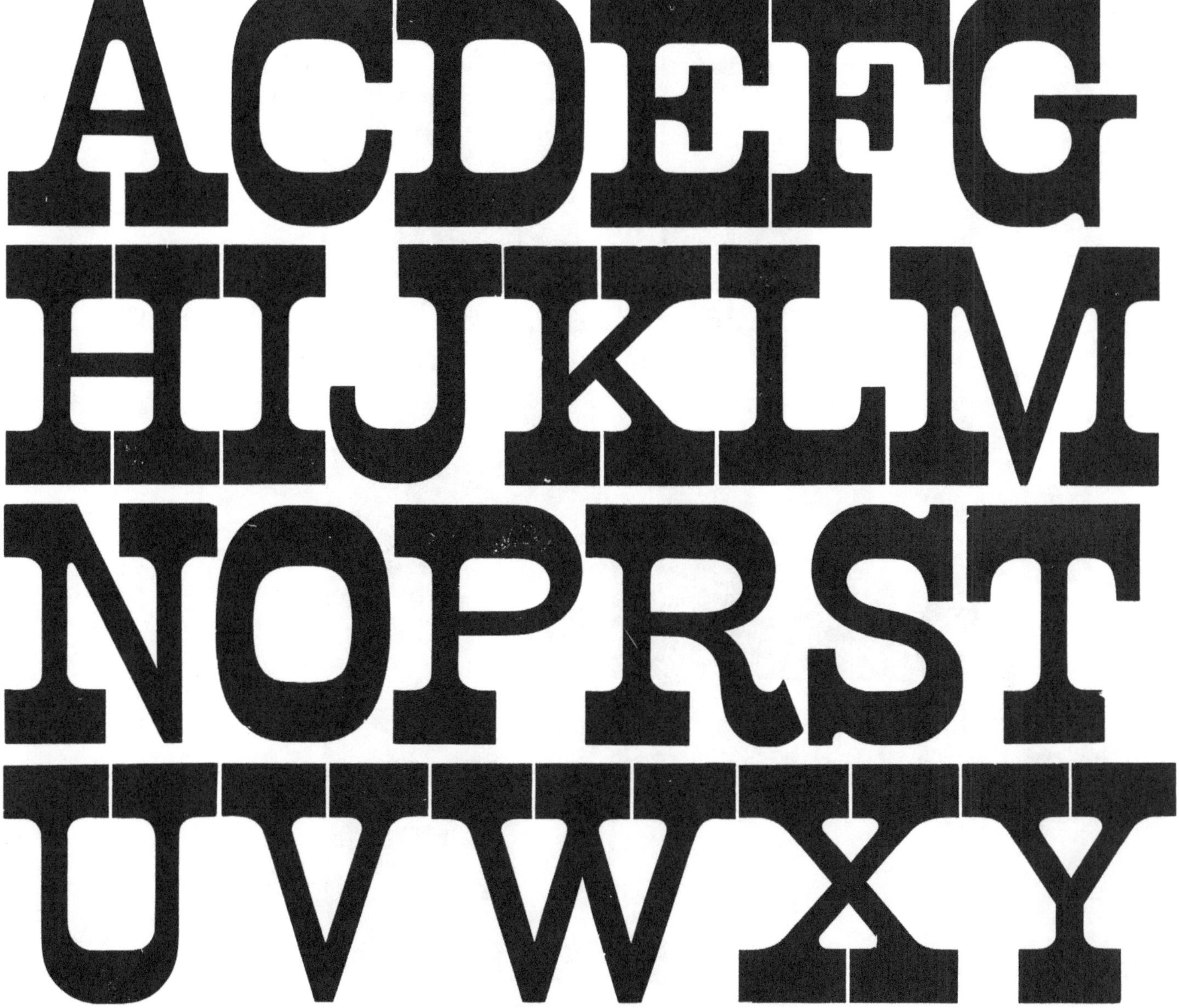

4.03.03.35 & 4.03.03.36
30 line [French Clarendon] cf. Hamilton: No. 116
Manufacturer and date unknown

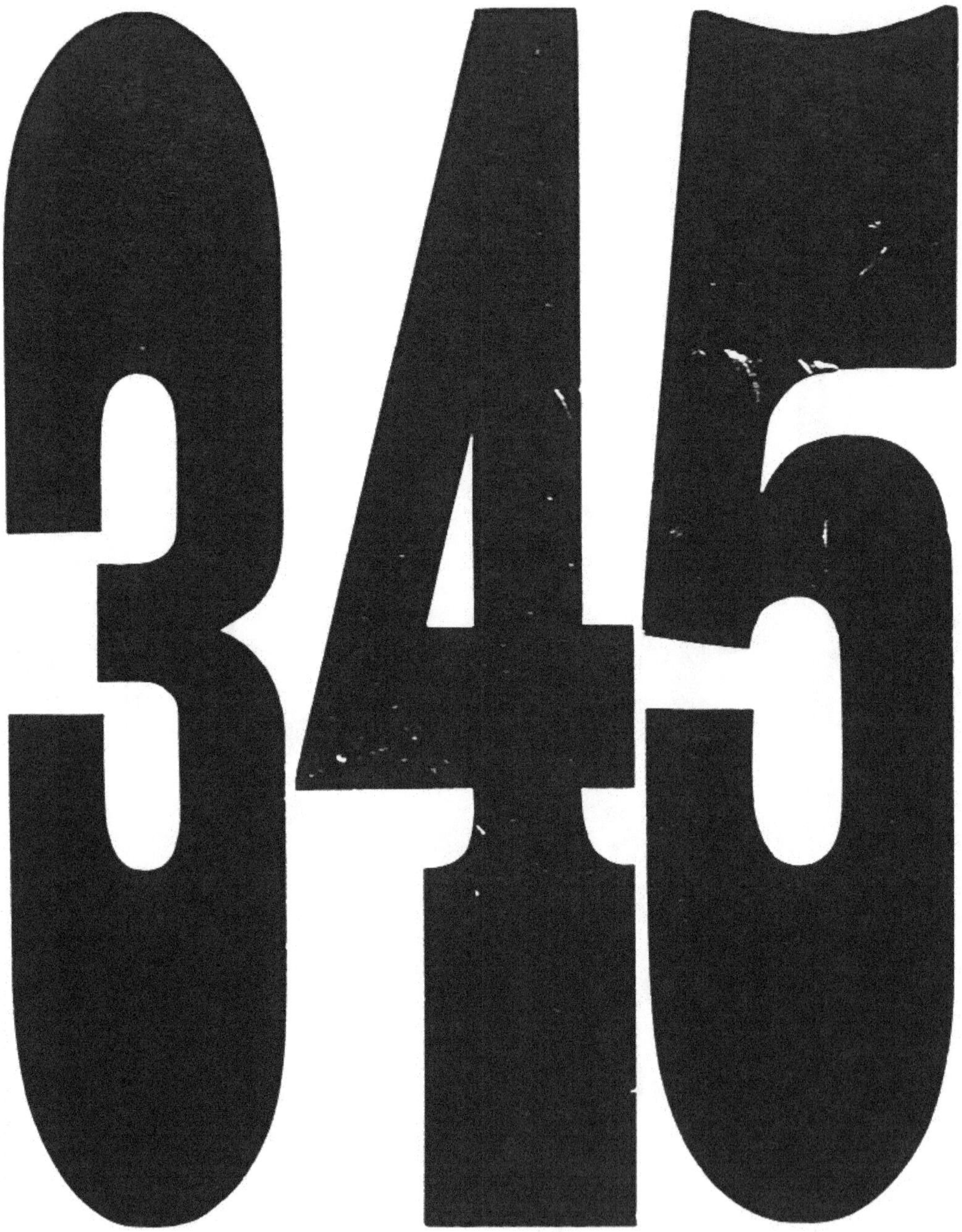

40 line [French Clarendon Condensed] cf. Hamilton: No. 24 [Actual size]

1234567

890

4.03.03.37
40 line [French Clarendon Condensed] cf. Hamilton: No. 24
Manufacturer and date unknown

NO

40 line No. 156 [Actual size]

ABCDEFG
NOPSTU
23456789

4.03.03.38 & 4.03.03.39
40 line No. 156
Hamilton Manufacturing Co., after 1891

YZ&$1

50 line [French Clarendon Condensed] cf. Page: Egyptian Extra Condensed [Actual size]

ABCDFGHI
JKLMNOP
QRSTUVW
XYZ&$12
3456780

4.03.03.40 & 4.03.03.41
50 line [French Clarendon Condensed] cf. Page: Egyptian Extra Condensed
Manufacturer and date unknown

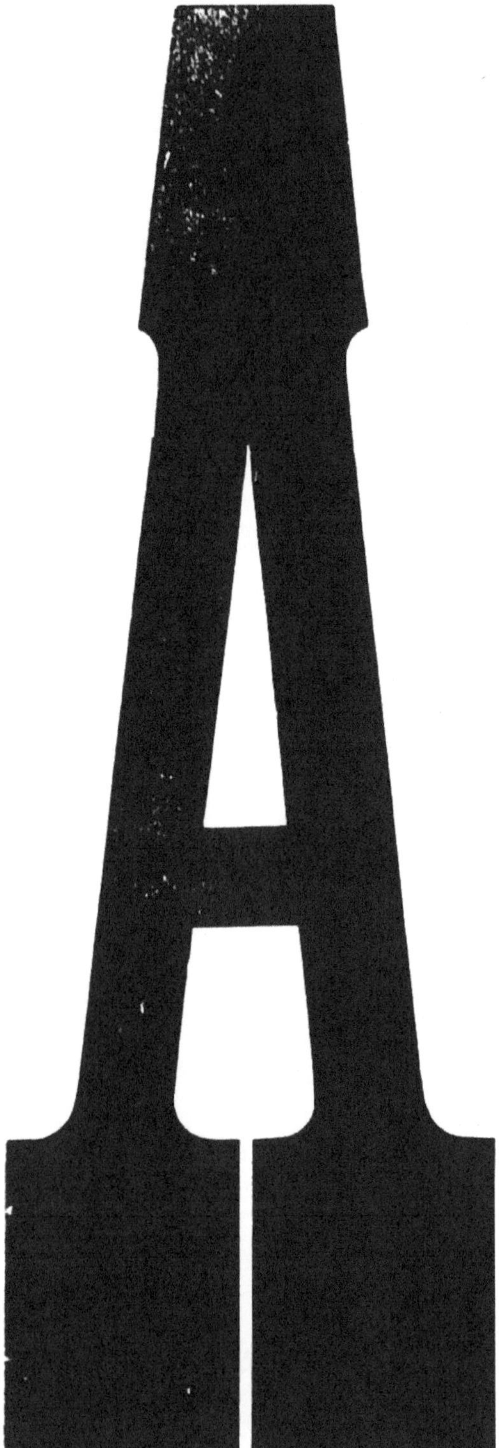

65 line Egyptian Extra Condensed
[This letter has been reduced to 70% of its actual size to fit the constraints of this book]

ABCDEFGHIJ
KLMNOPQRS
TUVWXY&Z
$123456780

4.03.03.42
65 line Egyptian Extra Condensed
William H. Page & Co., 1870 or later

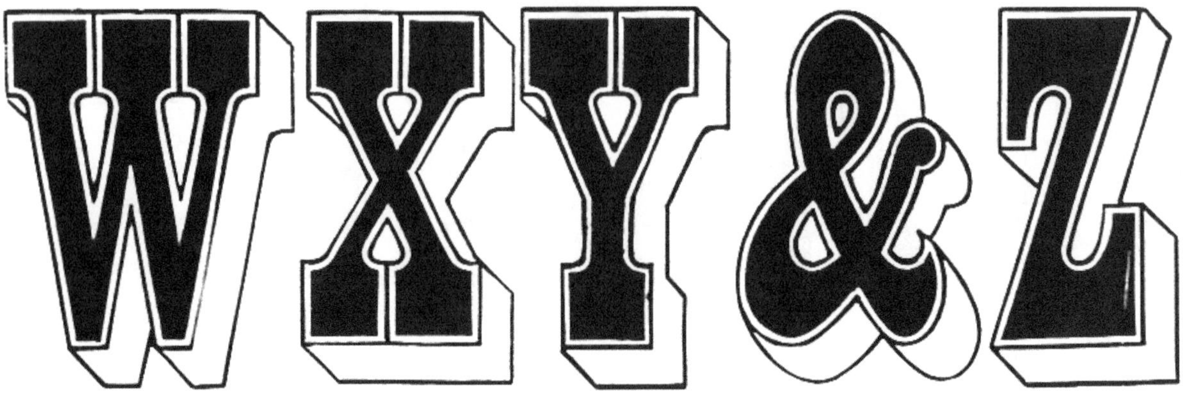

12 line Chromatic French Claredon Ornamented (first color-solid face) [Actual size]

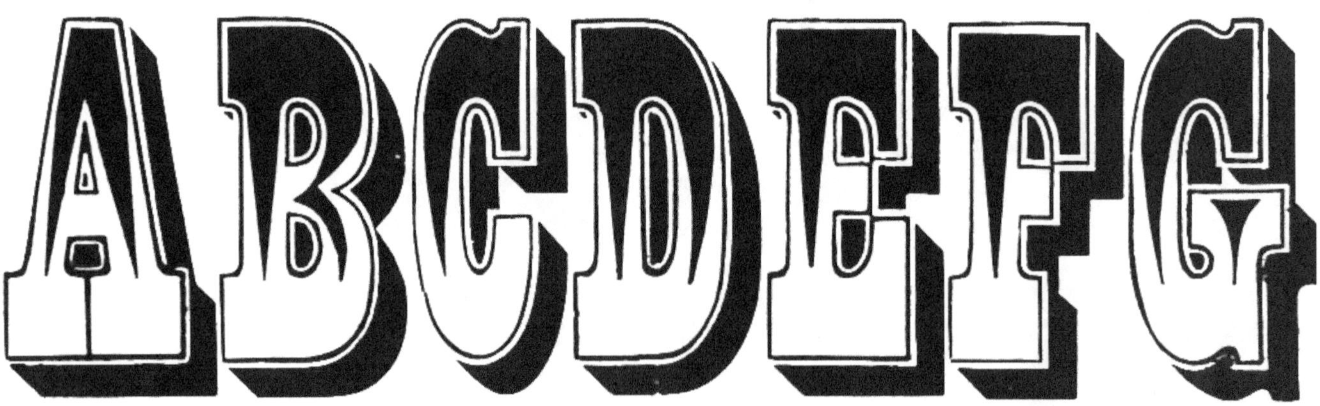

12 line Chromatic French Clarendon Ornamented (second color-ornamented face) [Actual size]

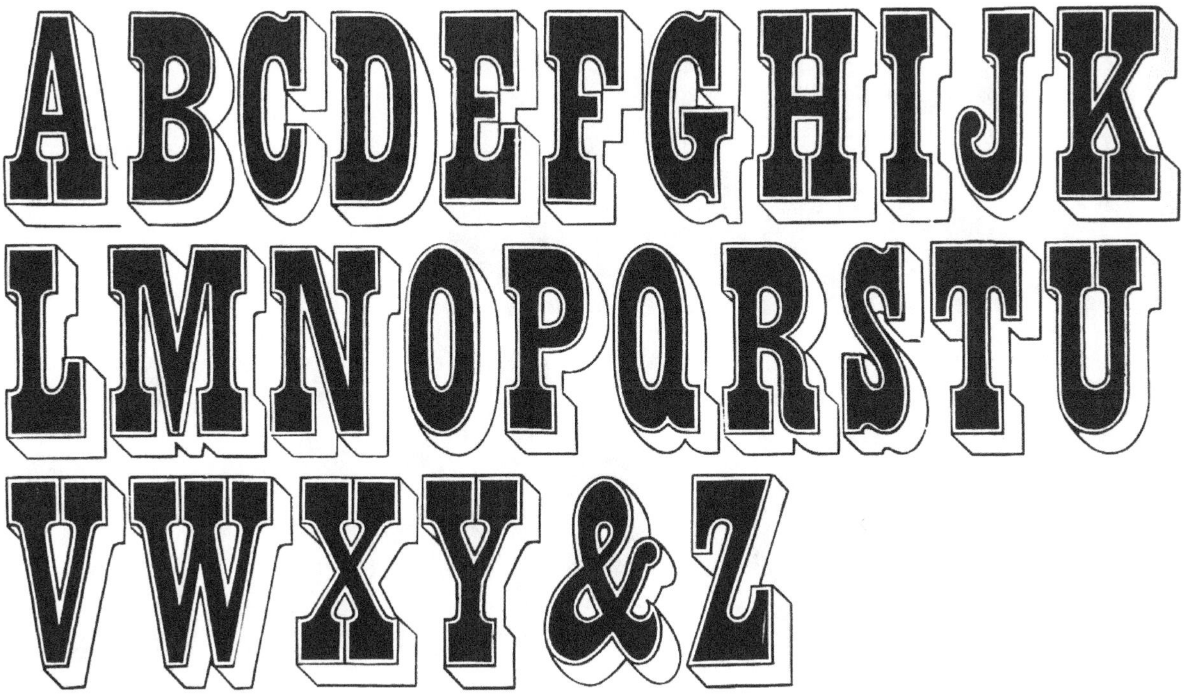

4.03.03.43
12 line Chromatic French Claredon Ornamented (first color-solid face)
William H. Page & Co., 1859 or later

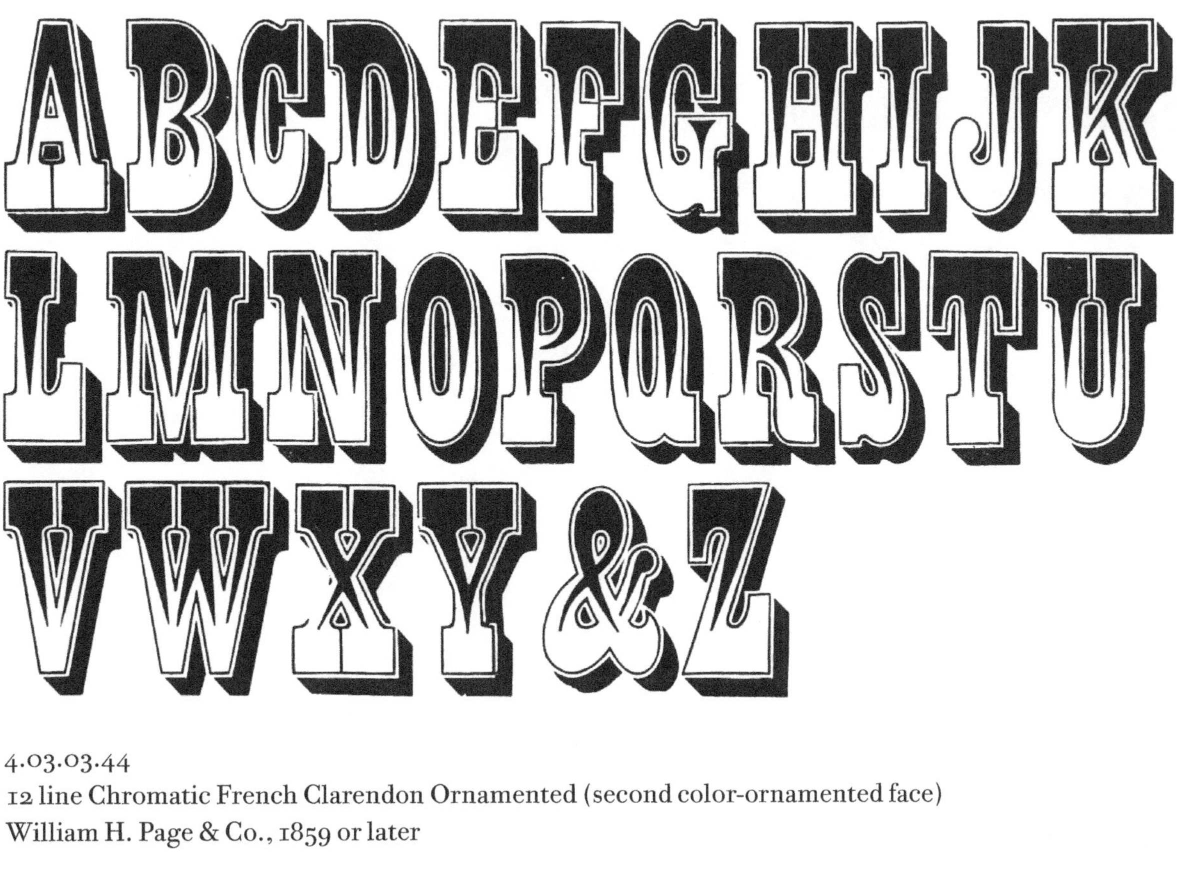

4.03.03.44
12 line Chromatic French Clarendon Ornamented (second color-ornamented face)
William H. Page & Co., 1859 or later

JKLMNOPQ

$123456 abcdefg

ff fi fl ffi ffl

10 line French Clarendon [Actual size]

ABCDEFGHIJKLMNOPQRST
UVWXY&Z $1234567890
abcdefghijklmnopqrstuvw
xyz ff fi fl ffi ffl

4.03.03.46
10 line French Clarendon
William H. Page & Co., 1859 or later

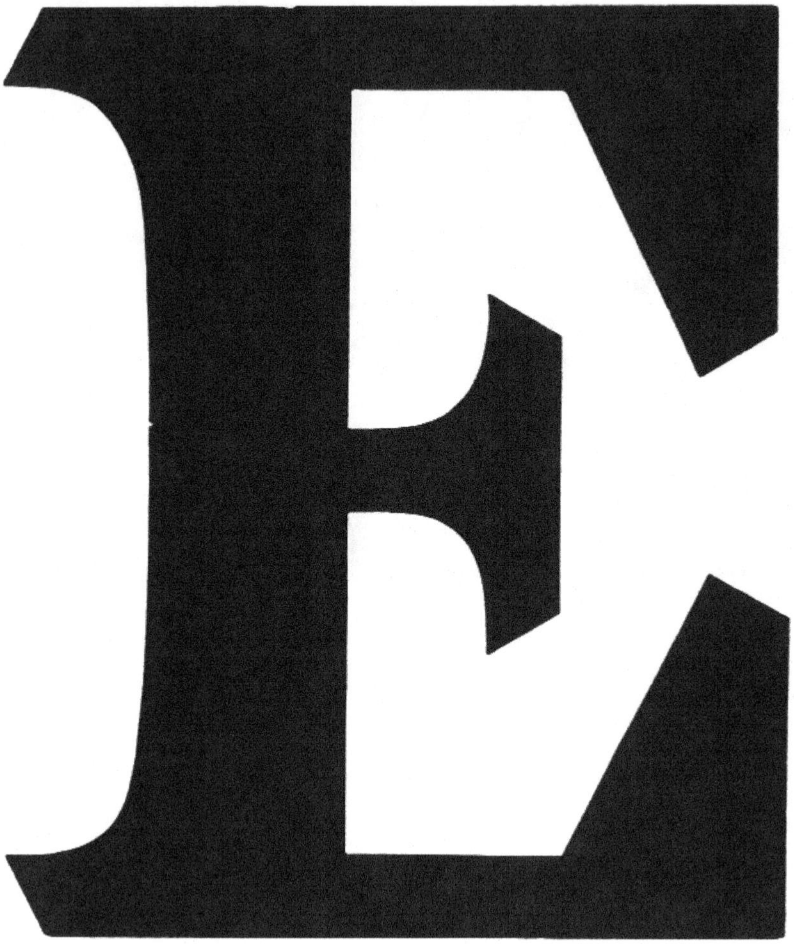

30 line Ætna Condensed [Actual size]

ABCD
EFGH
IJKL
MNOP
QRST
UVW
XY&Z

4.03.04.01 & 4.03.04.02
30 line Ætna Condensed
Morgans & Wilcox Mfg. Co., after 1881

ABC
WXY&Z
$123

10 line [Painter's Roman Condensed Open] cf. Heber Wells Roman Condensed No. 1 [Actual size]

ABCDEFGHIJK
LMNOPQRSTUV
WXY&Z
$1234567890

4.03.04.03
10 line [Painter's Roman Condensed Open] cf. Heber Wells Roman Condensed No. 1
Herber Wells, 1890–1898

GHIJ $1234

4 line [Antique Tuscan] cf. Hamilton No. 25 [Actual size]

PQR $23

4 line No. 15 [Actual size]

QRSTU

4 line [Antique Tuscan Expanded] cf. Page: Antique Tuscan Expanded [Actual size]

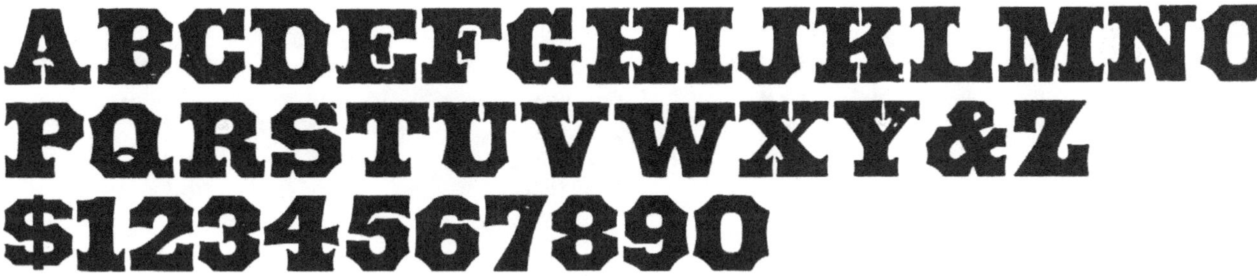

4.03.05.01
4 line [Antique Tuscan] cf. Hamilton No. 25
Manufacturer and date unknown

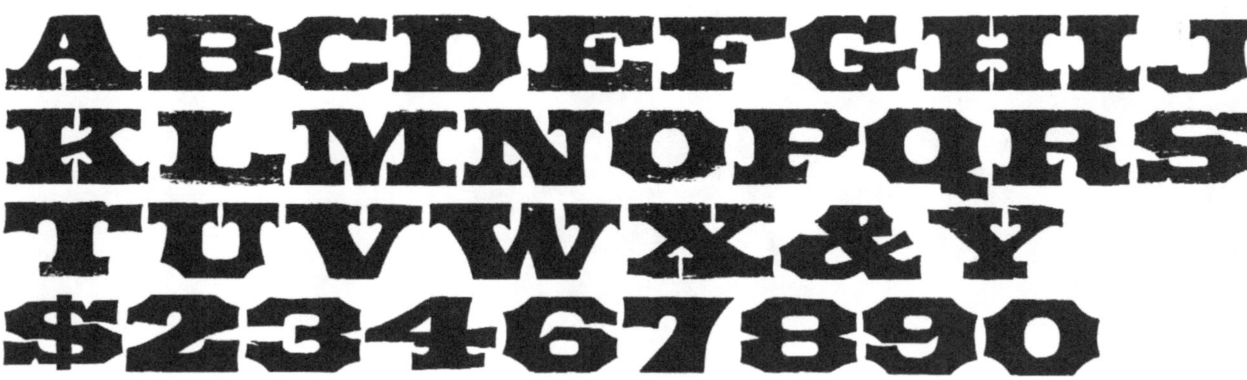

4.03.05.02
4 line No. 15
Hamilton Manufacturing Co., 1880-1889

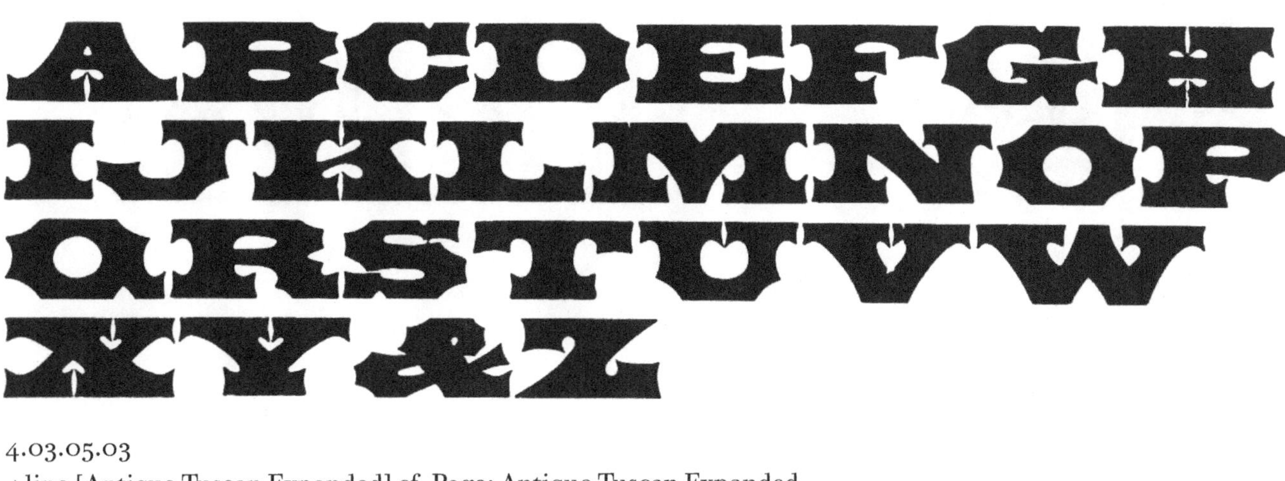

4.03.05.03
4 line [Antique Tuscan Expanded] cf. Page: Antique Tuscan Expanded
Manufacturer and date unknown

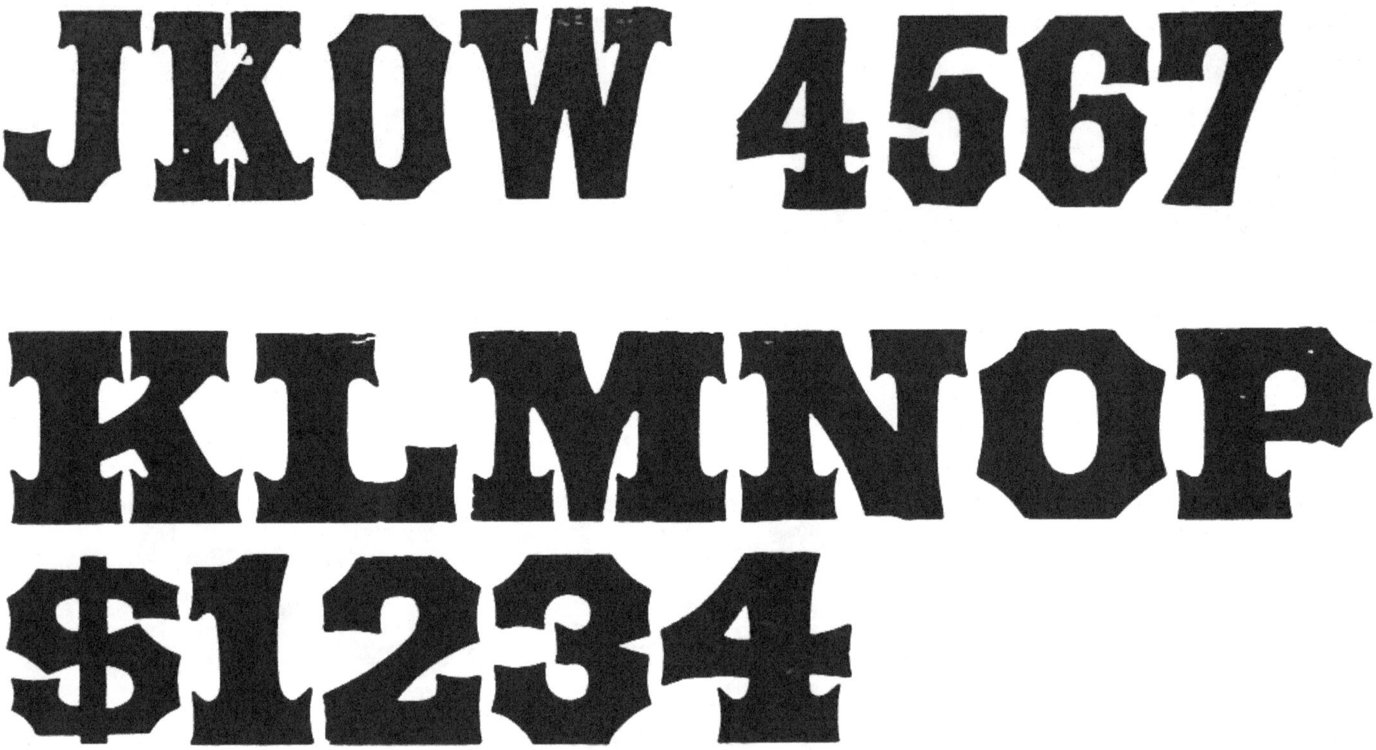

6 line No. 25 [Actual size]

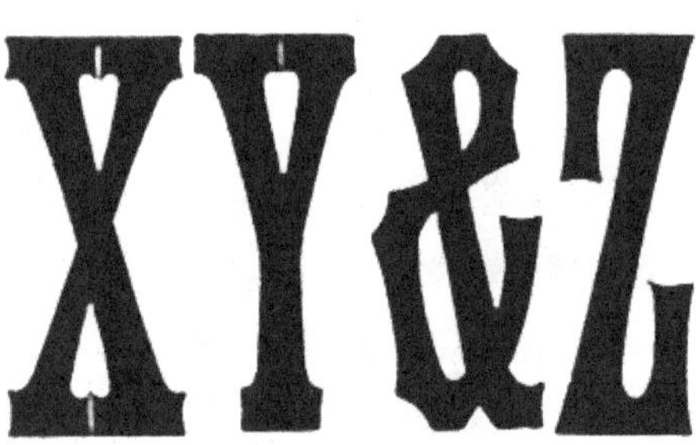

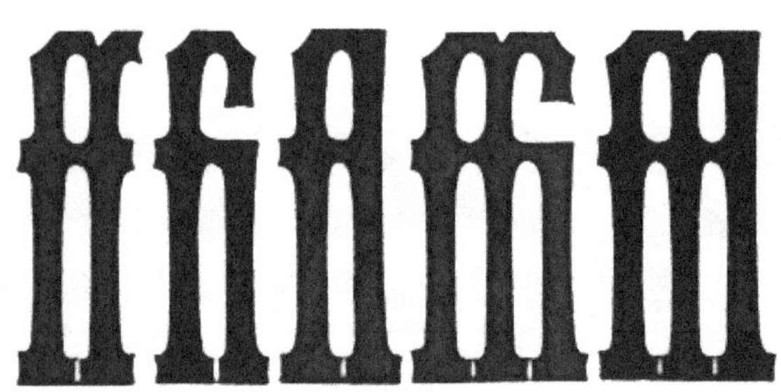

8 line Antique Tuscan Double Extra Condensed No. 1 [Actual size]

RDFGJKOW 1234567

4.03.05.04
6 line No. 48
Hamilton Manufacturing Co., 1880-1889

ABCDEFGHIJ
KLMNOPQRST
UVWXY&Z
$1234567890

4.03.05.05
6 line No. 25
Hamilton Manufacturing Co., 1880-1889

ABCDEFGHIJKLMNPRSTUVW
XY&Z ff fi fl ffi ffl
abcdefghijklmnopqrstuvwxyz

4.03.05.06
8 line Antique Tuscan Double Extra Condensed No. 1
William H. Page & Co., 1857-1859

QRSTUV
abcde

8 line [Antique Tuscan] cf. Page: Antique Tuscan Condensed [Actual size]

ABC MNO

10 line Antique Tuscan Extra Condensed [Actual size]

CEGHIJKLNOP
QRSTUVWX&Y
abcdefghijlmno
pqrstuvwxyz fi

4.03.05.07
8 line [Antique Tuscan] cf. Page: Antique Tuscan Condensed
Manufacturer and date unknown

ABCDEFGHIJKL
MNOPRSTUW
XY&Z

4.03.05.08
10 line Antique Tuscan Extra Condensed
William H. Page & Co, 1959 or later

PQRSTUV

10 line [Antique Tuscan Condensed] cf. Page: Antique Tuscan Extra Condensed [Actual size]

ABCD

12 line [Antique Tuscan] cf. Page: Antique Tuscan Condensed [Actual size]

ABCDFGIJKLNO
PQRSTUVWXY

4.03.05.09
10 line [Antique Tuscan Condensed] cf. Page: Antique Tuscan Extra Condensed
Manufacturer and date unknown

ABCDEFG
HIJKLMS
NOPQRT
UVWXYZ

4.03.05.10
12 line [Antique Tuscan] cf. Page: Antique Tuscan Condensed
Manufacturer and date unknown

FGH

15 line [Antique Tuscan] cf. Page: Antique Tuscan Condensed [Actual size]

Z8

12 line [Antique Tuscan] cf. Page: Antique Tuscan Condensed [Actual size]

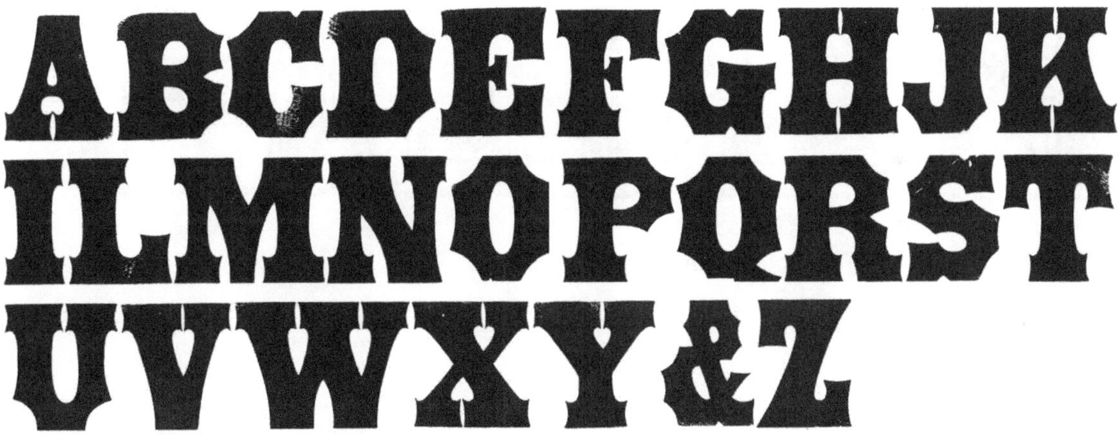

4.03.05.11
15 line [Antique Tuscan] cf. Page: Antique Tuscan Condensed
Manufacturer and date unknown

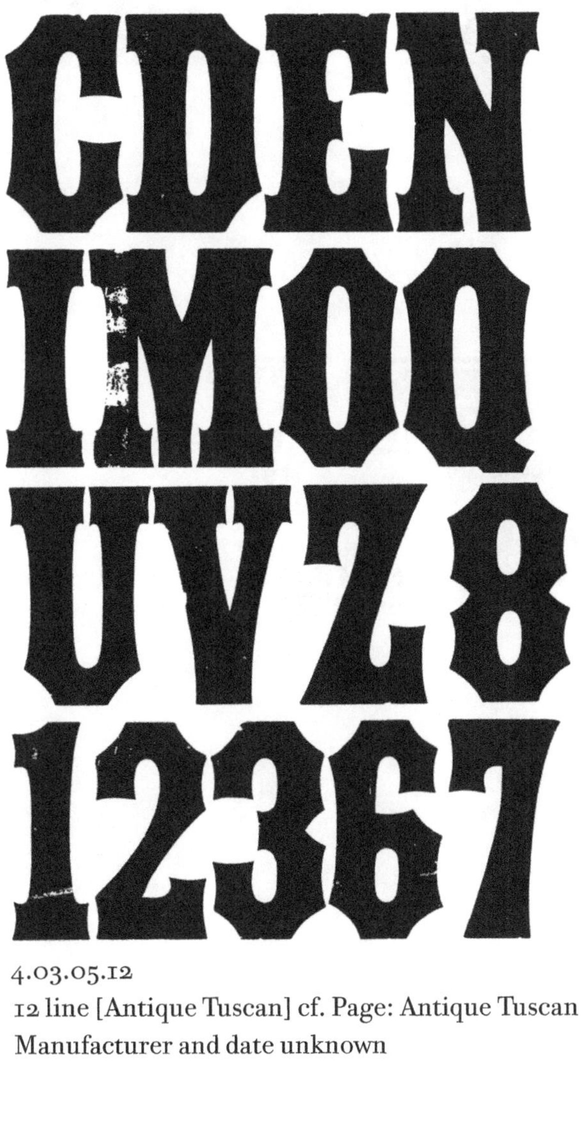

4.03.05.12
12 line [Antique Tuscan] cf. Page: Antique Tuscan Condensed
Manufacturer and date unknown

JKLMN

6 line Chromatic Antique Tuscan Shade Nos. 1 & 2 (one color only) [Actual size]

WXY&Z!

6 line Chromatic American (one color only) [Actual size]

&ÆŒ!

8 line [Antique Tuscan Outlined] cf. Hamilton: No. 416 [Actual size]

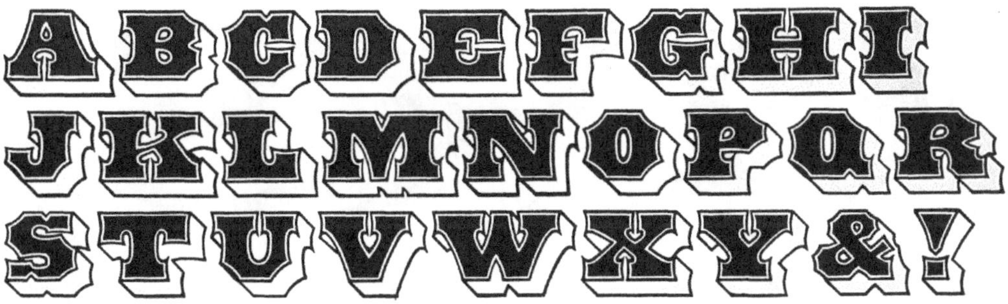

4.03.05.13
6 line Chromatic Antique Tuscan Shade Nos. 1 & 2 (one color only)
William H. Page & Co., 1857–1859

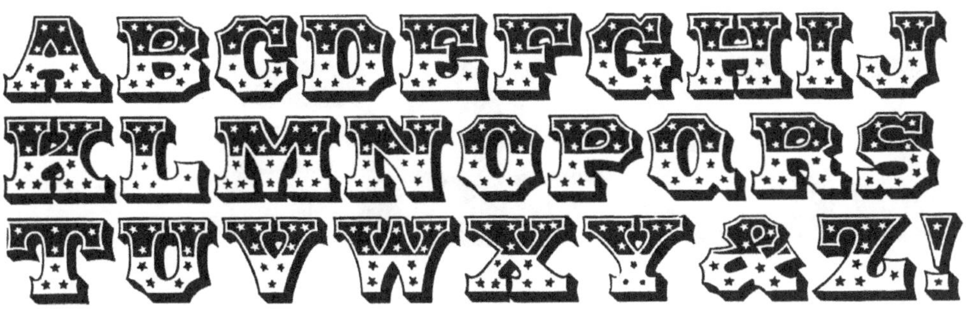

4.03.05.14
6 line Chromatic American (one color only)
William H. Page & Co., 1857–1859

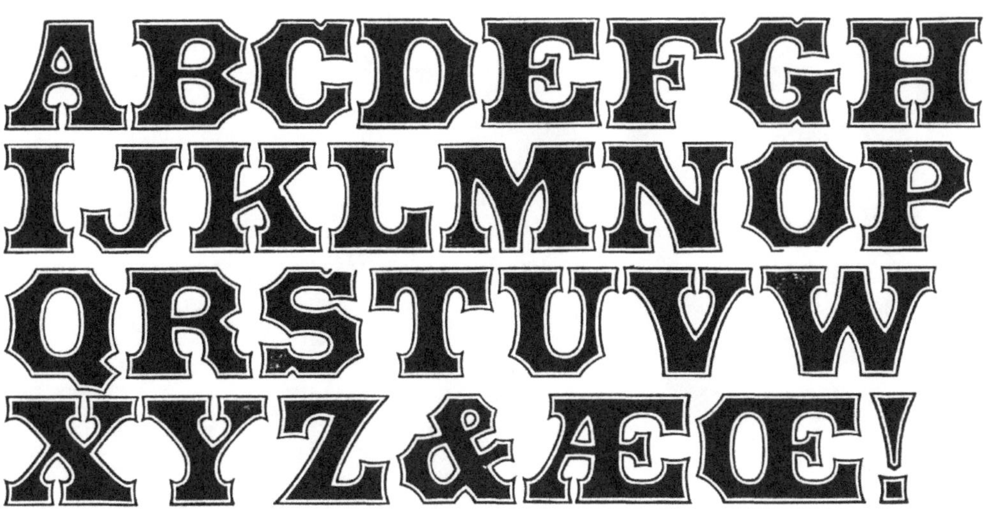

4.03.05.15
8 line [Antique Tuscan Outlined] cf. Hamilton: No. 416
Manufacturer and date unknown

OPQRS
hi jlmn
$12345

6 line DeVinne [Actual size]

ABCDEFGHI
JLMOPQRS
TUVWYZ
abcdefhijlmn
oprstuvwxyz
$1234567890

4.04.01.01
6 line DeVinne
Morgans & Wilcox Mfg. Co., after 1881

ABCDEFGHI
fghiklmnopq
$1234567890

8 line [DeVinne Extra Condensed] cf. Hamilton: No. 638 [Actual size]

ABCDEFGHIJKLMN
OPQRSSTUVWXYZ
abcdefghiklmnopqrs
stuvwxyz&
$1234567890

4.04.01.02
8 line [DeVinne Extra Condensed] cf. Hamilton: No. 638
Manufacturer and date unknown

NOPQR
abcdefg
$123456

8 line [DeVinne] cf. Hamilton: No. 627 [Actual size]

ABCEFGHIJK
LMMNOPQR
SSTUVWX
Y&Z
abcdefghijlmn
oprsstuvwxz
$1234567890

4.04.01.03
8 line [DeVinne] cf. Hamilton: No. 627
Manufacturer and date unknown

STU
Y&Z
$123

12 line [DeVinne] cf. Hamilton: No. 627 [Actual size]

CEFGHIJ
LNOQRS
STUVW
XY&Z
$1234567
890

4.04.01.04
12 line [DeVinne] cf. Hamilton: No. 627
Manufacturer and date unknown

NOPRST

fghij $346

15 line [DeVinne Double Extra Condensed] cf. Hamilton: No. 640 [Actual size]

ABCDEFHIJLM
NOPRSTVWXZ
abcdefghijlmnoq
stuwyz
$34678 90

4.04.01.05
15 line [DeVinne Double Extra Condensed] cf. Hamilton: No. 640
Manufacturer and date unknown

STUVWXY&Z
abcde $123456

4 line [DeVinne Italic] cf. Hamilton: No. 652 [Actual size]

ABC
fg $1

12 line [Roman Italic] cf. Hamilton: No. 644 [Actual size]

ABCDEFGHIJKLMNOPQR
STUVWXY&Z
abcdefghijklmnopqrstuvw
xyz $1234567890

4.04.01.06
4 line [DeVinne Italic] cf. Hamilton: No. 652
Manufacturer and date unknown

ABCEF
GHIJLM
NOPRST
UVW&Y
abcdefghi
jklmnopqr
stuvwxyz
$123456
7890

4.04.01.07
12 line [Roman Italic] cf. Hamilton: No. 644
Manufacturer and date unknown

TUVWXY&Z
hijklm $1234

6 line No. 654 [Actual size]

ABC xyz

15 line No. 640 [Actual size]

ABCDEFGHIJKLMNO
PQRSSTUVWXY&Z
abcdefghijklmnopqrss
tuvwxyz $1234567890

4.04.01.08
6 line No. 654
Hamilton Manufacturing Co., after 1891

ABCDEFGHIJK
LMNOPQRS
TUVWXY&Z
abcdefghijklmn
opqrstuvwxyz
$1234567890

4.04.01.09
15 line No. 640
Hamilton Manufacturing Co., after 1891

NOPQ

5 line No. 96 [Actual size]

ABCDEF $123456

8 line No. 2089 [Actual size]

JKfg

10 line No. 2087 [Actual size]

ABCDEFGHIJK
LMNOPQRSTU
VWXY&Z

4.04.02.01
5 line No. 96
Hamilton Manufacturing Co., after 1880–1889

ABCDEFGHIJKLMNOPQRSTU
VWXY&Z $1234567890

4.04.02.02
8 line No. 2089
American Wood Type Co. (Conn.), after 1883

ABCDEF
GHIJKL
MNOPQR
STUVWX
Y&Z
abcdefghij
klmnopqrs
tuvwxyz
$1234567
890

4.04.02.03
10 line No. 2087
American Wood Type Co. (Conn.), after 1883

MOPRS

12 line No. 500 [Actual size]

NQ gik

15 line No. 506 [Actual size]

BEFGIJLMOPRS
UVWYZ

4.04.02.04
12 line No. 500
William H. Page & Co., 1887-1891

FGJNQSVW
Xbcdegiklno
qrsuvwz

4.04.02.05
15 line No. 506
Hamilton Manufacturing Co., 1891-1906

FGHIJK

QRSTU

WXY&Z

8 line No. 514 [Actual size]

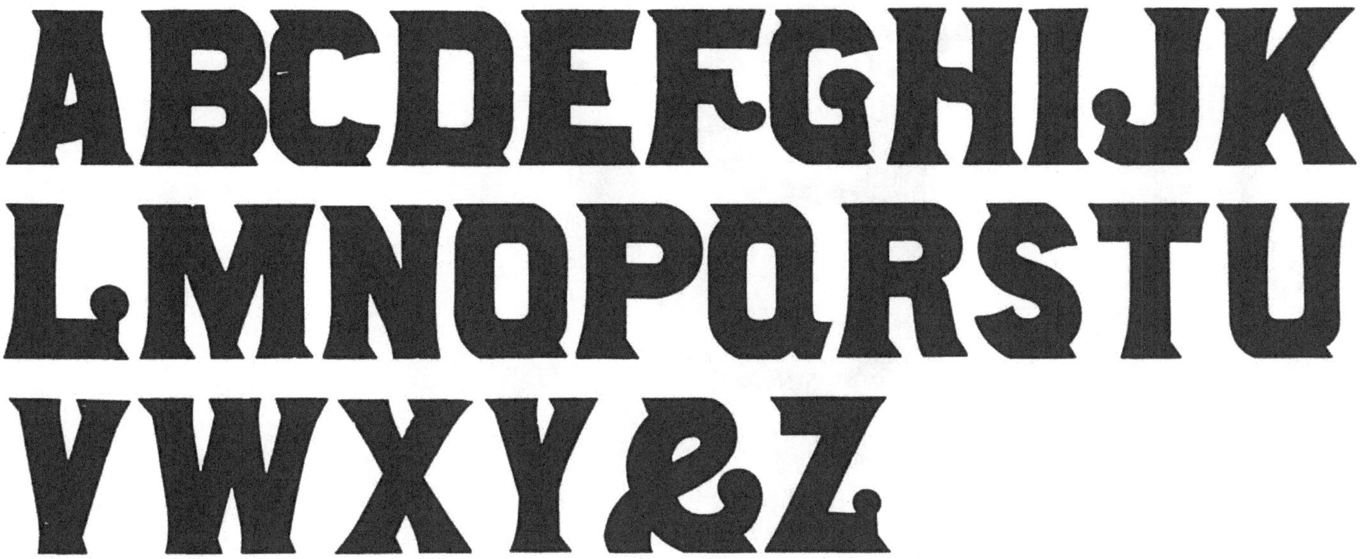

4.04.03.01
8 line No. 514
Hamilton Manufacturing Co., 1891-1906

ABC
MNO
1234

12 line No. 784, Goudy Extra Bold [Actual size]

ABCDEF
GHIJKL
MNOPQ
RSTUV
WXY&Z
1234567890

4.05.01.01
12 line No. 784, Goudy Extra Bold
Hamilton Manufacturing Co., after 1891

PQRSTU
aabc
fghhijkl
$l23456

6 line [Roman "Antiqued"] cf. Hamilton: No. 661, Plymouth [Actual size]

ABCDEFGHIJK
LMNOPQRSTU
VWXYZ
aabcdefghhijkl
mmnnopqrstu
uvwxyz
$1234567890

4.05.02.01
6 line [Roman "Antiqued"] cf. Hamilton: No. 661, Plymouth
Manufacturer and date unknown

WXY&Z
$1234567

8 line [Cooper Black Condensed] cf. Hamilton: No. 780 [Actual size]

4

25 line [Roman] [Actual size]

ABCDEFGHIJKL
MNOPQRSTUV
WXY&Z
$1234567890

4.05.02.02
8 line [Cooper Black Condensed] cf. Hamilton: No. 780
Manufacturer and date unknown

245
678

4.05.02.03
25 line [Roman]
Manufacturer and date unknown

1

60 line [Roman] [This letter has been reduced to 75% of its actual size to fit the constraints of this book]

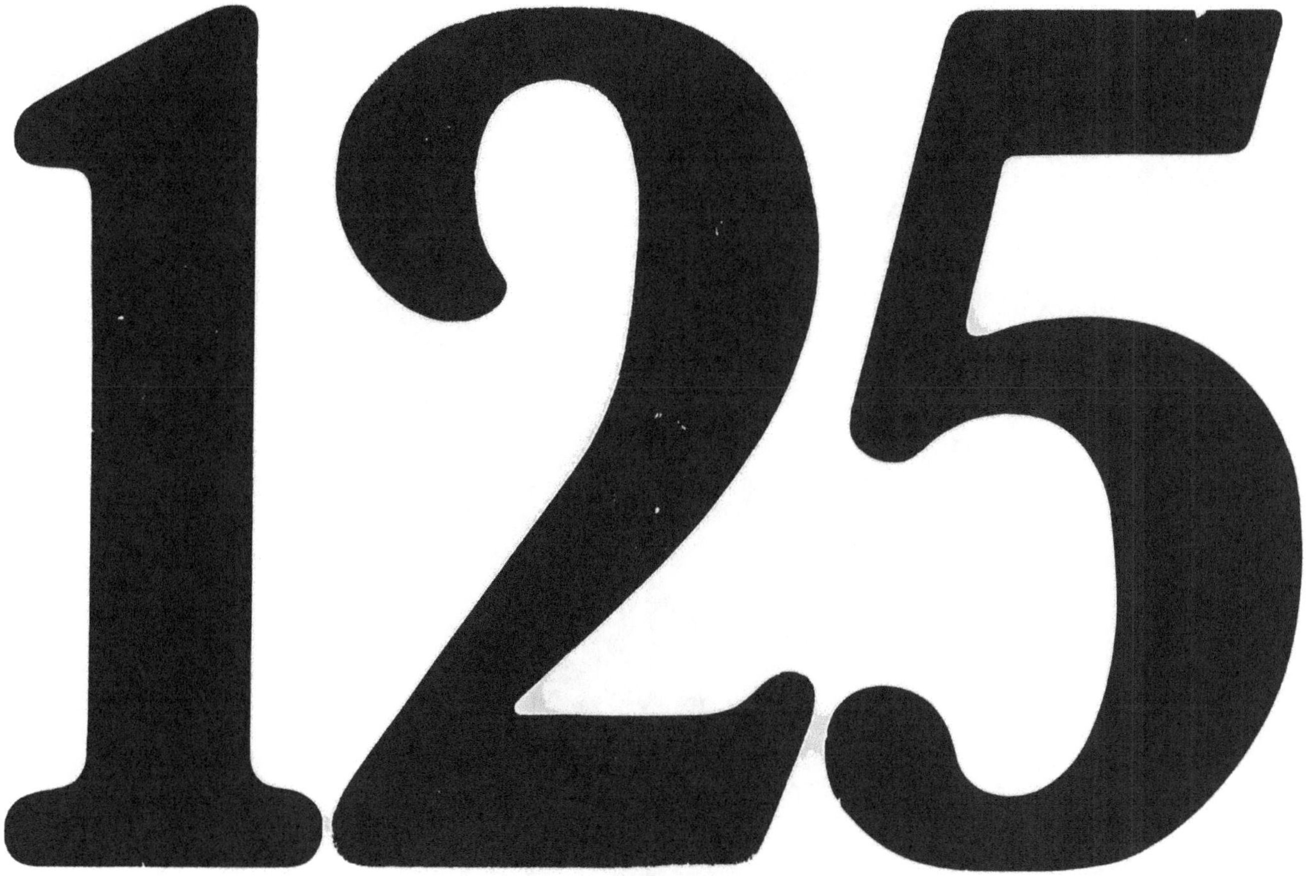

4.05.02.04
60 line [Roman]
Manufacturer and date unknown

Y

60 line [Roman] [This letter has been reduced to 55% of its actual size to fit the constraints of this book.]

[Large specimens of 72 line [Roman] and 96 line [Roman] are shown on the following pages: 194 & 195.]

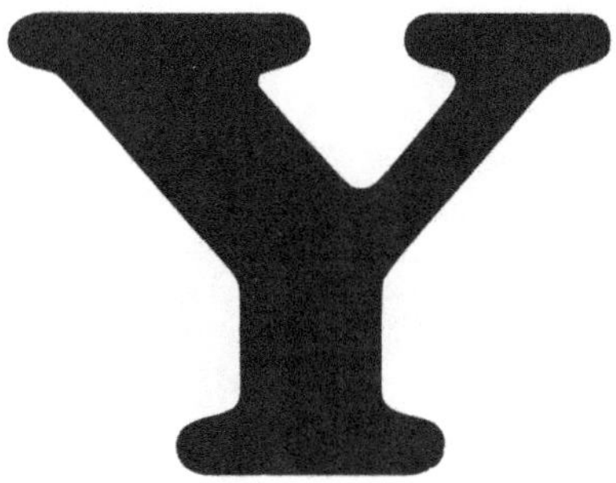

4.05.02.05
60 line [Roman]
Manufacturer and date unknown

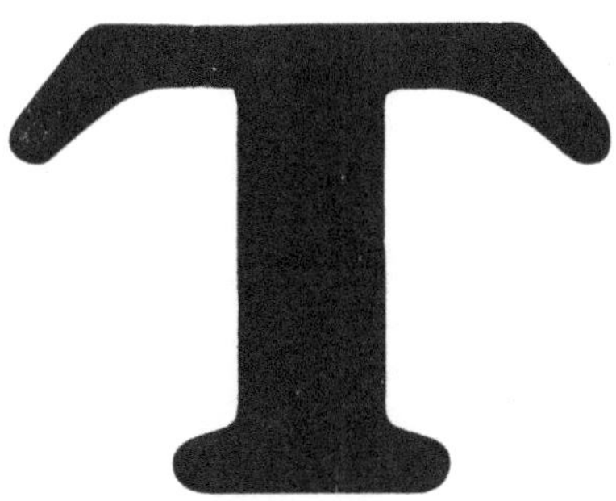

4.05.02.06
72 line [Roman]
Manufacturer and date unknown

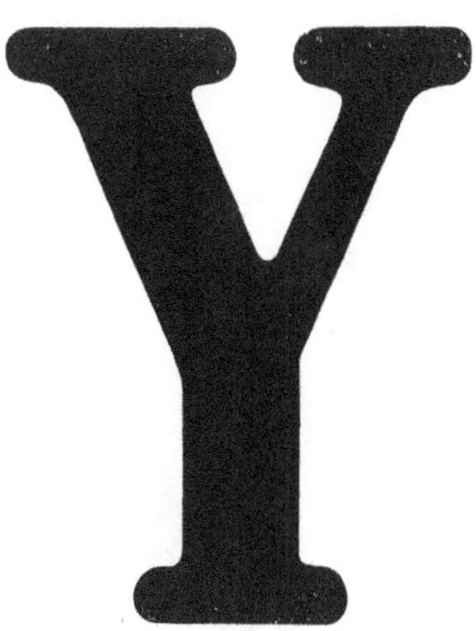

4.05.02.07
96 line [Roman]
Manufacturer and date unknown

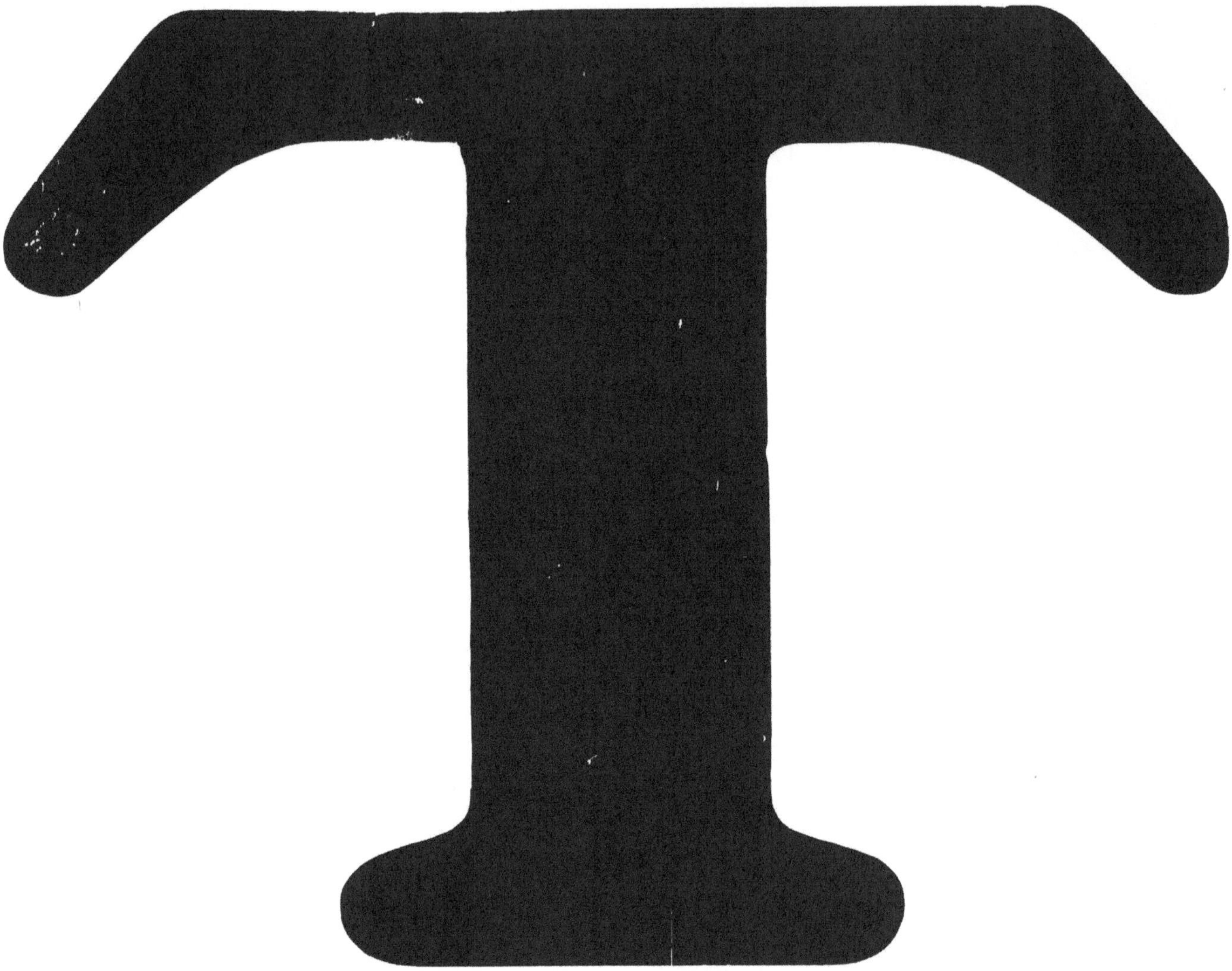

72 line [Roman] [This letter has been reduced to 45% of its actual size to fit the constraints of this book.]

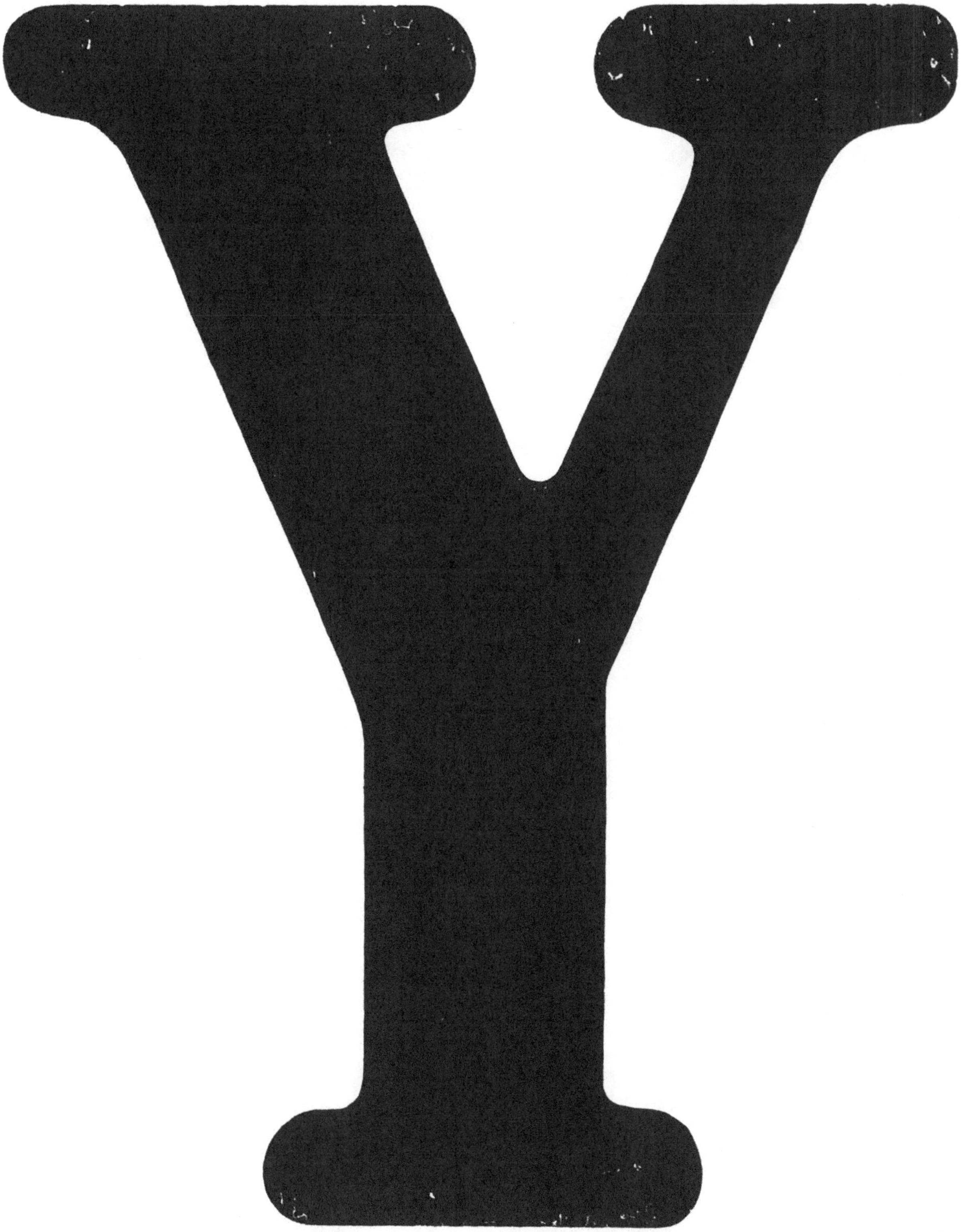

96 line [Roman]
[This letter has been reduced to 45% of its actual size to fit the constraints of this book.]

ABCDE
MNOPR

8 line [Antique Tuscan] cf. Hamilton: No. 6025, Special [Actual size]

GIKLO

8 line No. 59 [Actual size]

ABCDEFGIKL
MNOPRSTV
WY

4.06.01.01
8 line [Antique Tuscan] cf. Hamilton: No. 6025, Special
Manufacturer and date unknown

GIKLORSVWX

4.06.01.02
8 line No. 59
Hamilton Manufacturing Co., 1880–1889

JKLM

PQST

20 line No. 59 [Actual size]

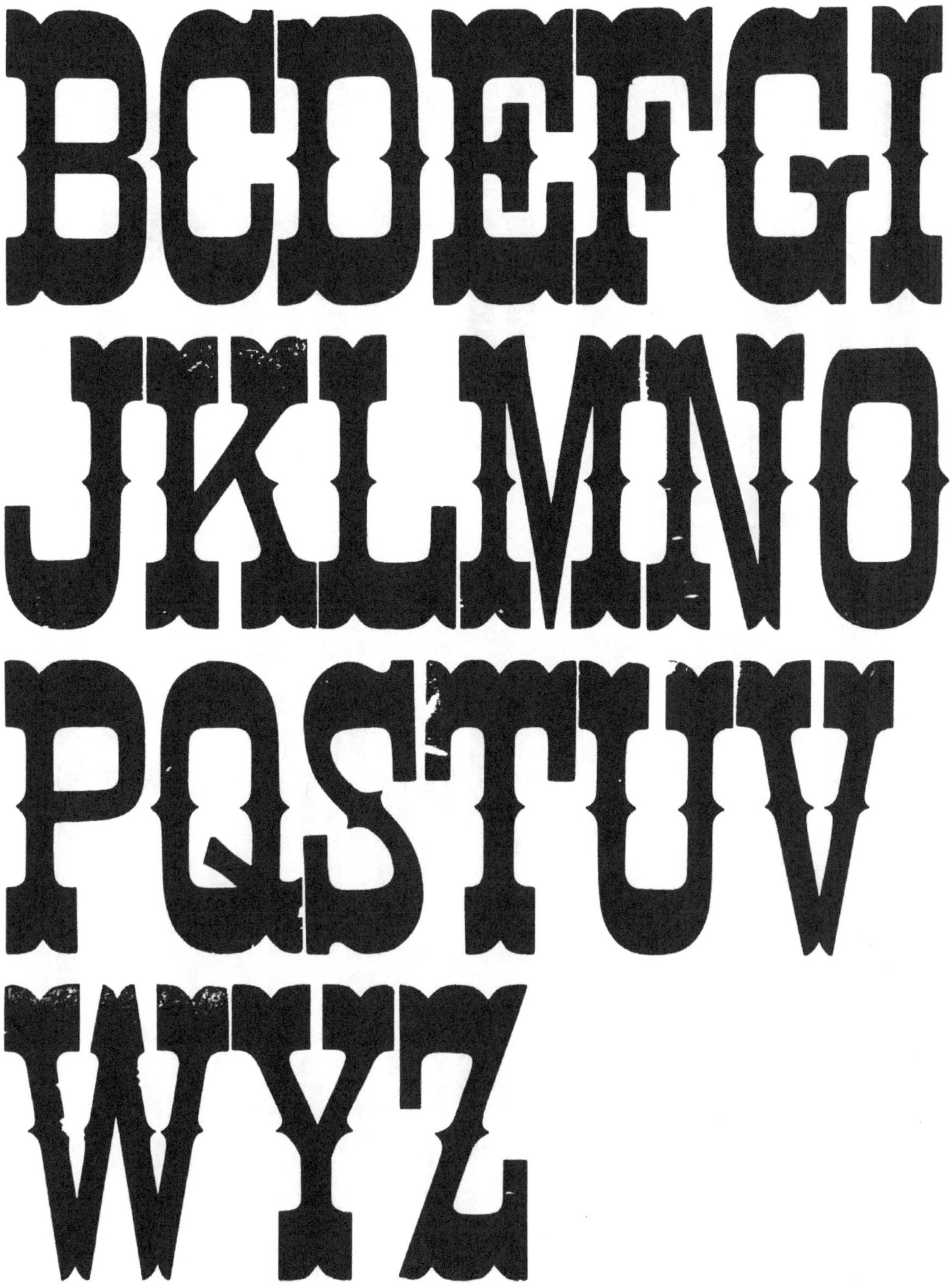

4.06.01.03
20 line No. 59
Hamilton Manufacturing Co., 1880–1889

STUVWXY&Z
fghijkl ff fi ffi fl
$12345

6 line Antique Tuscan No. 11 [Actual size]

WXY&Z
ff fi ffi fl

abcdefghij
$1234567

10 line Antique Tuscan No. 9 [Actual size]

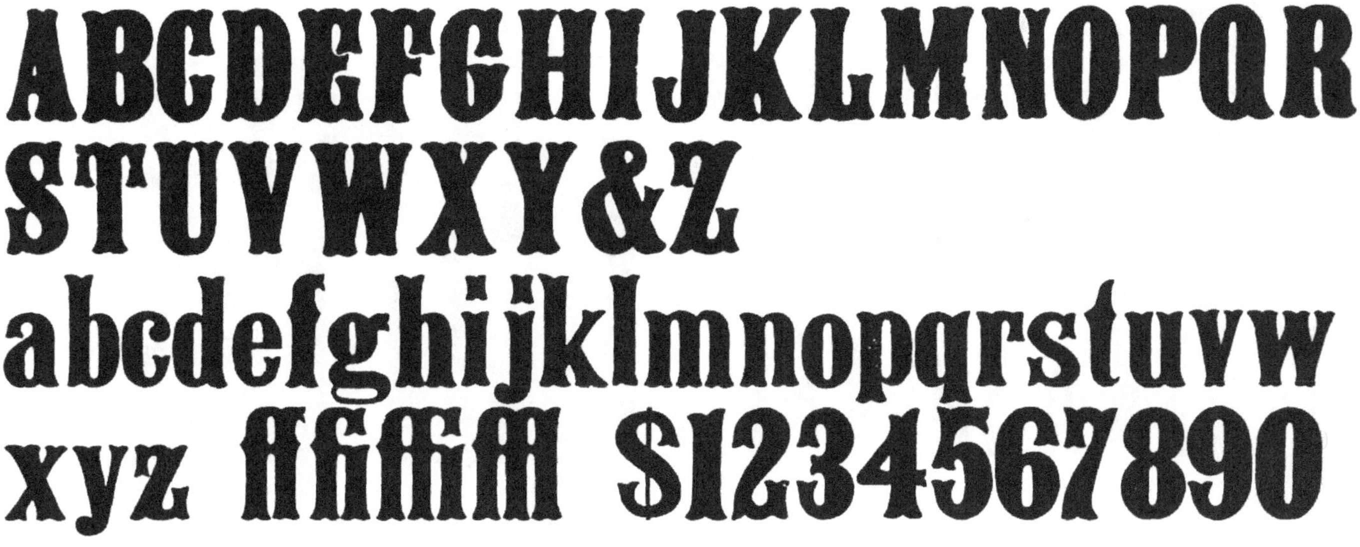

4.06.02.01
6 line Antique Tuscan No. 11
William H. Page & Co., 1857–1859

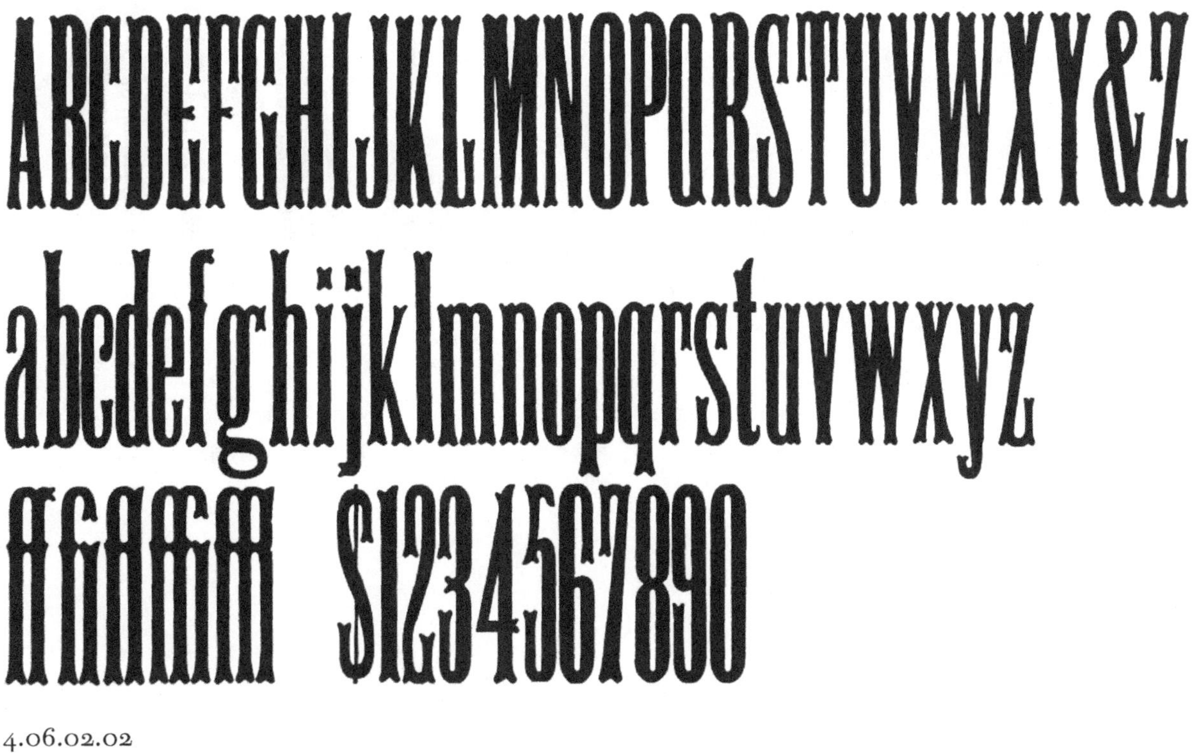

4.06.02.02
10 line Antique Tuscan No. 9
William H. Page & Co., 1857–1859

YZ&ÆŒ ghijkl

æœfffifl $12345

15 line [Tuscan Extra Condensed] cf. Page: Antique Tuscan No. 9 [Actual size]

ABCDEFGHIJKLMNOPRSTU

VWXYZ&ÆŒ

abcdefghijklmnopqrstuvw

xyzæœff fi fl ffi ffl

$1234567890

4.06.02.03
15 line [Tuscan Extra Condensed] cf. Page: Antique Tuscan No. 9
Manufacturer and date unknown

FGHIKLM
OPQRST
abcdefgh
lmnpqr
$2345780

4 line Runie Expanded [Actual size]

ABCDEFGHIKLM
OPQRSTUVWXYZ
abcdefghijklmnpqr
stuvwxyz
$2345780

4.06.03.01
4 line Runie Expanded
Vanderburgh, Wells & Co., 1867-1890

RSTVWXY&Z

6 line [Antique Tuscan] cf. Hamilton: No. 325 [Actual size]

ABDFGHIJKLMNOP

8 line [Antique Tuscan Condensed] cf. Hamilton No. 321 [Actual size]

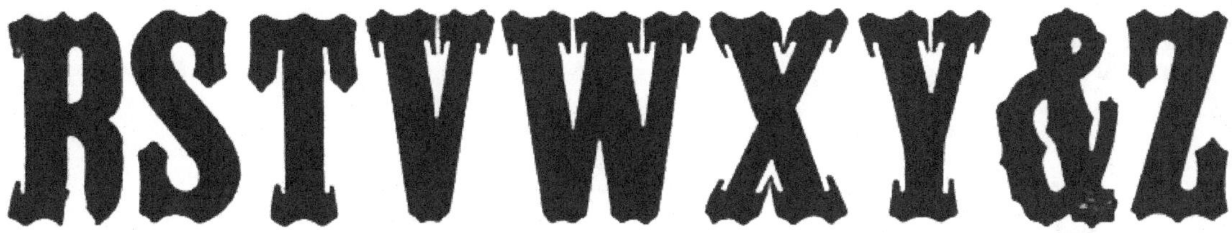

4.06.04.01
6 line [Antique Tuscan] cf. Hamilton: No. 325
Vanderburgh, Wells & Co., 1867–1890

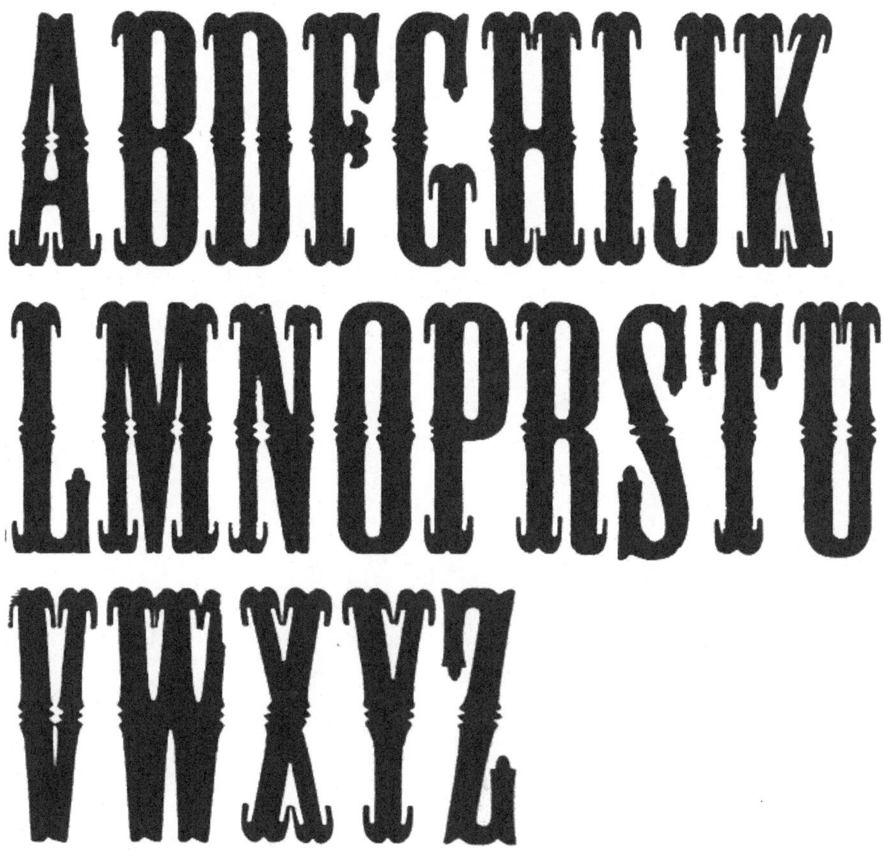

4.06.04.02
8 line [Antique Tuscan Condensed] cf. Hamilton No. 321
Manufacturer and date unknown

AEKLPT

7 line [Tuscan Condensed] cf. Page: Armenian [Actual size]

AEKLPTUWY&Z

4.06.05.01
7 line [Tuscan Condensed] cf. Page: Armenian
Manufacturer and date unknown

ABCD

15 line No. 515 [Actual size]

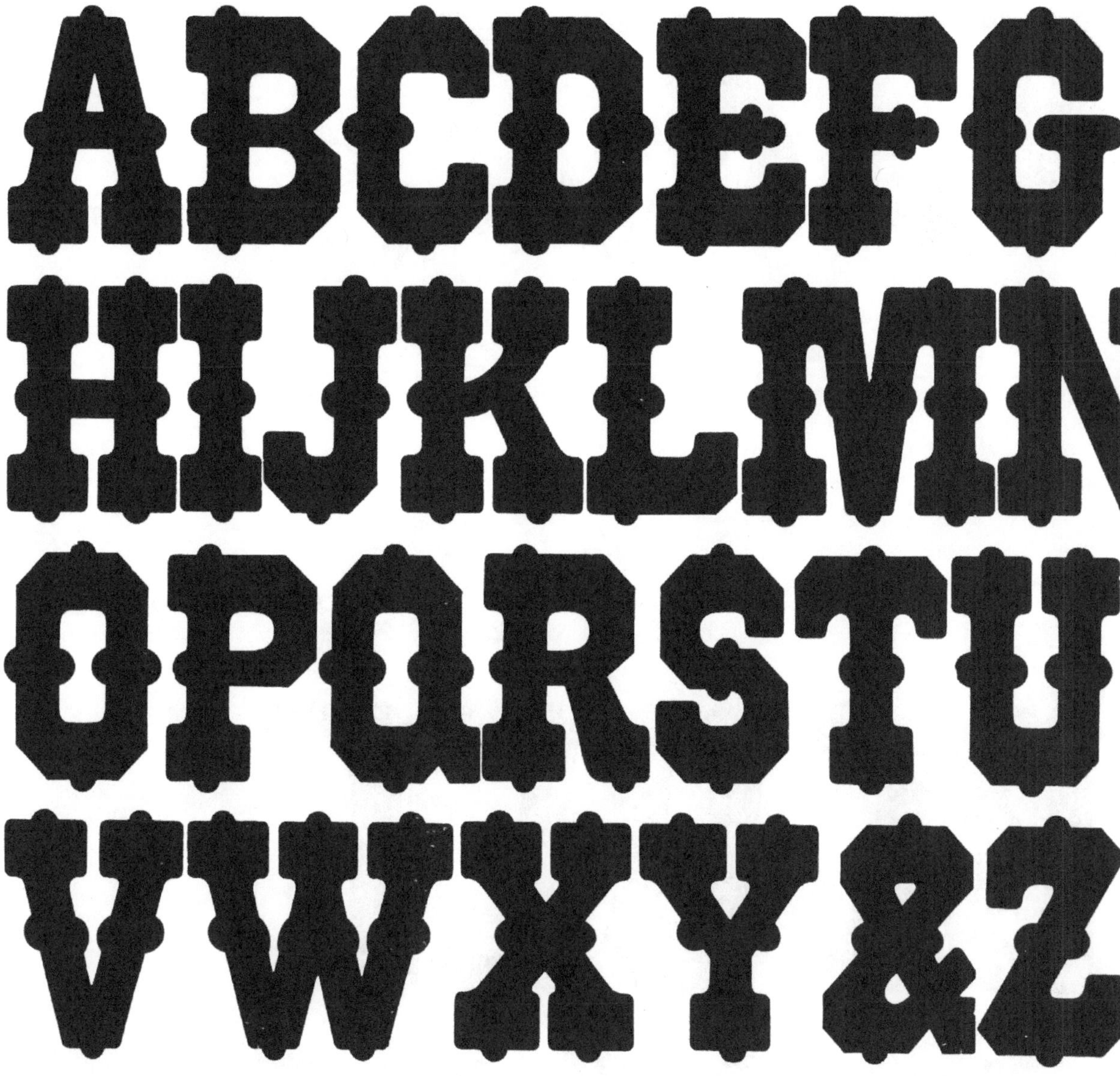

4.07.01.01
15 line No. 515
William H. Page & Co., 1887–1891

XYZ&Æ

8 line [Gothic Tuscan] cf. Hamilton: No. 20 [Actual size]

ABCDEF
$1234567

10 line [Gothic Tuscan Condensed] cf. Hamilton: No. 20 [Actual size]

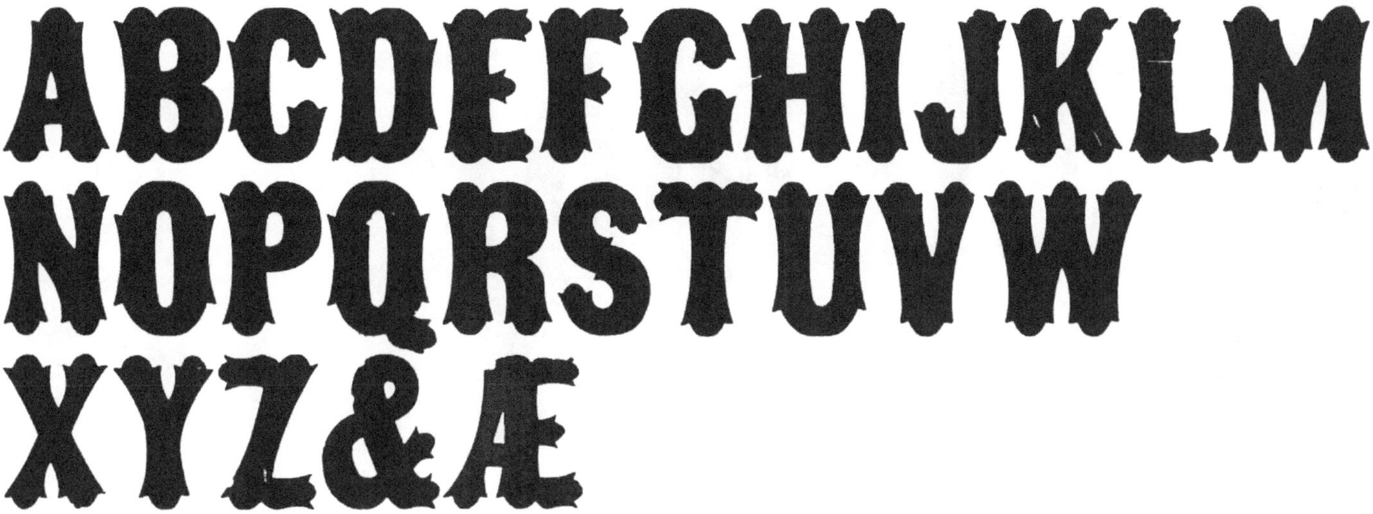

4.07.02.01
8 line [Gothic Tuscan] cf. Hamilton: No. 20
Manufacturer and date unknown

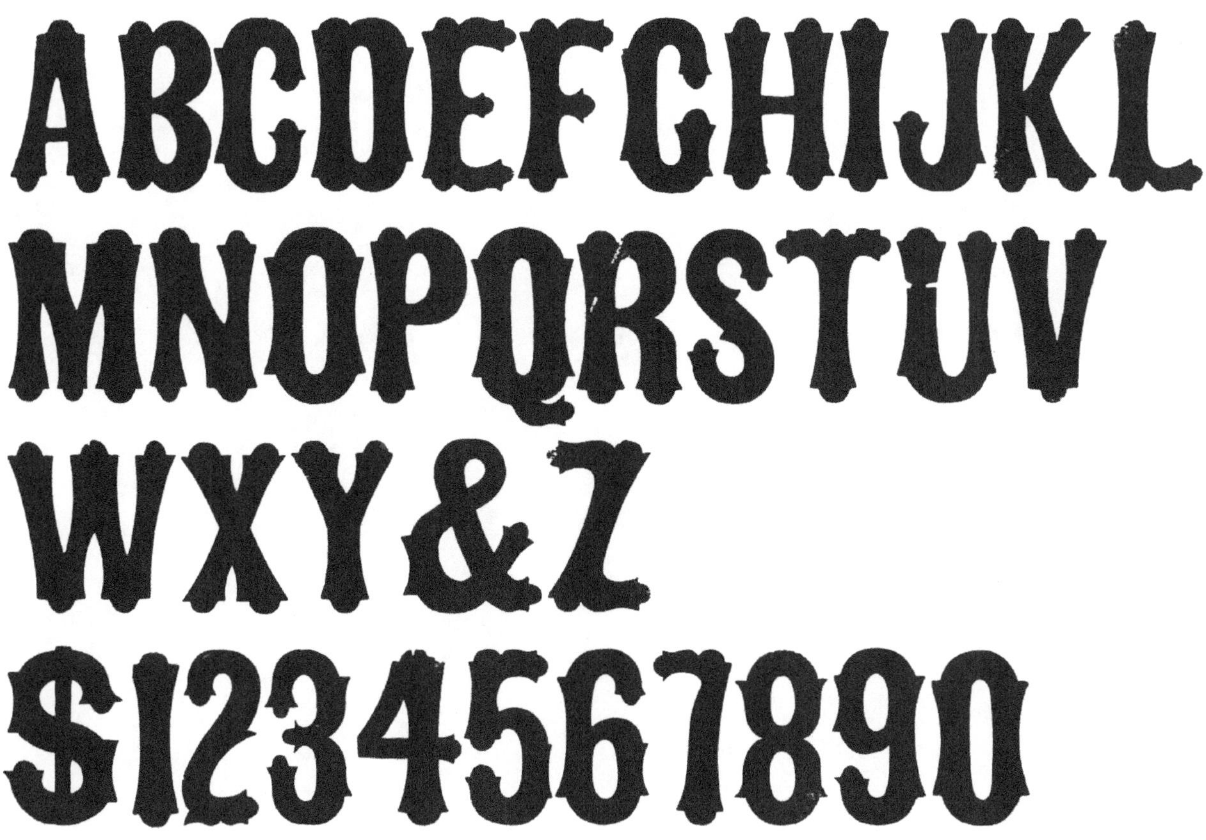

4.07.02.02
10 line [Gothic Tuscan Condensed] cf. Hamilton: No. 20
Manufacturer and date unknown

AEF JLMOP

8 line [Antique Tuscan] No. 10 [Actual size]

AEFJLMOPQRSTUVW
XYZ.

4.07.03.01
8 line [Antique Tuscan] No. 10
William H. Page & Co., 1859 or later

HIJKL

MNPQ XY&Z

10 line Persian [Actual size]

ABCDEFGHIJKLMNPQ
RSTUVWXY&Z

4.07.04.01
10 line Persian
Vanderburgh, Wells & Co., 1867–1890

ABCDEFGH
WXY&Z
fghijklmnopqrst
ﬀﬁﬂﬃﬄ

6 line Gothic Tuscan No. 3 [Actual size]

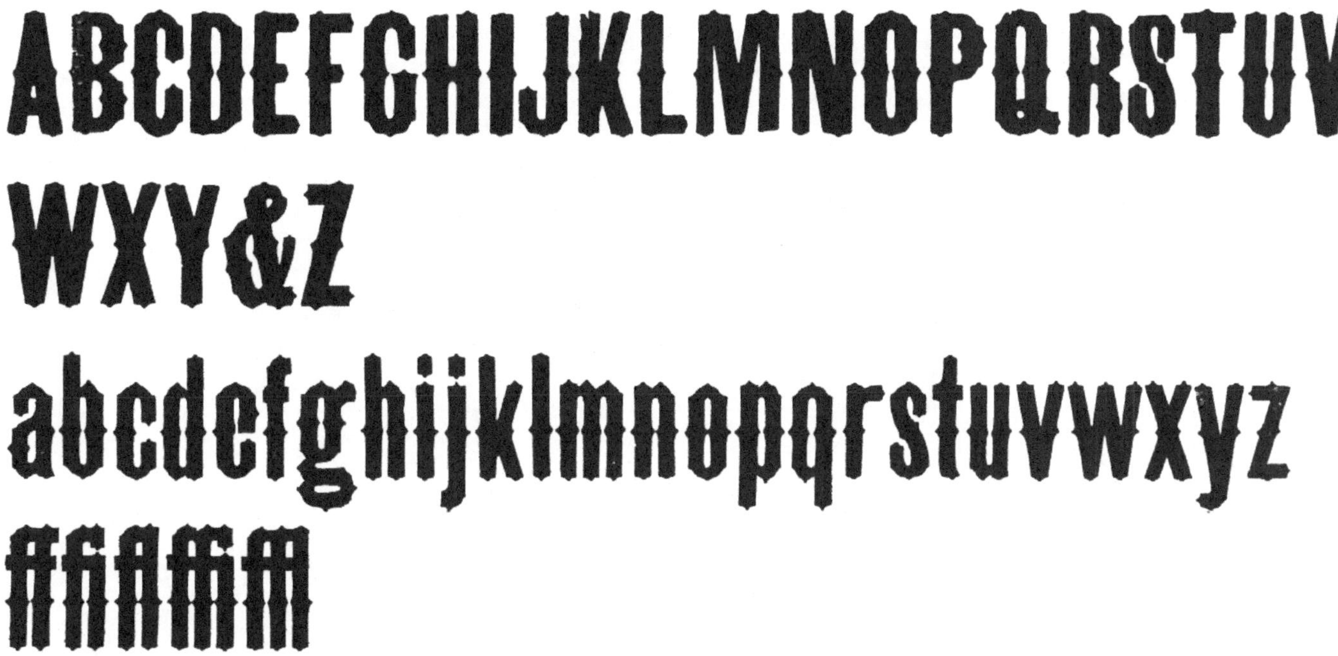

4.07.05.01
6 line Gothic Tuscan No. 3
William H. Page & Co., 1857–1859

Sans Serif Class

Typefaces that have no serifs or otherwise ornamented terminals, and are not classed as scripts.

MOPQRSTUVWXYZ

4 line Gothic Condensed No. 5 [Actual size]

ABCDEFGHIJK abcdefghijk

$1234567890 ff fi fl ffi ffl

5 line Gothic Extra Condensed Light Face [Actual size]

HIKLNOPRS $134

5 line No. 6243, Plain Gothic [Actual size]

OPQRSTUV $1234567

6 line No. 4050, Plain Gothic [Actual size]

ABCDEFGHIJKMOPQRSTUVWXYZ

5.01.01.01
4 line Gothic Condensed No. 5
Vanderburgh, Wells & Co., 1867–1890

ABCDEFGHIJKLMNOPQRSTUVWXY&Z
abcdefghijklmnoprstuvwxyz ff fi fl ffi ffl
$1234567890

5.01.01.02
5 line Gothic Extra Condensed Light Face
Morgans & Wilcox Mfg. Co., after 1881

ACEFGHIKLNOPRSTUVY $134

5.01.01.03
5 line No. 6243, Plain Gothic
Hamilton Manufacturing Co., after 1891

ABCDEFGHIJLMNOPQRSTUVWXY&Z
$1234567890

5.01.01.04
6 line No. 4050, Plain Gothic
Hamilton Manufacturing Co., after 1891

QRSTUVWXY
$12345678

5 line [Gothic Expanded] cf. Hamilton No. 5071 [Actual size]

ABCDEFG $123456

6 line No. 4006, Plain Gothic [Actual size]

LMOPQRS 1234567

6 line No. 4006, Plain Gothic [Actual size]

WXY&Z

6 line [Gothic Condensed] cf. Hamilton, No. 6243 [Actual size]

ABCDEFGHIJKLMNOP
QRSTUVWXY&Z
$1234567890

5.01.01.05
5 line [Gothic Expanded] cf. Hamilton No. 5071
Vanderburgh, Wells & Co., 1867–1890

ABCDEFGHIJKLMNOPQRSTUVWXY&Z
$1234567890

5.01.01.06
6 line No. 4006, Plain Gothic
Hamilton Manufacturing Co., after 1891

ABCDEFGHIJKLMOPQRSTVWY&Z
1234567890

5.01.01.07
6 line No. 4006, Plain Gothic
Hamilton Manufacturing Co., after 1891

ABCDEFGHIJKLMNOPQRSTUV
WXY&Z

5.01.01.08
6 line [Gothic Condensed] cf. Hamilton, No. 6243
Manufacturer and date unknown

DEFGHIJ $12345

klmnopq

6 line No. 22 [Gothic Expanded] cf. Hamilton No. 6245 [Actual size]

PQRSTU $12345

tuvwxyz ff fi fl ffi ffl

6 line No. 6234, Plain Gothic [Actual size]

ABCDEFGHI

6 line [Gothic] cf. Hamilton, No. 5969 [Actual size]

ABCDEFGHIJKLMNOPQRSTUV
WXY&Z $1234567890
abcdefghijklmnopqrstuvwxyz

5.01.01.09
6 line No. 22 [Gothic Expanded] cf. Hamilton No. 6245
Empire Type Foundry (Delevan, NY), 1918–1924

ABCDEFGHIJKLMNOPQRSTU
VWXY&Z $1234567890
abcdefghijklmnoprstuvwxyz
ff fi fl ffi ffl

5.01.01.10
6 line No. 6234, Plain Gothic
Hamilton Manufacturing Co., after 1891

ABCDEFGHIJKLMNOP
QRSTUVWXY&Z

5.01.01.11
6 line [Gothic] cf. Hamilton, No. 5969
Manufacturer and date unknown

OPQRSTUV
$12345678

6 line No. 5072, Plain Gothic [Actual size]

NOPRSTUVWXYZ

7 line [Gothic Extra Condensed] cf. Hamilton: No. 266 [Actual size]

FGIJKLMNPRS

7 line Gothic Extra Condensed [Actual size]

WXY&Z

8 line [Gothic Extra Condensed] cf. Hamilton, No. 81 [Actual size]

ABCDEFGHIJKLMN
OPQRSTUVWXY&Z
$1234567890

5.01.01.12 & 5.01.01.13
6 line No. 5072, Plain Gothic
Hamilton Manufacturing Co., after 1891

ABCDEFGHIJKLNOPRSTUVWXYZ

5.01.01.14
7 line [Gothic Extra Condensed] cf. Hamilton: No. 266
Manufacturer and date unknown

ABCDEFGIJKLMNPRSTUVW&Y

5.01.01.15
7 line Gothic Extra Condensed
William H. Page & Co., 1857–1859

ABCDEFGHIJKLMNOPQRSTUV
WXY&Z

5.01.01.16
8 line [Gothic Extra Condensed] cf. Hamilton, No. 81
Manufacturer and date unknown

JKLMN $1234

nopqrstuvwxyz

8 line No. 4006, Plain Gothic [Actual size]

TUVWXYZ

fgijkqrsvwyz

8 line [Gothic Condensed] cf. Hamilton, No. 6423 [Actual size]

ABCDEFGHIJKLMNOPQRSTU
VWXY&Z $1234567890
abcdefghijklmnopqrstuvwxyz

5.01.01.17
8 line No. 4006, Plain Gothic
Hamilton Manufacturing Co., after 1891

ABCDFGHJKLMNOPQS
TUVWXYZ
cdfgijkqrsvwyz

5.01.01.18
8 line [Gothic Condensed] cf. Hamilton, No. 6423
Manufacturer and date unknown

CDEFGH $1234

8 line [Gothic Condensed] cf. AWT (LI): Newstype [Actual size]

ABCDEF
aehimn $1234

8 line No. 6243 Plain Gothic [Actual size]

MNOPRST

8 line [Gothic Condensed] No. 5 [Actual size]

ABCDEFGHIJKLMNOPQRST
UVWXY&Z $1234567890

5.01.01.19
8 line [Gothic Condensed] cf. AWT (LI): Newstype
Manufacturerer and date unknown

ABCDEFGHIJKLMNOPQ
RSTUVWXY&Z
aehimnorst
$1234567890

5.01.01.20
8 line No. 6243 Plain Gothic
Hamilton Manufacturing Co., after 1891

ABCDEFGHIJLMNOPRST
UVWXYZ

5.01.01.21
8 line [Gothic Condensed] No. 5
Vanderburgh, Wells & Co., 1867–1890

WXY&Z

8 line No. 5072, Plain Gothic [Actual size]

ABCDEFGHIJKLM

10 line No. 81 [Actual size]

BDEFG $123

10 line [Gothic Extra Condensed] cf. Hamilton: No. 4006 [Actual size]

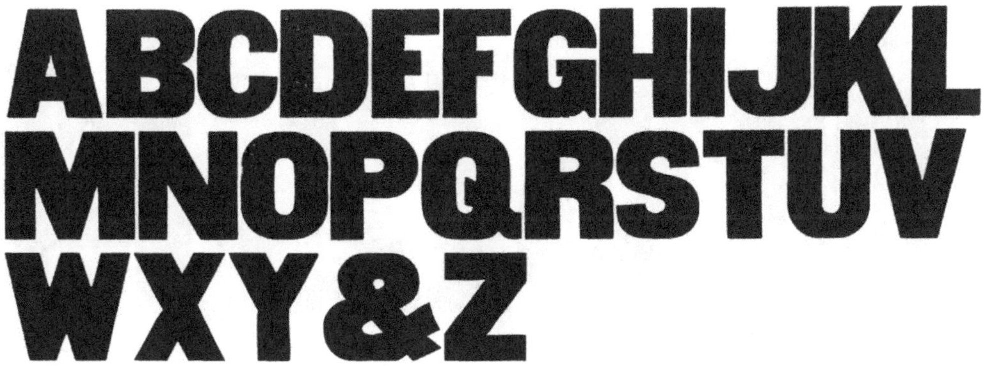

5.01.01.22
8 line No. 5072, Plain Gothic
Hamilton Manufacturing Co., after 1891

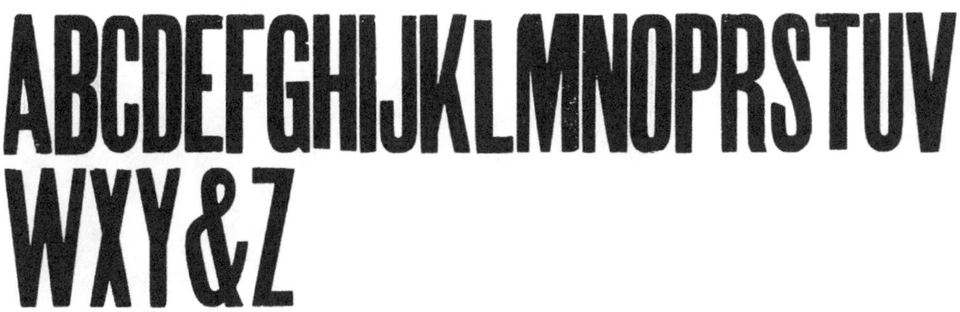

5.01.01.23
10 line No. 81
Hamilton Manufacturing Co., 1880–1889

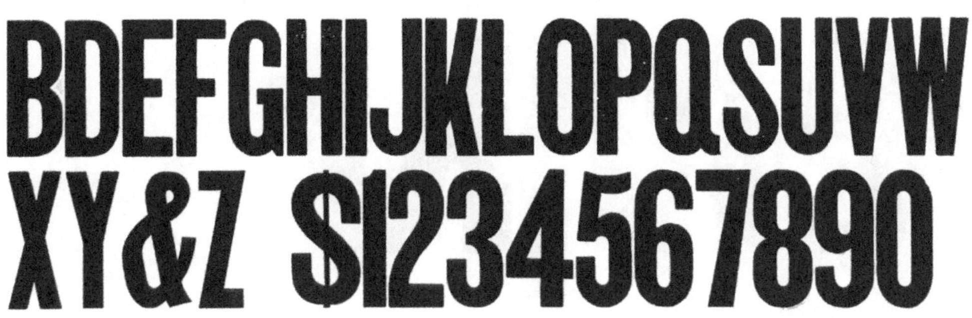

5.01.01.24
10 line [Gothic Extra Condensed] cf. Hamilton: No. 4006
Manufacturer and date unkown

JKLM $1234

10 line [Gothic Condensed] cf. AWT (LI): Newstype [Actual size]

NOP $123
cdefghijkl

10 line No. 6243, Plain Gothic [Actual size]

ABCDEFGHIJKLMNO
PQRSTUVWXY&Z
$1234567890

5.01.01.25
10 line [Gothic Condensed] cf. AWT (LI): Newstype
Manufacturer and date unknown

ABCDEFGHIJKLM
NOPQRSTUVWX
Y&Z
$1234567890
abcdefghijklmnopqrs
tuvwxyz

5.01.01.26
10 line No. 6243, Plain Gothic
Hamilton Manufacturing Co., after 1891

EFGHIJ
QRSTUV
WXY&Z

10 line No. 6011, Plain Gothic [Actual size]

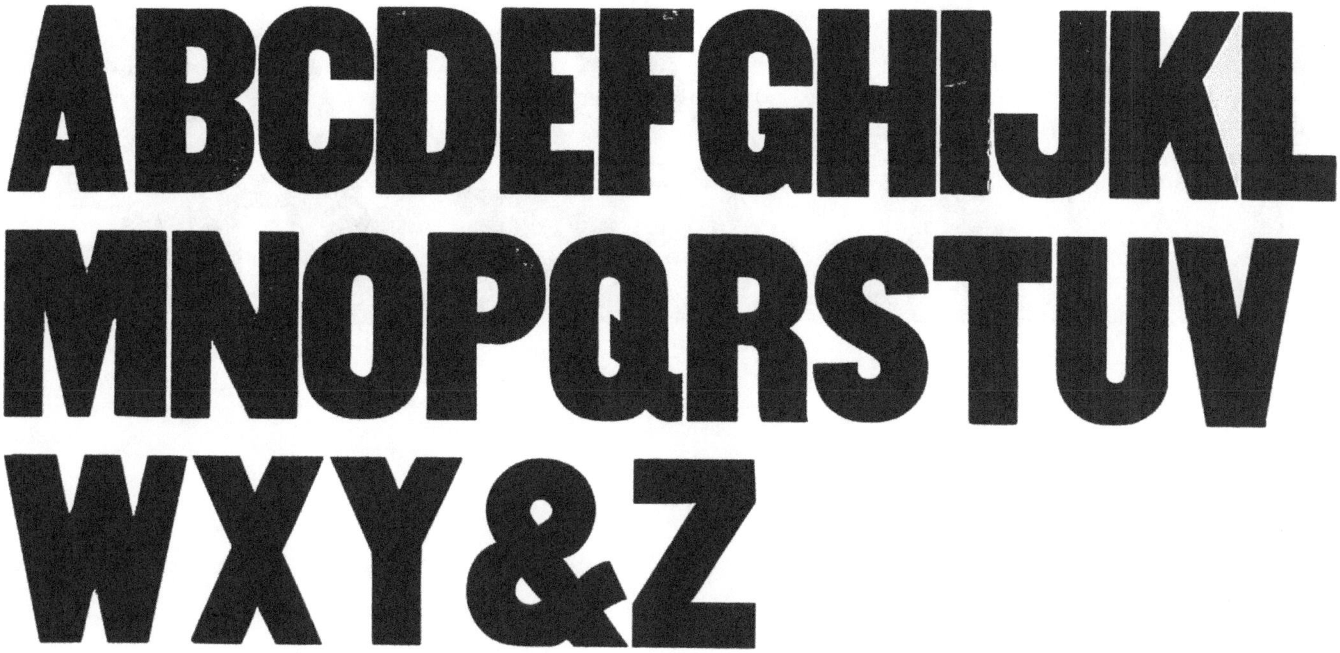

5.01.01.27
10 line No. 6011, Plain Gothic
Hamilton Manufacturing Co., after 1891

YZ&Æ

10 line [Gothic] cf. Hamilton No. 5072 [Actual size]

STUVW $1234

12 line [Gothic Extra Condensed] cf. Hamilton: No. 81 [Actual size]

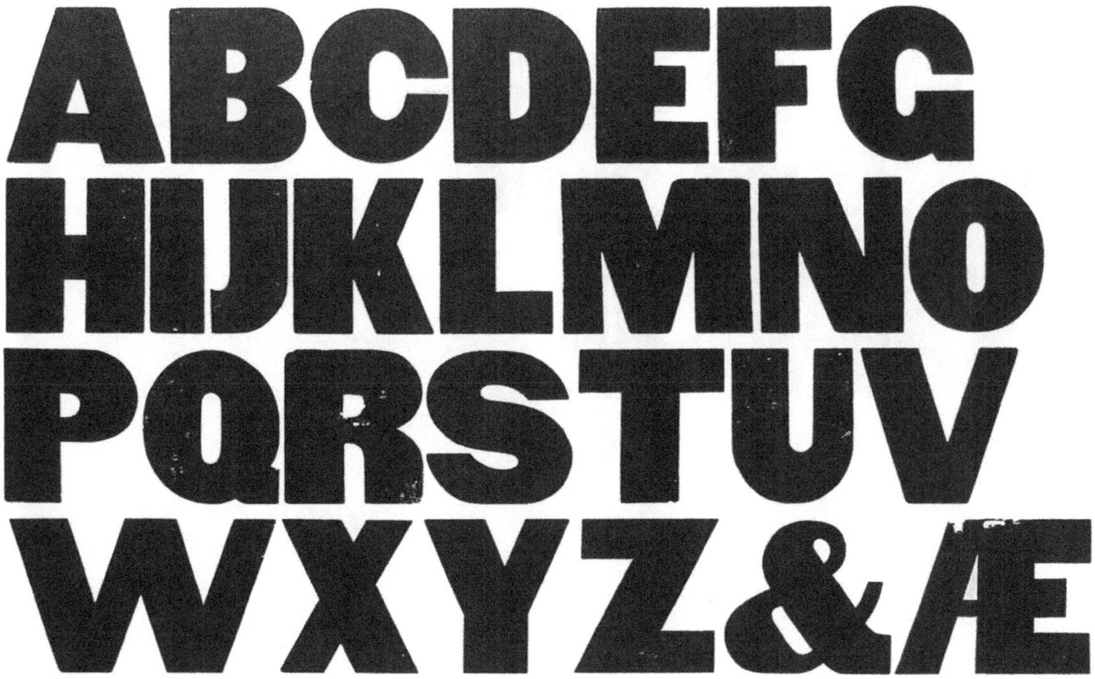

5.01.01.28
10 line [Gothic] cf. Hamilton No. 5072
Manufacturer and date unknown

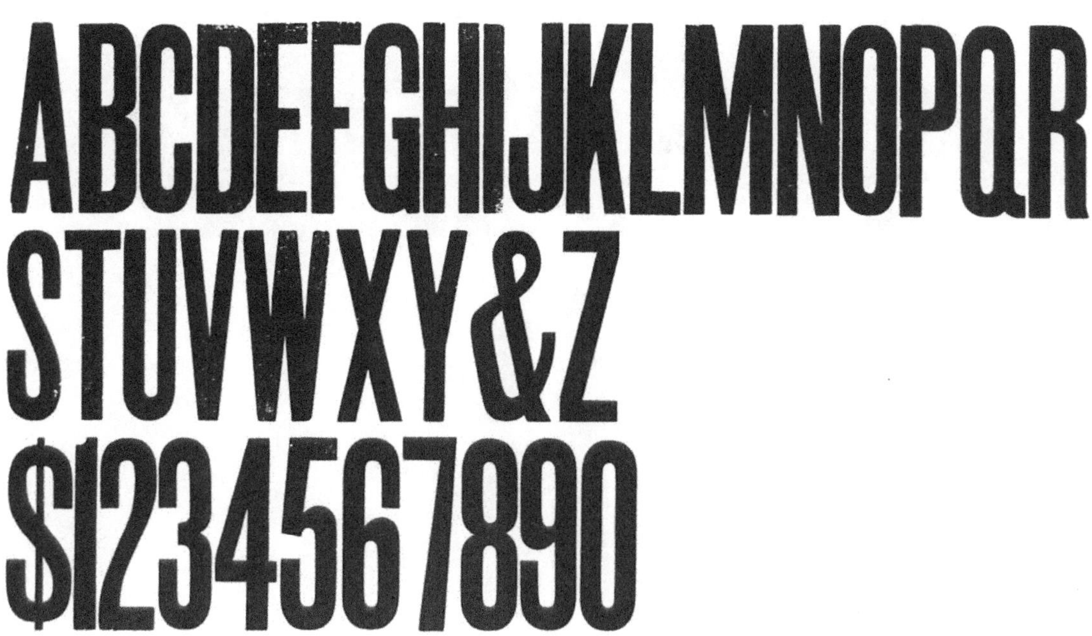

5.01.01.29
12 line [Gothic Extra Condensed] cf. Hamilton: No. 81
Manufacturer and date unknown

KLMNOP

12 line No. 20 [Gothic Condensed], cf. Hamilton: No. 81 [Actual size]

ABCDEFGHIJ

$123456

12 line No. 266, Plain Gothic [Actual size]

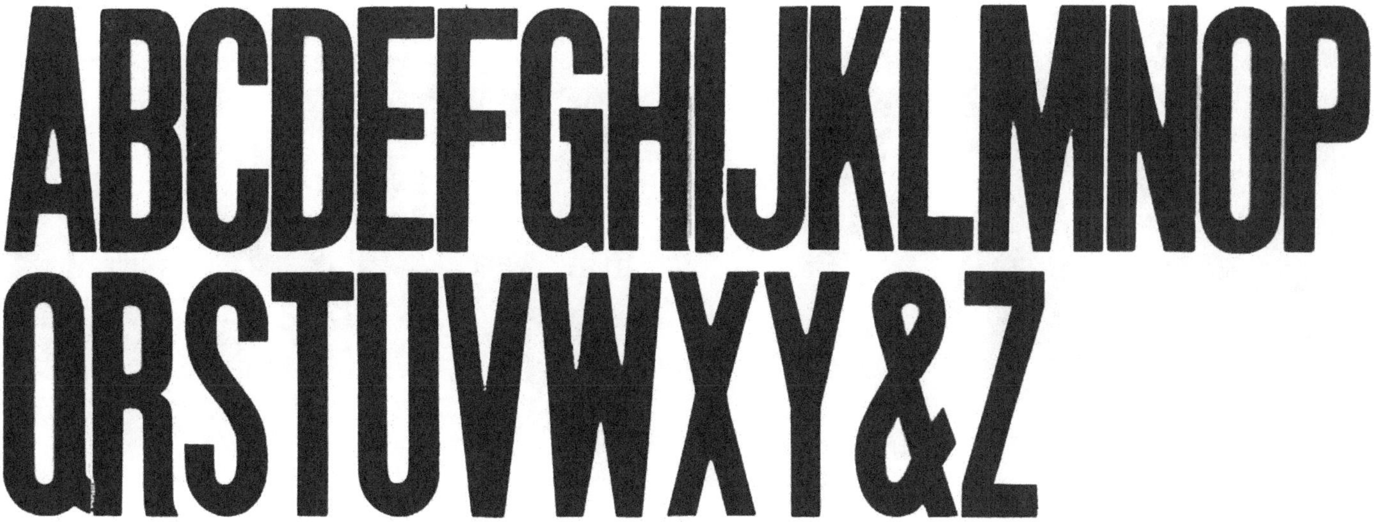

5.01.01.30
12 line No. 20 [Gothic Condensed], cf. Hamilton: No. 81
Empire Type Foundry (Delevan, NY), 1918–1924

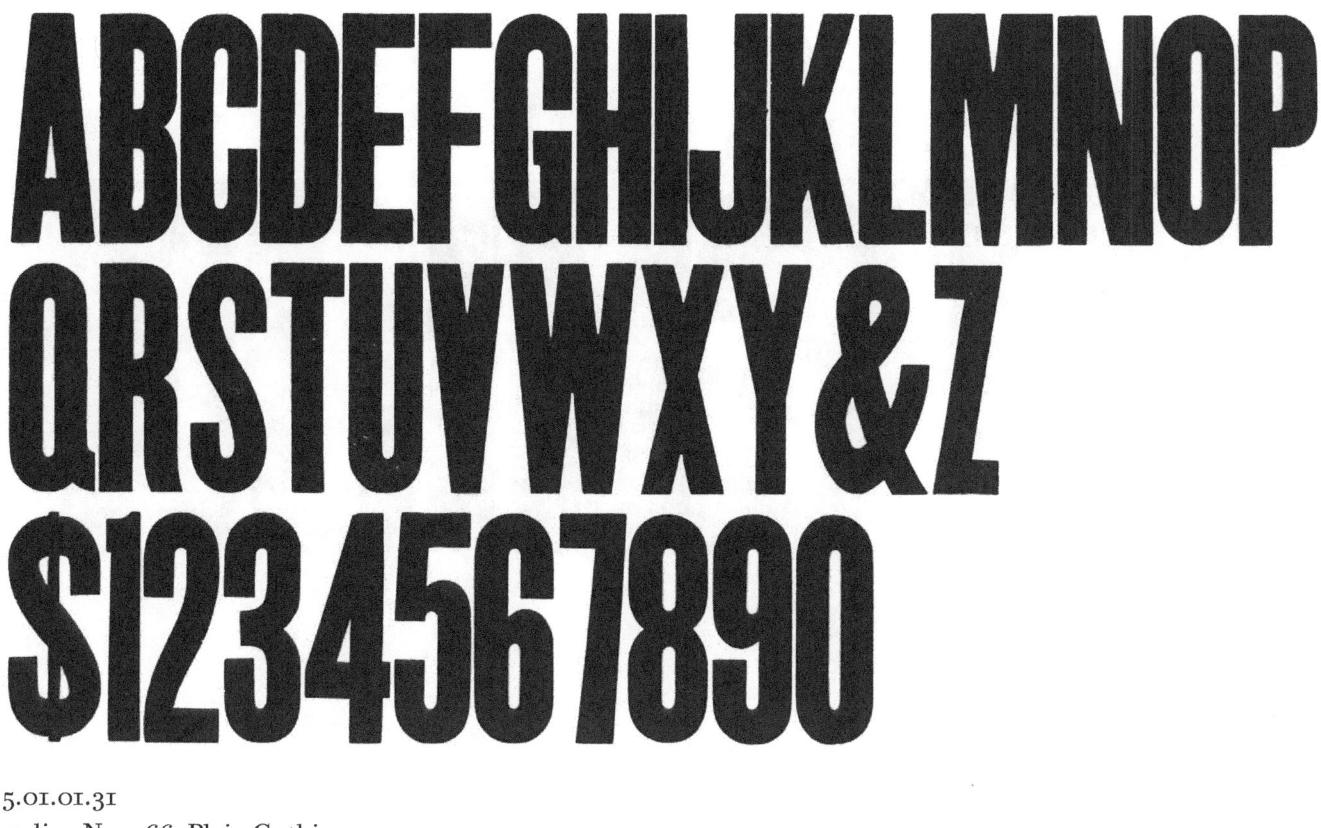

5.01.01.31
12 line No. 266, Plain Gothic
Hamilton Manufacturing Co., after 1891

WXY $123

12 line [Gothic Condensed], cf. AWT (LI): Newstype [Actual size]

DEFGHIJK

12 line Gothic Condensed No. 5 [Actual size]

ABCDEFGHIJKLM
NOPQRSTUVWXY
Z&$1234567890

5.01.01.32
12 line [Gothic Condensed], cf. AWT (LI): Newstype
Manufacturer and date unknown

ABCDEFGHIJKLM
NOPQRSTUVWX
Y&Z

5.01.01.33
12 line Gothic Condensed No. 5
Vanderburgh, Wells & Co., 1867–1890

Y&Z $123

14 line Gothic Extra Condensed No. 1 [Actual size]

ABCD $123

15 line [Gothic Extra Condensed] cf. Hamilton No. 81 [Actual size]

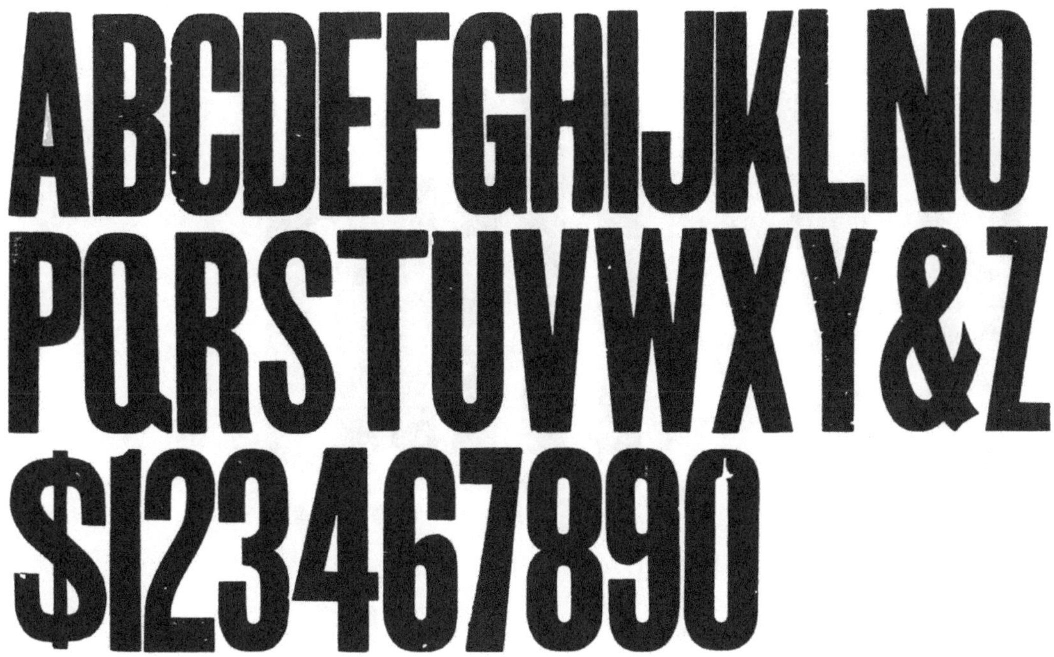

5.01.01.34
14 line Gothic Extra Condensed No. 1
Vanderburgh, Wells & Co., 1867–1890

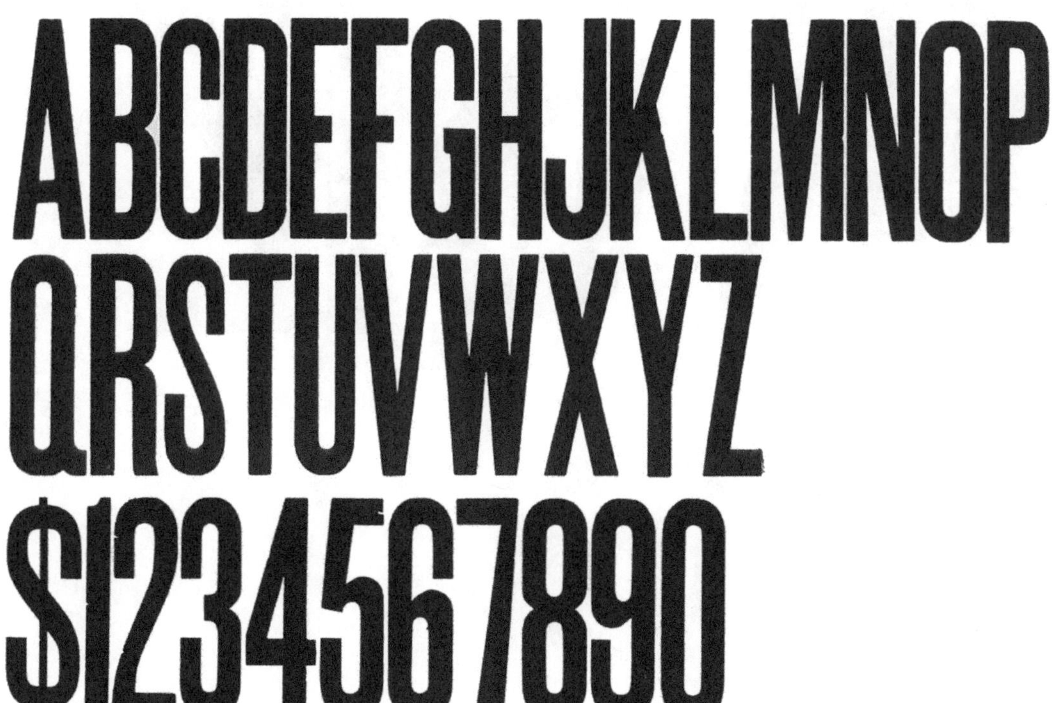

5.01.01.35
15 line [Gothic Extra Condensed] cf. Hamilton No. 81
Manufacturer and date unknown

KSVY fhig

15 line [Gothic Extra Condensed] cf. Hamilton No. 4006 [Actual size]

QRS $12

15 line No. 4006, Plain Gothic [Actual size]

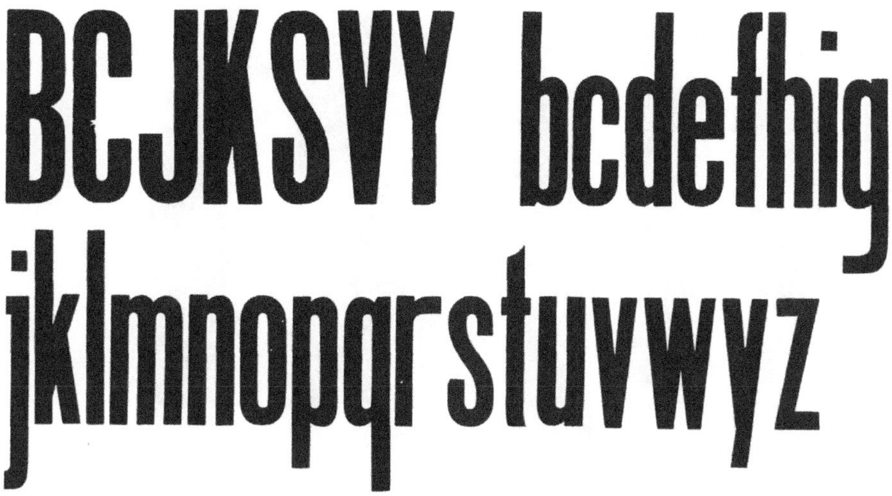

5.01.01.36
15 line [Gothic Extra Condensed] cf. Hamilton No. 4006
Manufacturer and date unknown

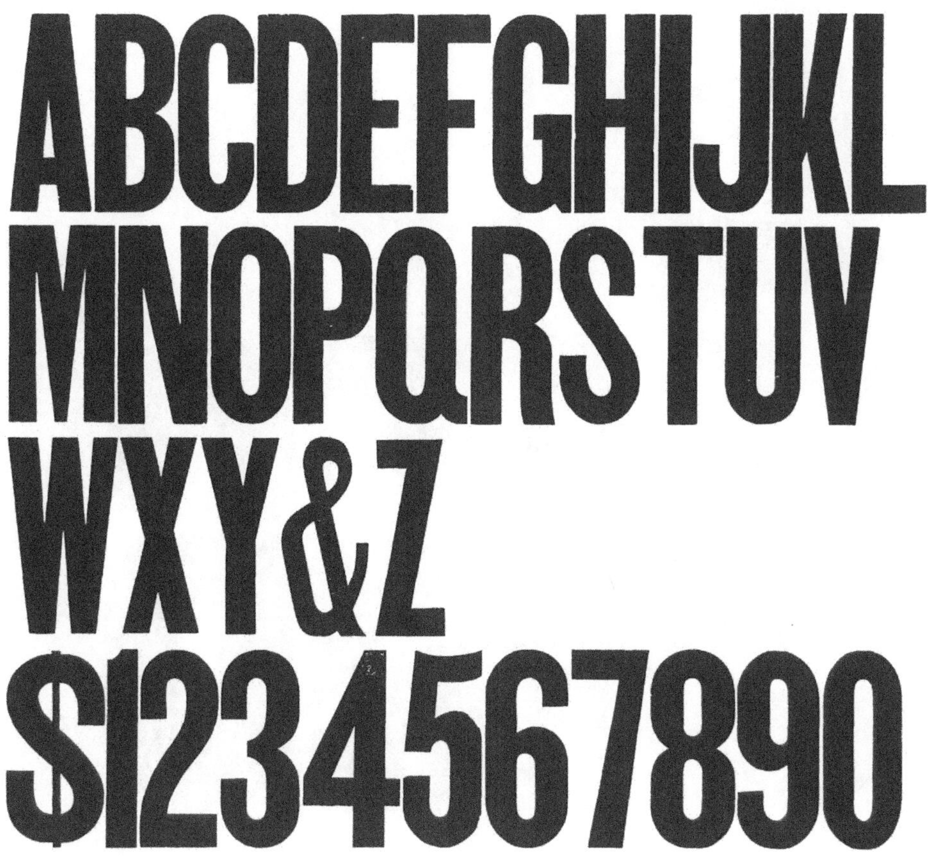

5.01.01.37 & 5.01.01.38
15 line No. 4006, Plain Gothic
Hamilton Manufacturing Co., after 1891

NOQRST

Y&Z

$123456

15 line No. 2066 [Actual size]

ABCDEFGHIJKL
NOQRSTUVWX
Y&Z
$1234567890

5.01.01.39
15 line No. 2066
American Wood Type Co. (Conn.), after 1883

XY&Z
$12

15 line No. 4045, Palin Gothic [Actual size]

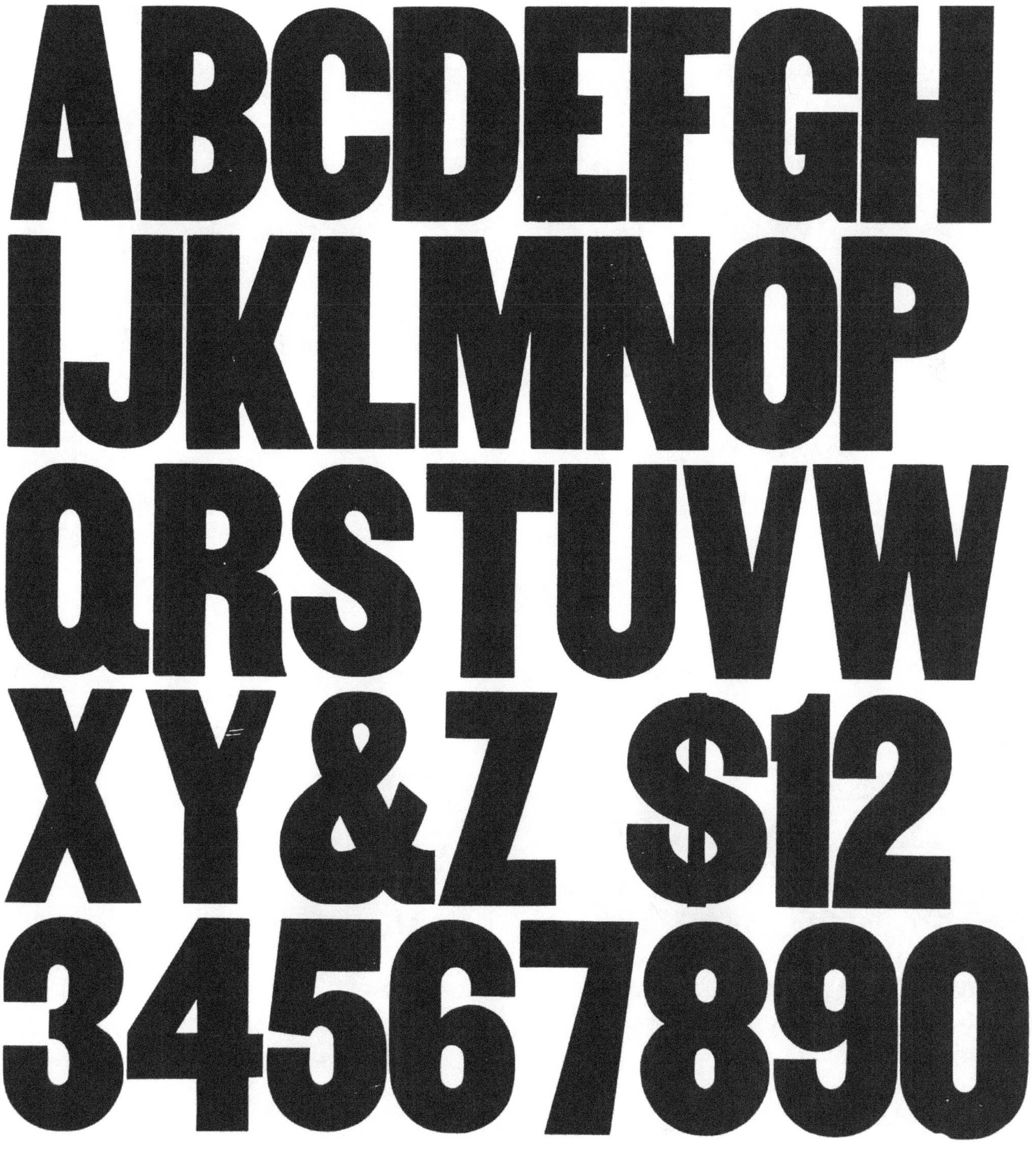

5.01.01.40 & 5.01.01.41
15 line No. 4045, Plain Gothic
Hamilton Manufacturing Co., after 1891

GH$1

15 line No. 6011, Plain Gothic [Actual size]

$12

15 line No. 2064 [Actual size]

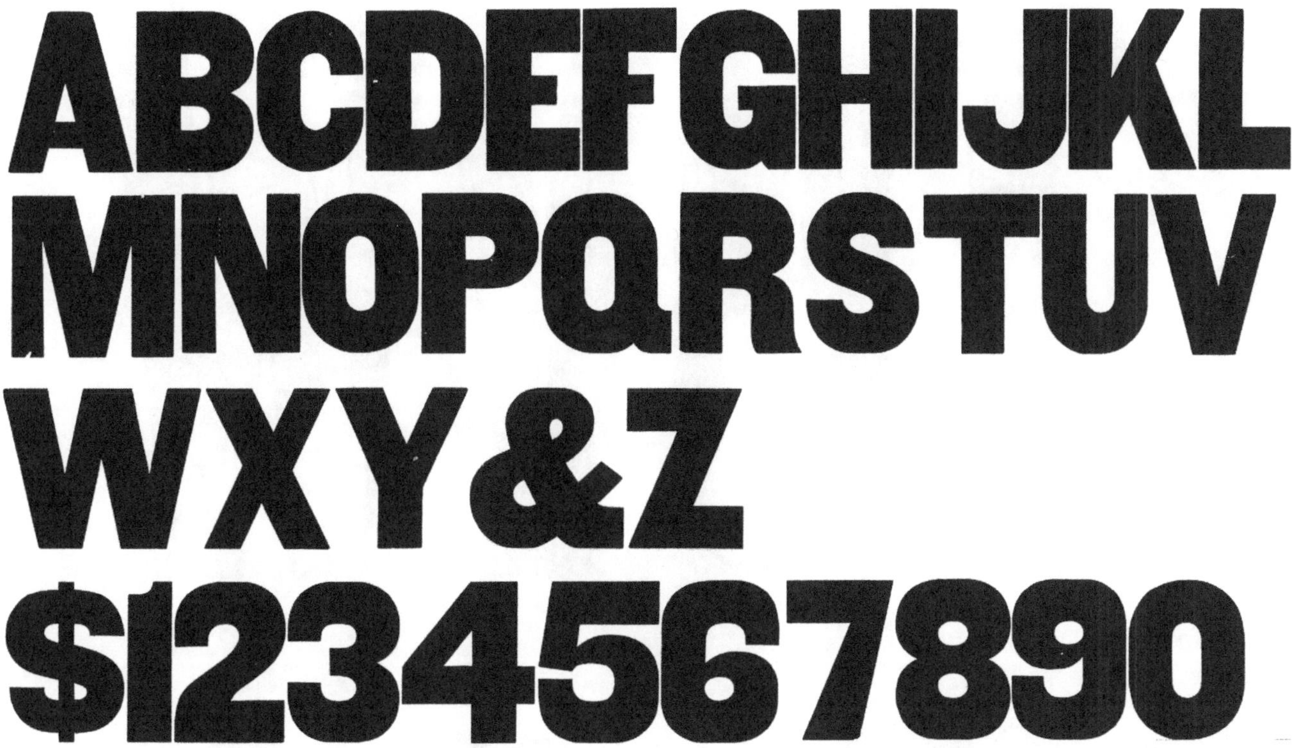

5.01.01.42 & 5.01.01.43
15 line No. 6011, Plain Gothic
Hamilton Manufacturing Co., after 1891

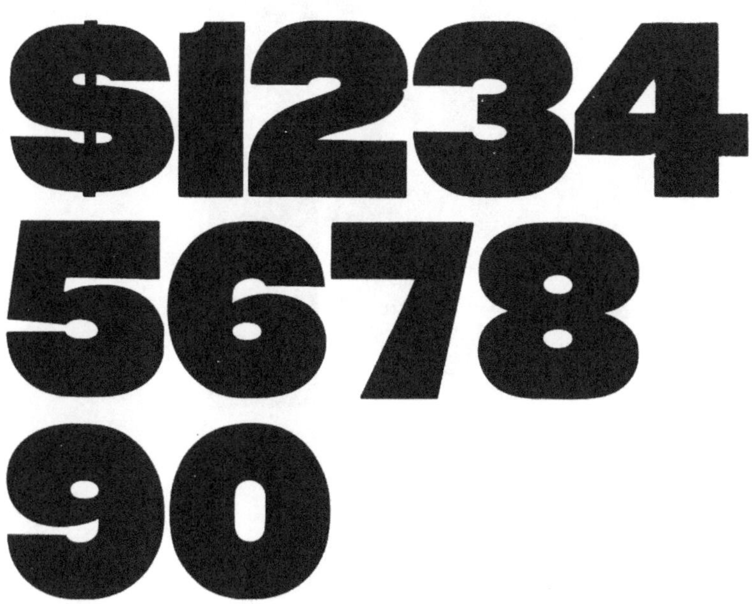

5.01.01.44
15 line No. 2064
American Wood Type Co., date unknown

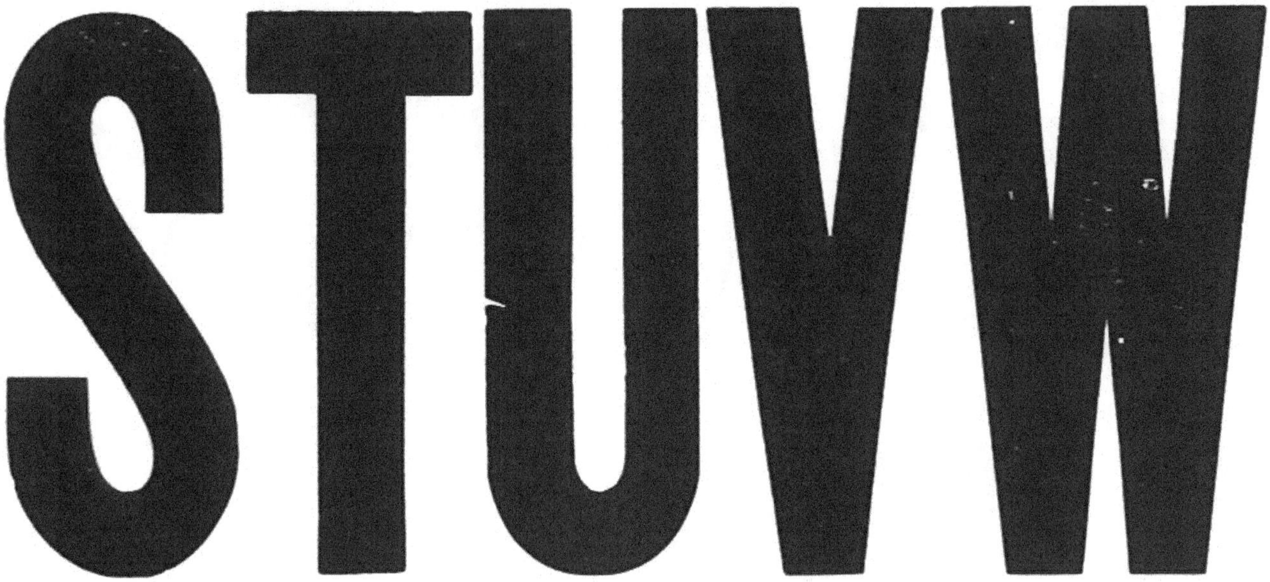

18 line Gothic Extra Condensed [Actual size]

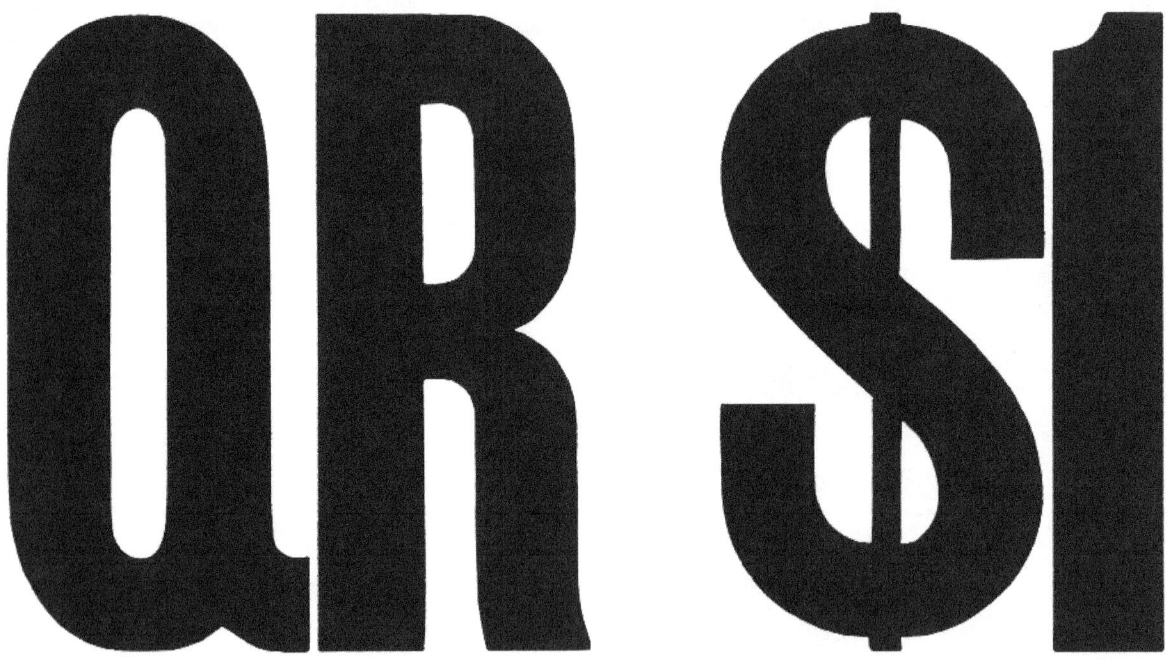

20 line No. 4006, Plain Gothic [Actual size]

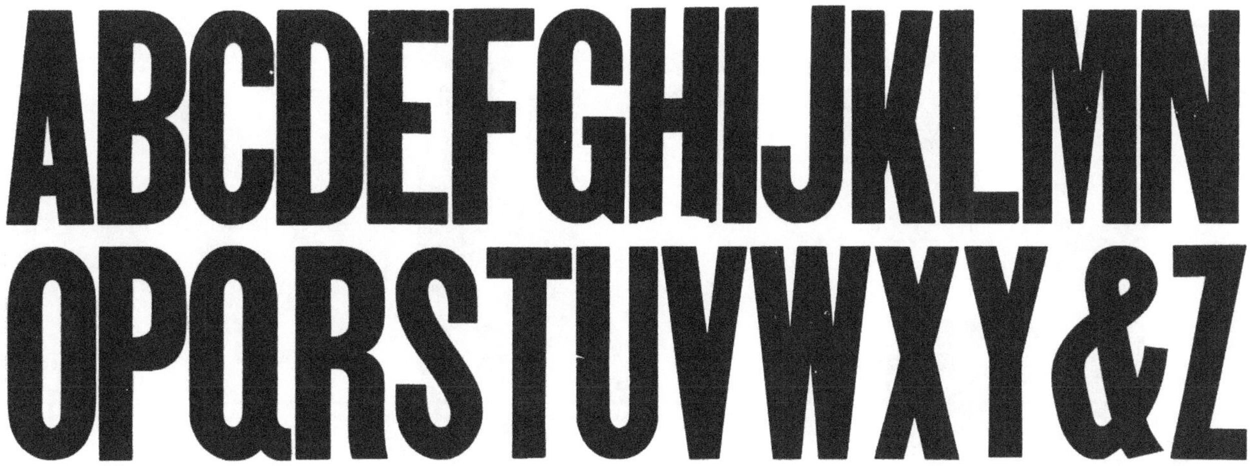

5.01.01.45
18 line Gothic Extra Condensed
William H. Page & Co., 1870 or later

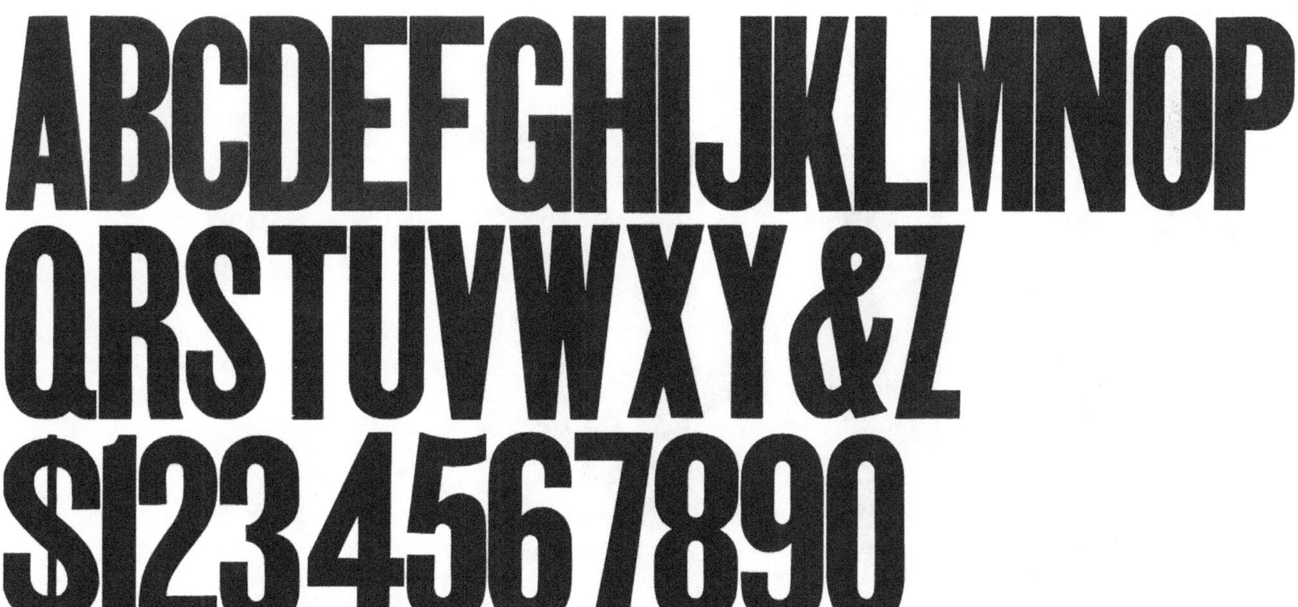

5.01.01.46 & 5.01.01.47
20 line No. 4006, Plain Gothic
Hamilton Manufacturing Co., after 1891

FG 4

18 line Gothic Extra Condensed [Actual size]

ABC

20 line Gothic Condensed Light Face [Actual size]

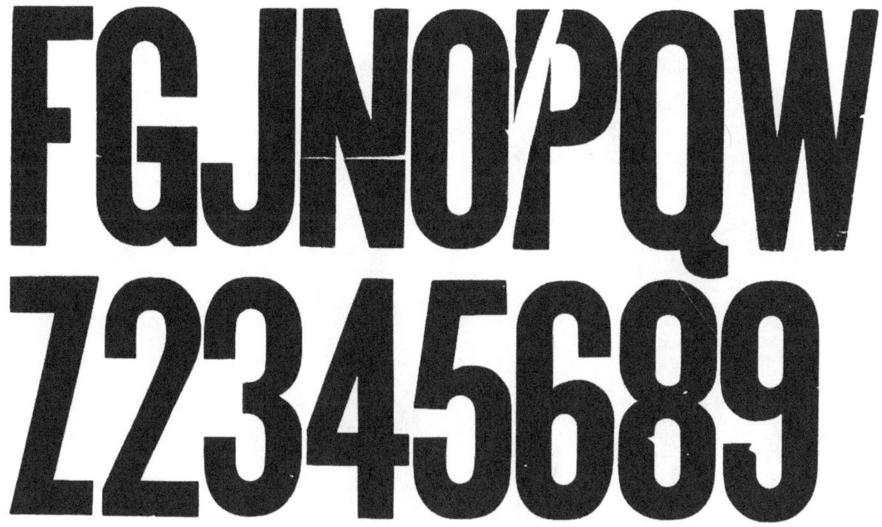

5.01.01.48
18 line Gothic Extra Condensed
William H. Page & Co., 1870 or later

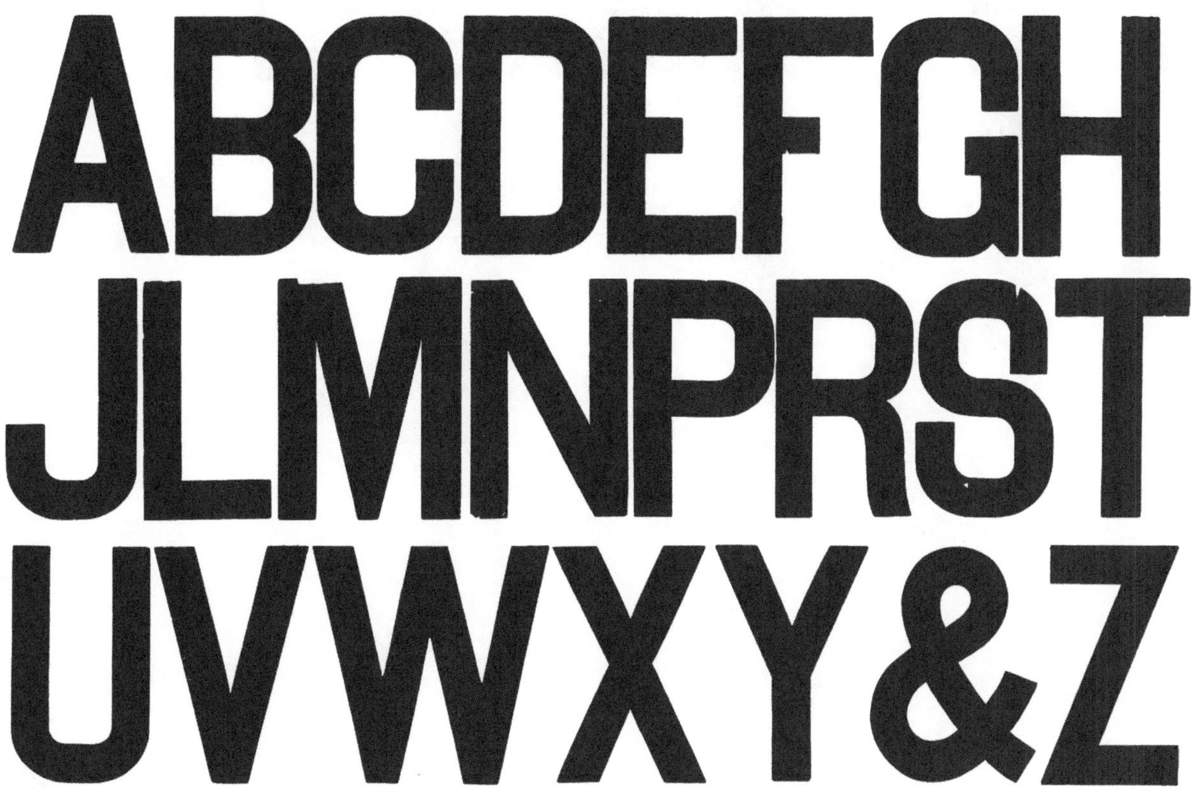

5.01.01.49
20 line Gothic Condensed Light Face
William H. Page & Co., 1857–1859

XY&Z

25 line [Gothic Extra Condensed] cf. Hamilton No. 81 [Actual size]

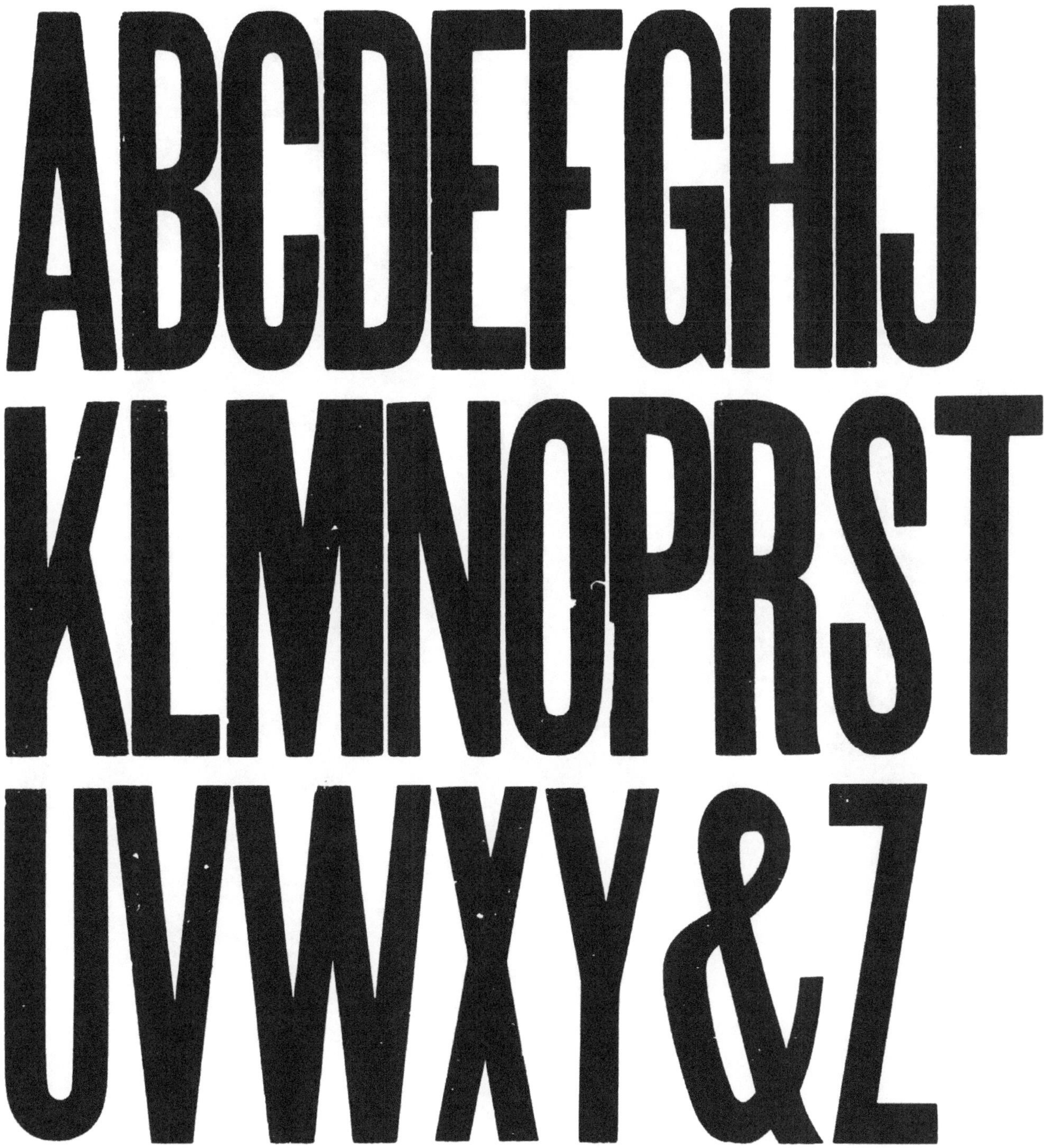

5.01.01.50
25 line [Gothic Extra Condensed] cf. Hamilton No. 81
Manufacturer and date unknown

456

30 line [Gothic Extra Condensed] cf. Hamilton No. 266 [Actual size]

123456
7890

5.01.01.51
30 line [Gothic Extra Condensed] cf. Hamilton No. 266
Manufacturer and date unknown

DEFGHIJKL
fghijklmnopqr
1234567890

5 line Doric Gothic Italic, No. 2275 [Actual size]

1234567890

6 line [Gothic Modulated Outline] [Actual size]

ABCDEFGHIJKLMNOQ
RSTUVWXYZ
abcdefghijklmnopqrst
uvwxyz
1234567890

5.01.01.52
5 line Doric Gothic Italic, No. 2275
Tubbs & Company, circa 1900

1234567890

5.01.01.53
6 line [Gothic Modulated Outline]
Manufacturer and date unknown

ABCDEFGHI stuvwxz

5 line [Gothic Condensed] cf. Hamilton: No. 720, Unit Gothic [Actual size]

JKLMNOPQRSTUV

$1234567890

12 line No. 722, Unit Gothic [Actual size]

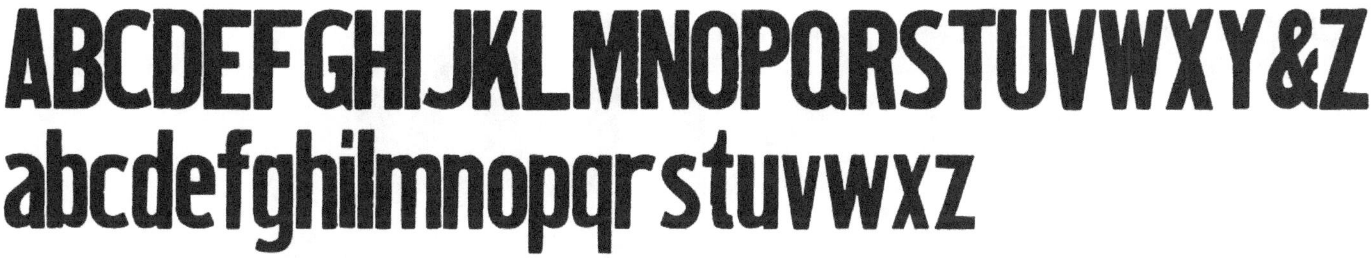

5.01.02.01
5 line [Gothic Condensed] cf. Hamilton: No. 720, Unit Gothic
Manufacturer and date unknown

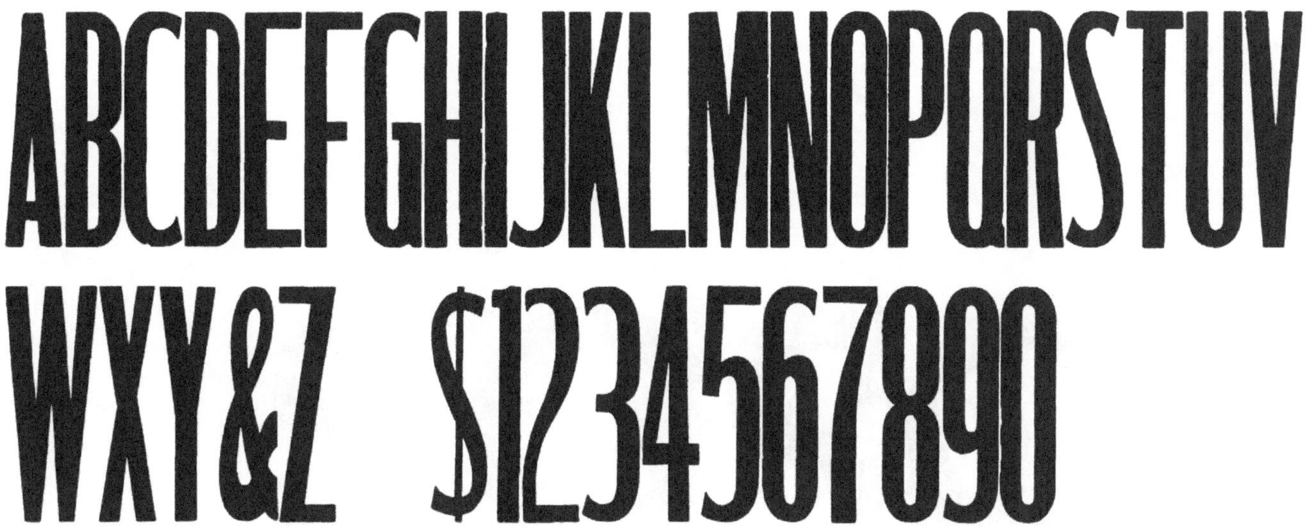

5.01.02.02
12 line No. 722, Unit Gothic
Hamilton Manufacturing Co., after 1891

PQRSTUV
abcdef 7890

6 line [Gothic] cf. AWT(LI): Mode Medium [Actual size]

NOPQR

8 line [Gothic] cf. AWT(LI): Mode Medium [Actual size]

ABCDEFGHIJKLMNO
PQRSTUVWXY&Z
abcdefghijklmnopqrstu
vwxyz $1234567890

5.01.03.01
6 line [Gothic] cf. AWT(LI): Mode Medium
Manufacturer and date unknown

ABCDEFGHIJKL
MNOPQRSTUV
WXY&Z

5.01.03.02
8 line [Gothic] cf. AWT(LI): Mode Medium
Manufacturer and date unknown

TUVWXY&Z
$1234567

5 line [Angled Gothic] cf. Hamilton: No. 3080 [Actual size]

RSTUVWX
12345678

6 line [Angled Gothic] cf. Hamilton: No. 3080 [Actual size]

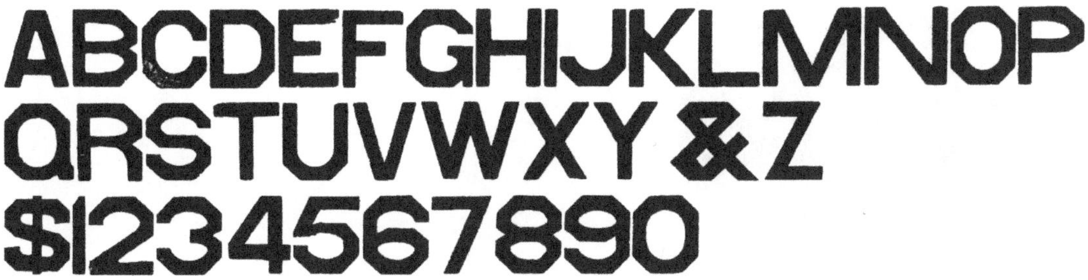

5.01.04.01
5 line [Angled Gothic] cf. Hamilton: No. 3080
Manufacturer and date unknown

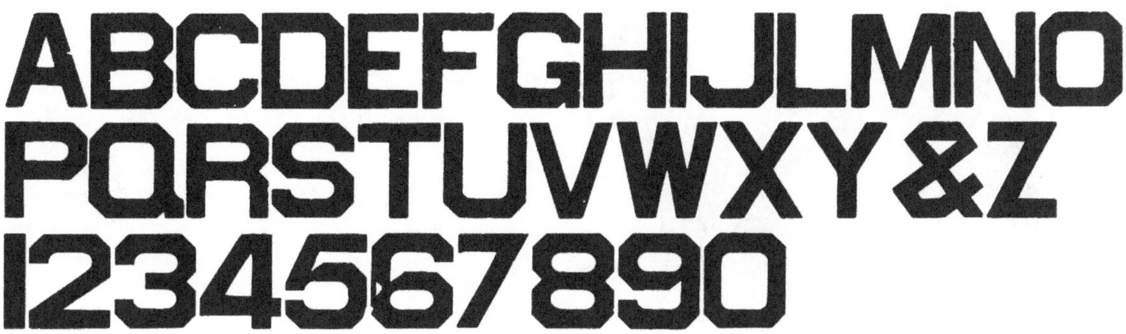

5.01.04.02
6 line [Angled Gothic] cf. Hamilton: No. 3080
Manufacturer and date unknown

L&

50 line [Angled Gothic Condensed] cf. Hamilton: No. 3080 [Actual size]

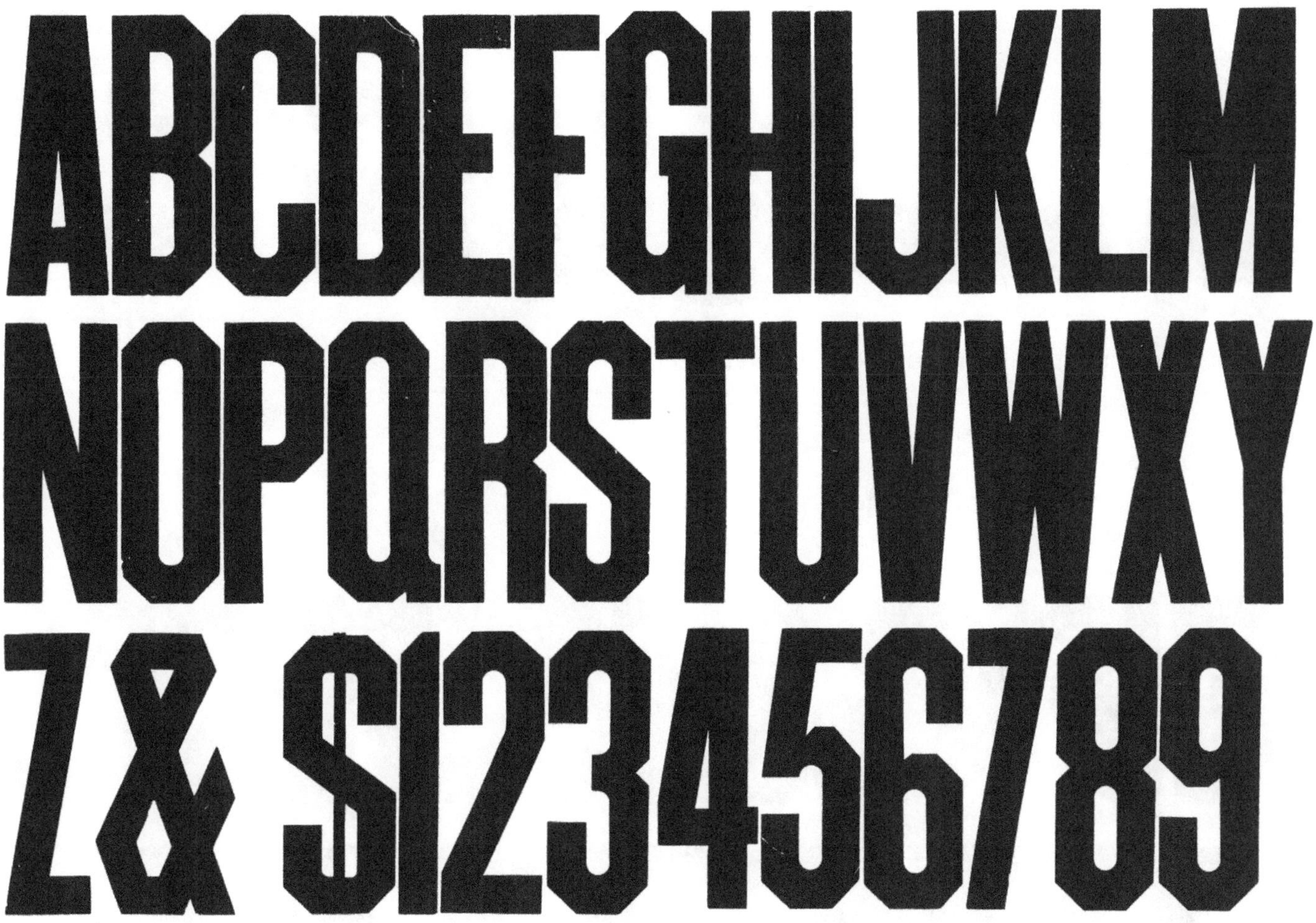

5.01.04.03, 5.01.04.04 & 5.01.04.05
50 line [Angled Gothic Condensed] cf. Hamilton: No. 3080
Manufacturer and date unknown

HIJKL fffiflffiffl
abcdefg $1234

4 line [Rounded Gothic] cf. Page: Gothic Round [Actual size]

EFGHIJKL
QRSTUV

7 line [Rounded Gothic] cf. Page: Gothic Round [Actual size]

ABCDEFGHIJKLMNOPQR
STUVWXY&Z ff fi fl ffi ffl
abcdefghijklmnopqstuvwx
yz $1234567890

5.02.01.01
4 line [Rounded Gothic] cf. Page: Gothic Round
Manufacturer and date unknown

ABCDEFGHIJKL
MNOPQRSTUV
WXY&Z

5.02.01.02
7 line [Rounded Gothic] cf. Page: Gothic Round
J.G. Cooley, 1859–1868

ABCDE

10 line [Rounded Gothic] cf. Page: Gothic Round [Actual size]

FIJKL

10 line [Rounded Gothic] cf. Page: Gothic Round [Actual size]

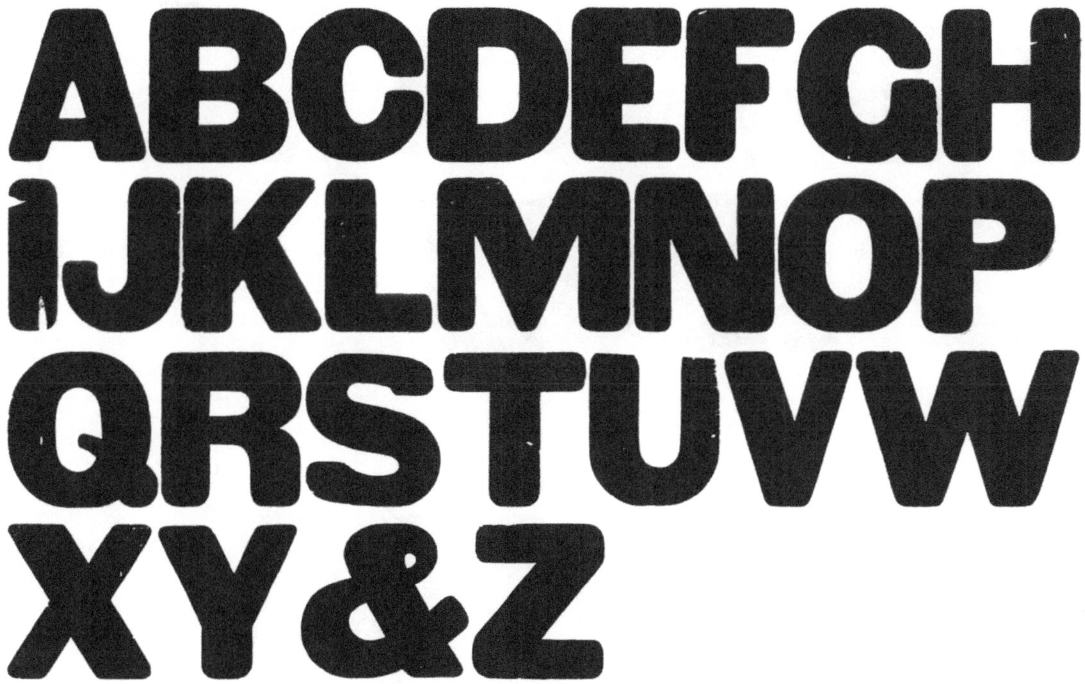

5.02.01.03
10 line [Rounded Gothic] cf. Page: Gothic Round
J.G. Cooley, 1859–1868

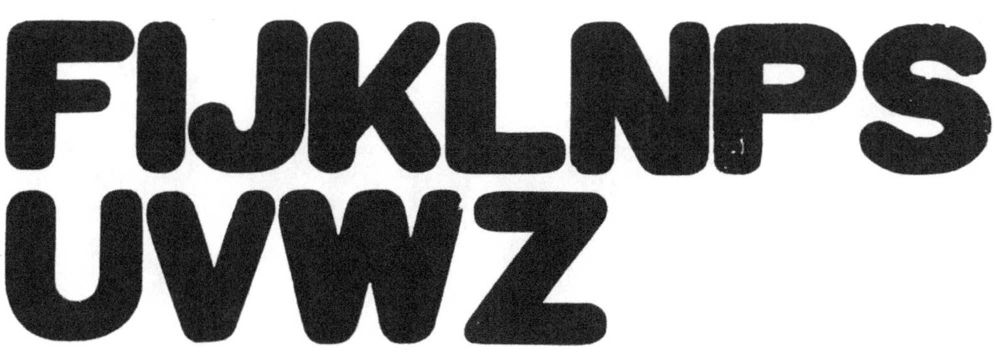

5.02.01.04
10 line [Rounded Gothic] cf. Page: Gothic Round
Manufacturer and date unknown

RSTUVWXYZ
$1234567

5 line No. 507 [Actual size]

DEFGH 1234

6 line No. 509 [Actual size]

WYZ efgh
459

8 line No. 507 [Actual size]

ABCDEFGHIJKLMNOPQ
RSTUVWXYZ
$1234567890¢

5.03.01.01
5 line No. 507
William H. Page & Co., 1887–1891

ABCDEFGHIKLMNOPQRS
TUVWYZ 1234567890

5.03.01.02 & 5.03.01.03
6 line No. 509
William H. Page & Co., 1887–1891

ABCDFGIJLPQSU
WYZ cbefghikm
pqrstuvwxz 459

5.03.01.04
8 line No. 507
Hamilton Manufacturing Co., 1891–1906

XY&Z

12 line No. 508 [Actual size]

MObo1

12 line No. 507 [Actual size]

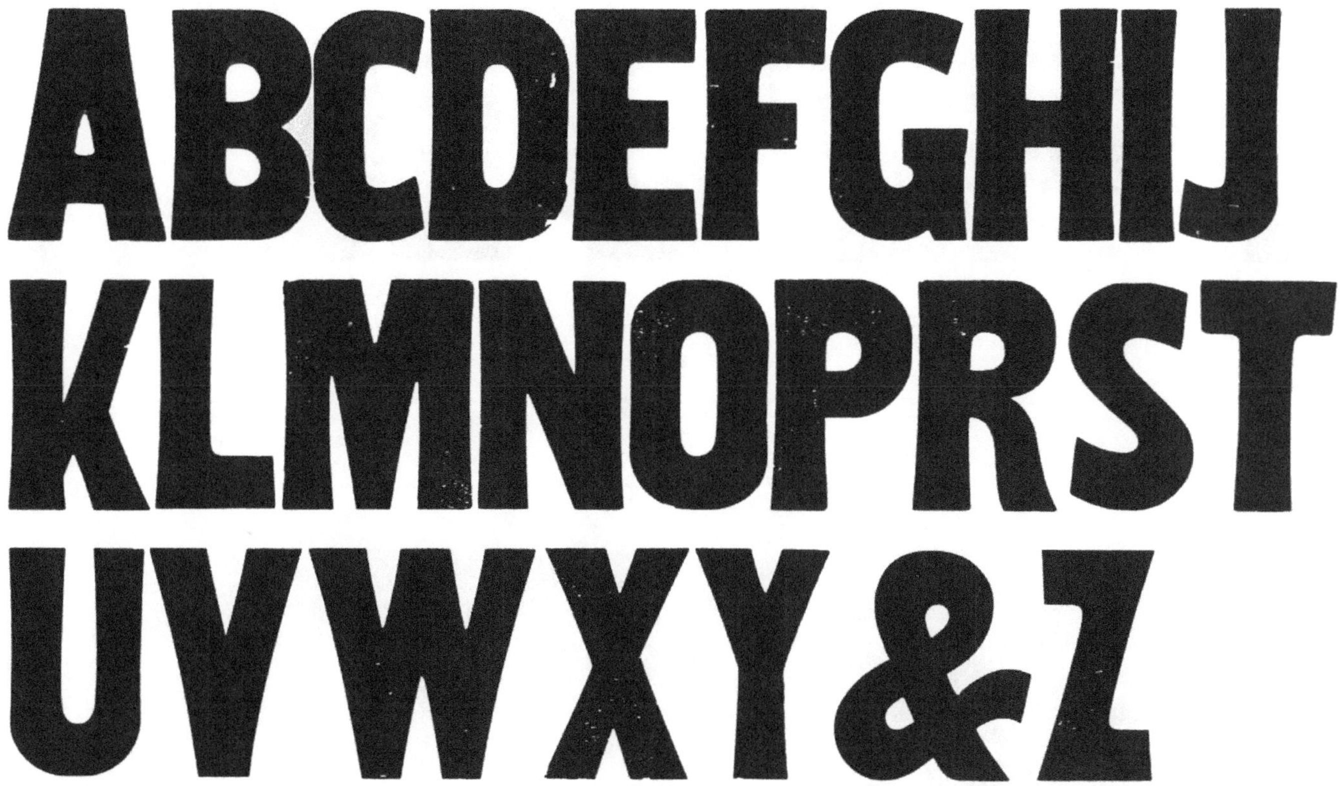

5.03.01.05
12 line No. 508
Hamilton Manufacturing Co., 1891–1906

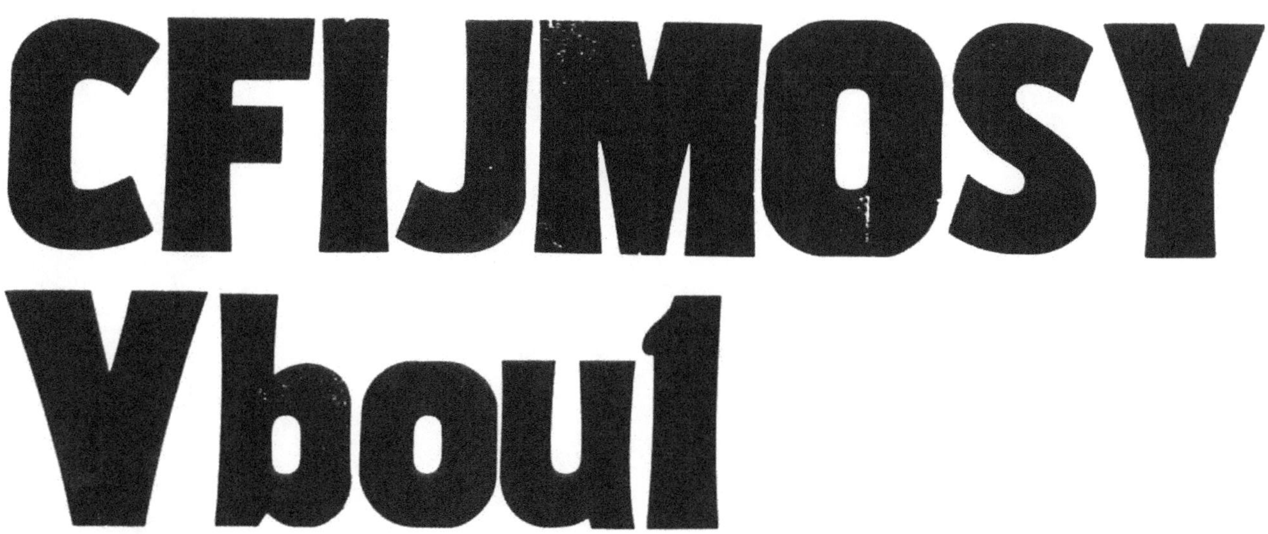

5.03.01.06
12 line No. 507
William H. Page & Co., 1887–1891

FGIJK

8 line Gothic Tuscan [Actual size]

RSTU

9 line Gothic Tuscan [Actual size]

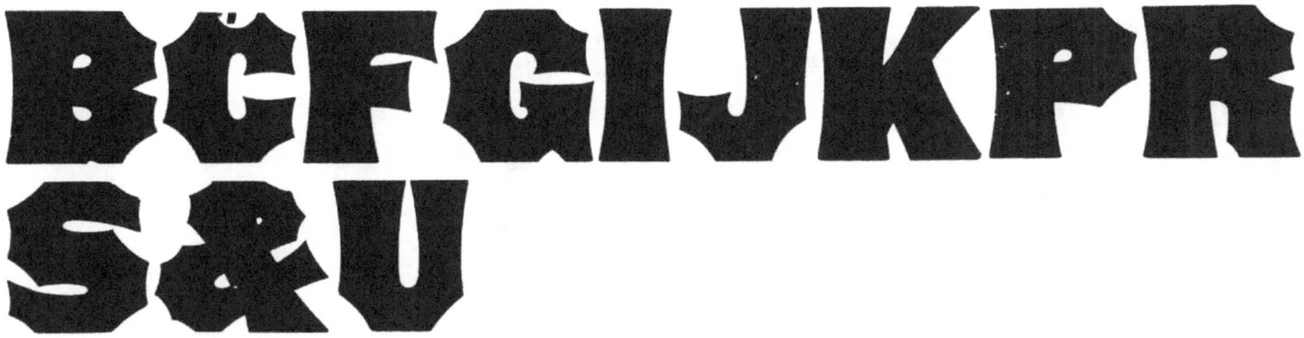

5.03.02.01
8 line Gothic Tuscan
William H. Page & Co., 1857–1859

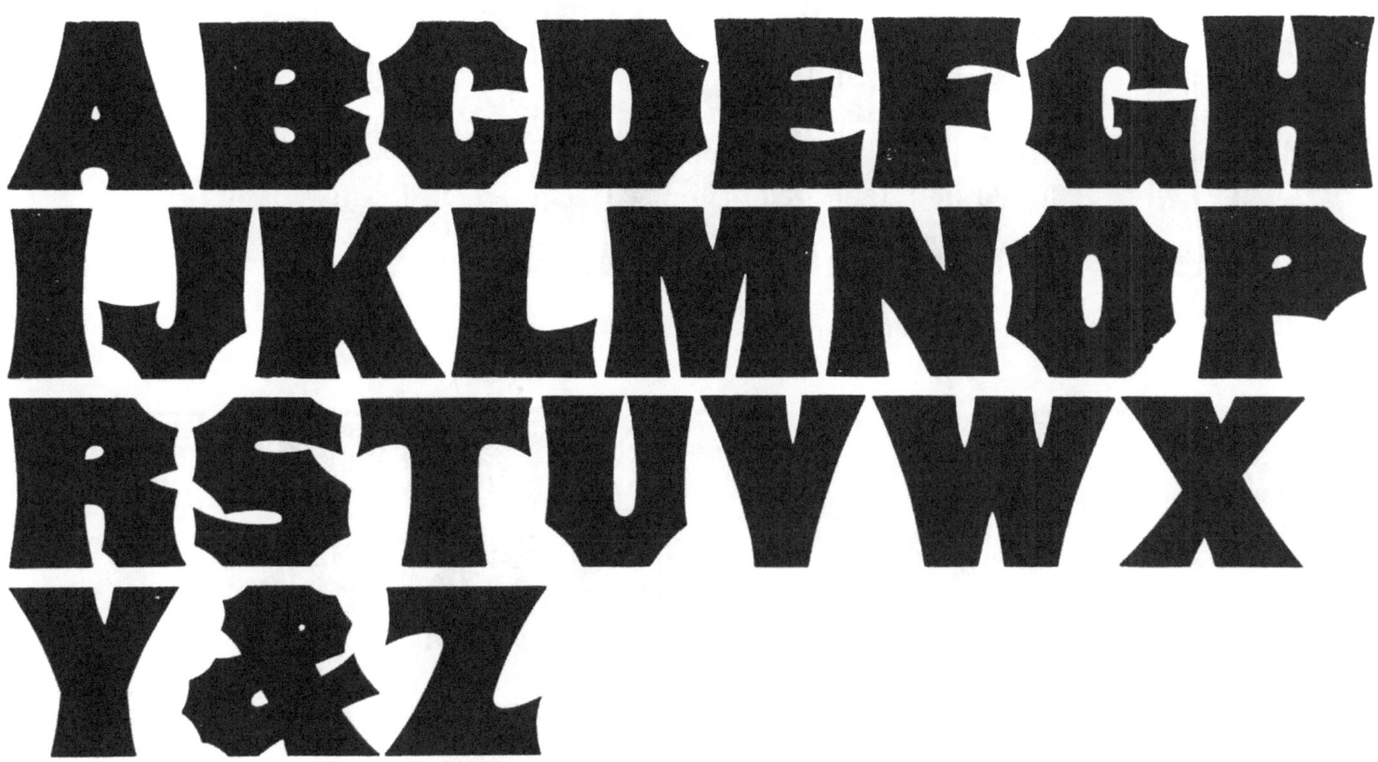

5.03.02.02
9 line Gothic Tuscan
William H. Page & Co., 1857–1859

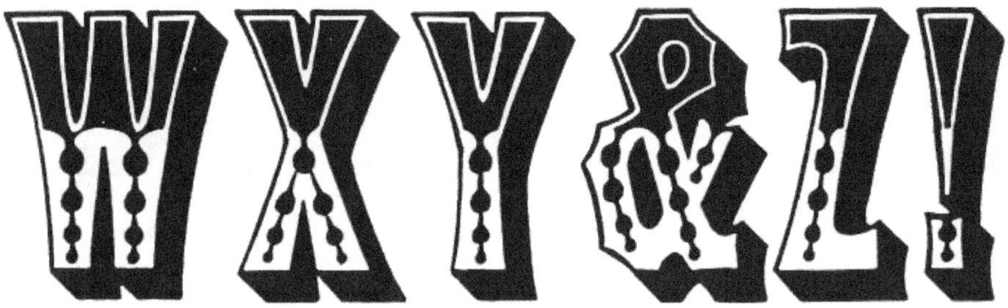

8 line Ornate [Actual size]

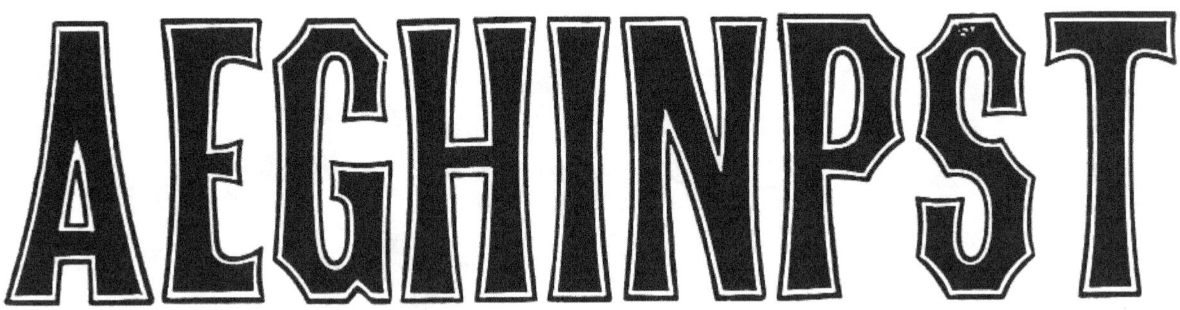

9 line [Gothic Tuscan Outlined] cf. Hamilton: No. 412 [Actual size]

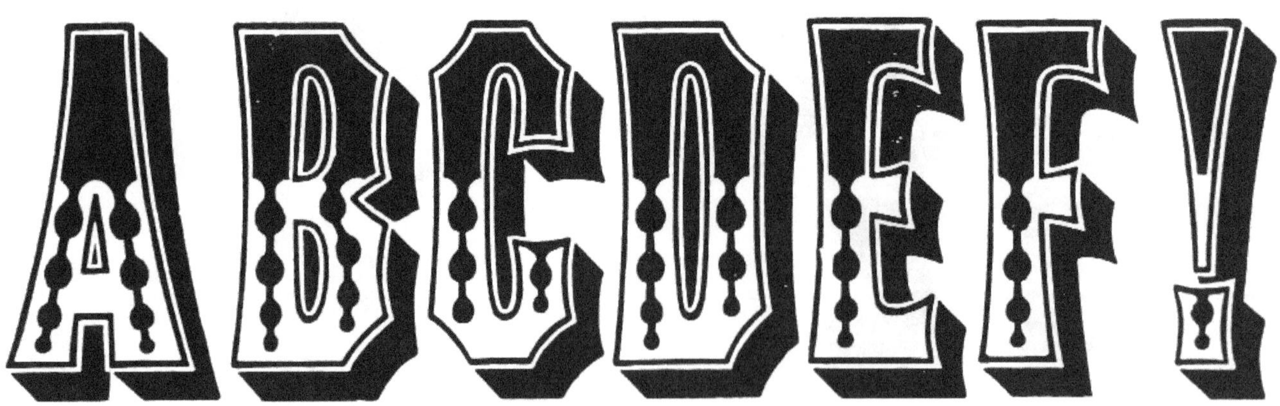

12 line Ornate No. 2 [Actual size]

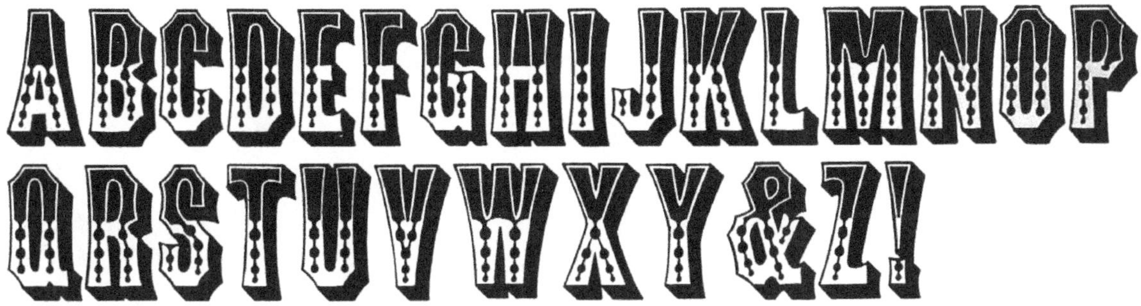

5.03.02.03
8 line Ornate
William H. Page & Co., 1857–1859

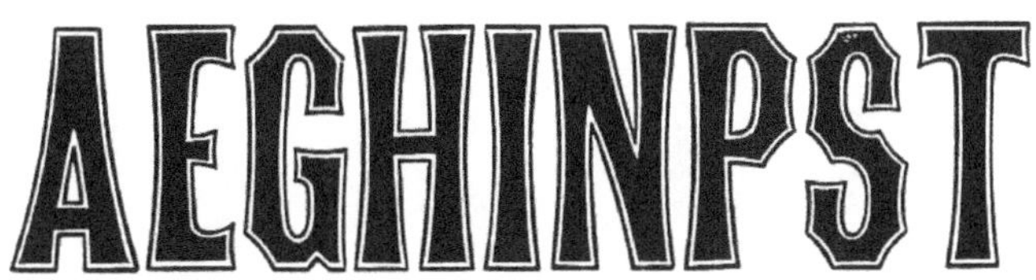

5.03.02.04
9 line [Gothic Tuscan Outlined] cf. Hamilton: No. 412
Manufacturer and date unknown

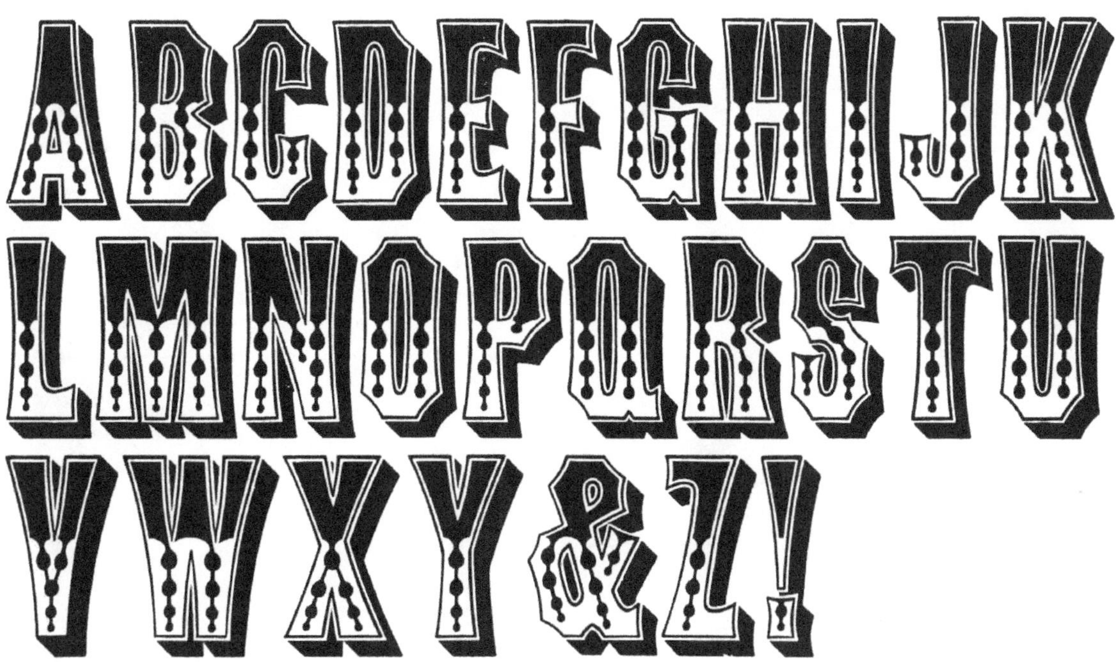

5.03.02.05
12 line Ornate No. 2
William H. Page & Co., 1857–1859

Script Class

Typefaces that are designed to appear as handwriting.

DEFGHIJKLM

abcdefghijklmnop

$123456789&0

4 line [Script] cf. Hamilton: Kaufmann Bold, No. 831 [Actual size]

ABCDEFGHIJKLMNOP
QRSTUVWXYZ
abcdefghijklmnopqrstuvwxyz
$123456789&0

6.01.01.01
4 line [Script] cf. Hamilton: Kaufmann Bold, No. 831
Manufacturer and date unknown

Miscellaneous Class

Typefaces that are highly stylized or decorated, and which do not fit into other classes.

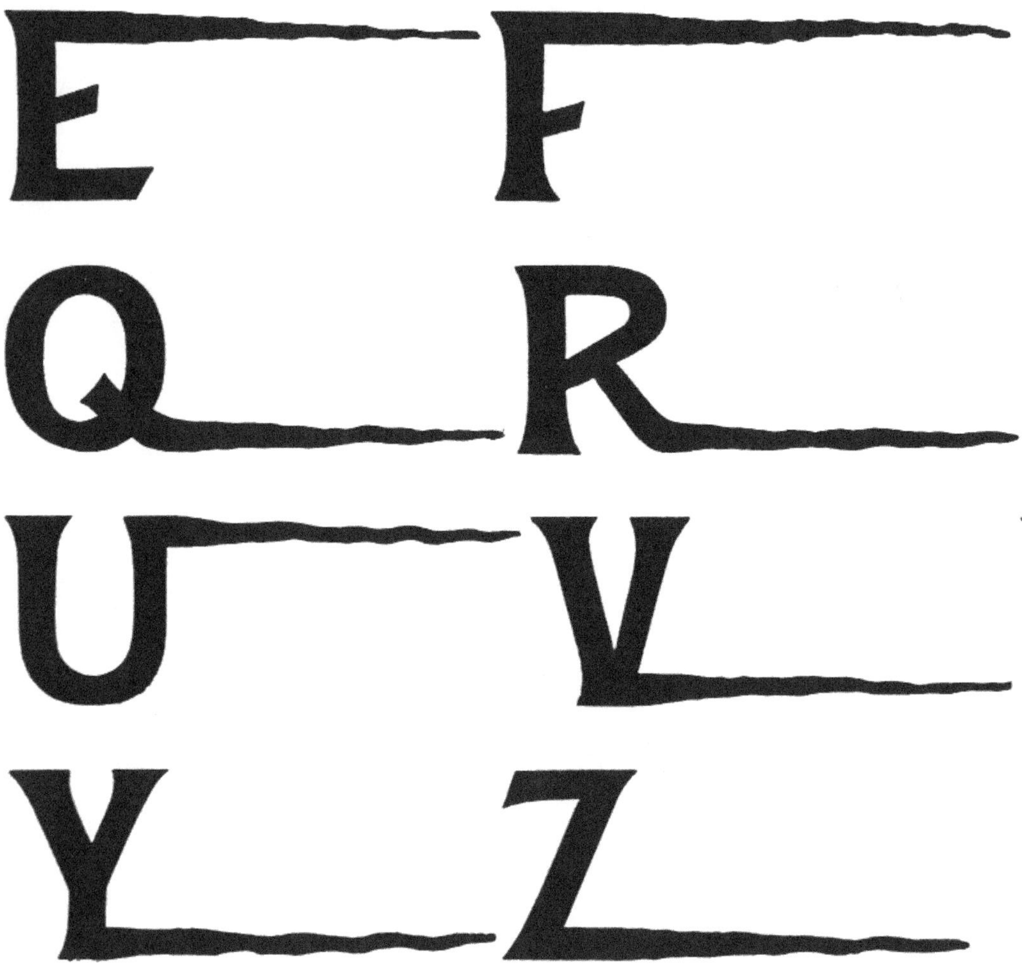

6 line [Ornamented] cf. Hamilton: No. 227 [Actual size]

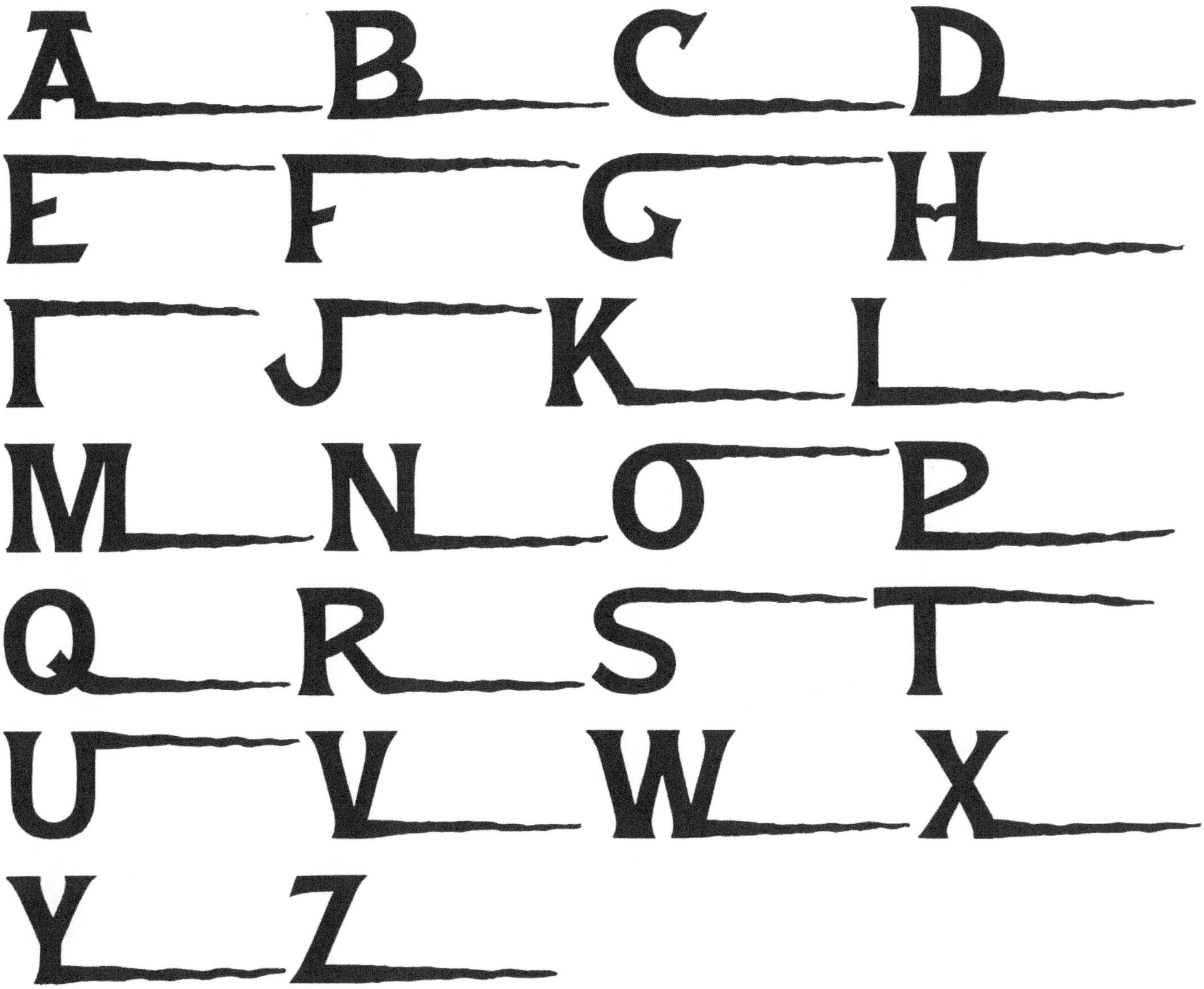

7.01.01.01
6 line [Ornamented] cf. Hamilton: No. 227
Manufacturer and date unknown

Decorative Wood Type

Miscellaneous decorative borders and ornaments.

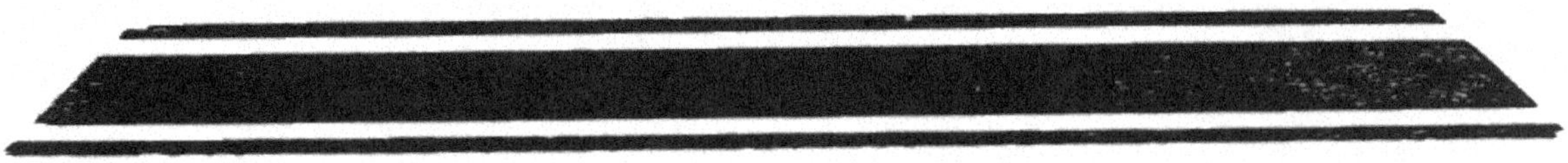

Wood rules [Actual size]

Star rules [Actual size]

End wood border [Actual size]

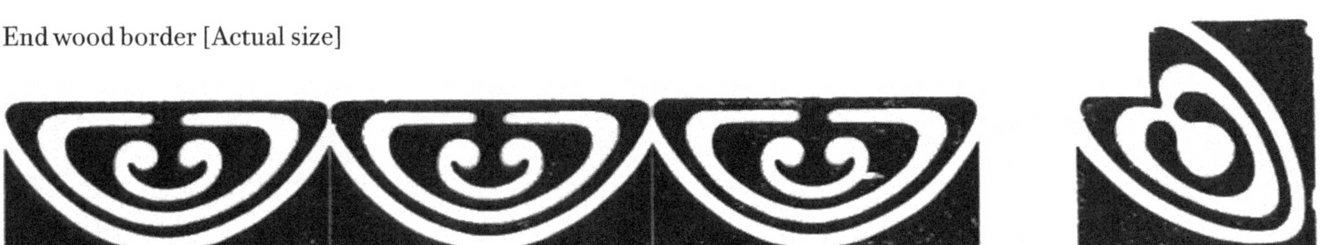

Routed border [Actual size]

[All of the above were made and sold by most manufacturers of wood type.]

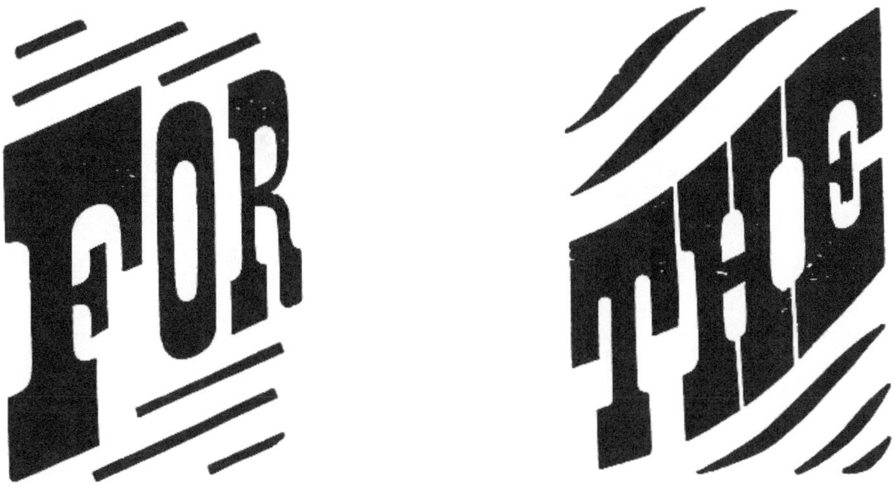

Catchwords [Actual size]

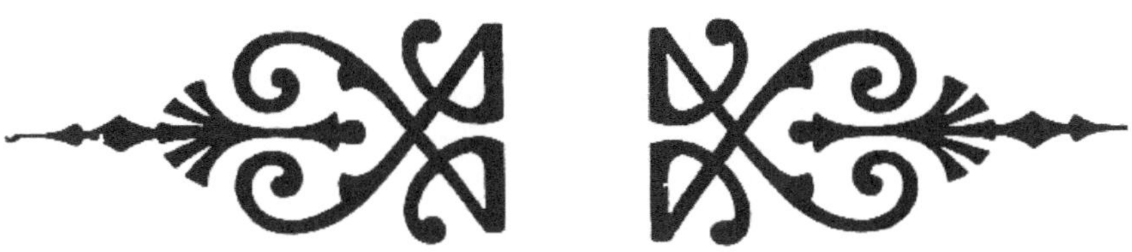

Fancy ornaments [Actual size]

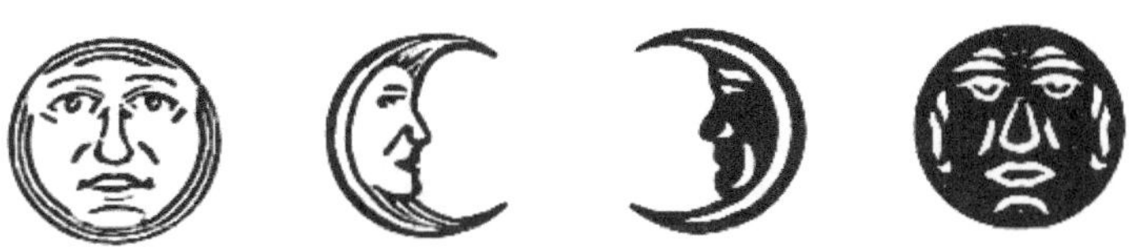

Moon phases [Actual size]

Wood pointers and florentine ornament [Actual size]

[All of the above were made and sold by most manufacturers of wood type.]

List of Manufacturers

Bibliography

Adobe Systems Incorporated. *Adobe Wood Type 1*. Mountain View, CA: 1990.

A Typographical Journey Through the Inland Printer, 1883–1900. Compiled by Maurice Annenberg. Baltimore, MD: Maran Press. 1977.

Annenberg, Maurice. *Specimens of Wood Type Presented to the School of Library Service Columbia University*. New York, NY: The Book Arts Press, 1980.

Clement, Walter and Robertson, Ian. *Alphabets and Others*. Nostasulga, AL: The Armstrong Press and Fairhope, AL: The Slow Loris Press, 1998.

Gaskell, Phillip. "Nomenclature for Roman Type," *Visible Language*, X: 1 Winter, 1976. pp. 41-51.

Grastorf, Dennis J. *Wood Type of the Angelica Press*. New York, NY: The Angelica Press, 1975.

Hamilton Mfg. Co. *Specimens of [Large] Wood Type*. Two Rivers, WI: Hamilton Mfg. Co., 1892.

Hamilton Mfg. Co. *Specimens of New Process Wood Type*. Two Rivers, WI: Hamilton Mfg. Co., 1892.

Hamilton Mfg. Co. *Hamilton's Wood Type Catalog No. 14*, 1899-1900. Two Rivers, WI: Hamilton Mfg. Co., 1900.

Hamilton Mfg. Co. *Hamilton's Wood Type; New Gothic Faces in Wood Type*. Two Rivers, WI: Hamilton Mfg. Co., 1901.

Hamilton Mfg. Co. *Specimens of wood type, wood ornaments, flourishes, dashes silhouettes, catch-words, corners, fractions, calendars, and borders*. Catalogue No. 16. Two Rivers, WI: Hamilton Mfg. Co.,1906.

Harris, Elizabeth M. *The Fat and the Lean: American Wood Type in the 19th Century*. The National Museum of American History, Smithsonian Institution, Washington, D.C.: 1983.

Johnson, A. F. *Type Designs: Their History and Development*. London: Grafton & Co., 1934.

Kelly, Rob Roy. *American Wood Types, 1828–1900*. Volume One [Portfolio]. Kansas City, MO: Printed by Rob Roy Kelly, 1964.

Kelly, Rob Roy. *American Wood Type 1828–1900*. New York, NY: Van Nostrand Reinhold, 1969.

Kelly, Rob Roy, ed. *Wood Type Alphabets: 100 Fonts*. New York, NY: Dover Publications, 1977.

Lawson, Alexander S. "Wood Type-Story of Printers' Craft." *Printing Impressions*. February 1970.

Long, Robert P. *Wood Type and Printing Collectibles*. East Meadow, NY: Robert P. Long, 1980.

Morgans & Wilcox Mfg. Co., *Specimen Book of Wood Type*. Middletown, NY: Morgans & Wilcox, 1882.

Saxe, Stephen O. "The Romance of Wood Type," *Fine Print on Type: The Best of Fine Print Magazine on Type and Typography*. San Francisco, CA: Fine Print and Bedford Arts, 1989.

Specimen Book of Wood Type from the Collection of the Silver Buckle Press. Introduction by Rob Roy Kelly. Madison, WI: Silver Buckle Press, 1999.

Specimens of Wood Type held at the Alembic Press. Oxford: Alembic Press, 1993.

Thorp, Joseph. "Towards a Nomenclature for Letter Forms." *The Monotype Recorder*. Vol. 30, no. 240, April-May, 1931. pp.9–19.

Wall, David P. "A Catalogue of the Wood Type at Rochester Institute of Technology." (Master's Thesis, School of Printing Management and Sciences, RIT), 1992.

Wm. H. Page Wood & Co. *Specimens of Wood Type, Borders, Rules, & c.* Greenville, CT: Wm. H. Page & Co., 1859.

Wm. H. Page & Co. *Specimens of Chromatic Wood Type, Borders, &c.* Greenville, CT: Wm. H. Page & Co., 1874.

Wm. H. Page & Co. *Pages Wood Type Album.* Vol. 1, nos. 1–3, April-October, 1879. Norwich, CT: Wm. H. Page & Co. , 1879.

Wm. H. Page & Co. *Specimens of Machine Cut Wood Type!* Norwich, CT: Wm. H. Page Wood Type Co., 1890.

Woodtype [portfolio] Design Program, Indiana University, Bloomington, IN, 1966.

Vanderburgh, Wells & Co. *Specimens of Wood Type, Borders, Rules, &c.* New York, NY: Vanderburgh, Wells & Co., 1877.

Colophon

This book was created as a companion piece to David P. Wall's letterpress type specimen portfolio of wood type in the Cary Graphic Art Collection, produced in 1992. The cover and layout were designed by graduate assistants of the Cary Collection, Candice Reese and Jackie Clements.

Type specimens shown throughout the book were derived from digital photographs of the original letterpress type specimen portfolio, which were then corrected in Adobe Photoshop CS3 by Megan Miller. Each typeface image was then modified as necessary to fit the parameters of this book and placed into Adobe InDesign CS3, where the layout and typography were completed. All body copy was set in 12 pt. Bodoni Twelve ITC Book OS with captions set in 10 pt. Bodoni Twelve ITC Book. Headings appear in 30 pt. Bodoni Twelve ITC Book SC and are accompanied by Adobe Wood Type Ornaments.